Travel With
Great Writers

Travel With Great Writers

An Informal Literary Guide to Europe

edited by

Robert Hector

Nash Publishing, Los Angeles

Grateful acknowledgment is made to the following: The chapter on bullfighting is reprinted by permission of Charles Scribner's Sons from *Death in the Afternoon* by Ernest Hemingway, copyright © 1932, Charles Scribner's Sons. The chapters from "Andalusia" by Somerset Maugham are through the courtesy of Doubleday and Co.; the essay on Madame Tussaud by Max Beerbohm is through the courtesy of Dodd Mead and Co. Mary McCarthy's chapter on Florence from *The Stones of Florence* is reprinted by permission of Harcourt Brace Jovanovich Inc. J.B. Priestley's "The British Museum" is reprinted by the permission of A.D. Peters and Co.

Library of Congress Catalog Card Number: 74-83036
International Standard Book Number: 0-8402-1357-3

Published simultaneously in the United States and Canada by Nash Publishing Corporation, 9255 Sunset Boulevard Los Angeles, California 90069

Printed in the United States of America

First Printing

Preface

Many of the world's greatest writers have written superlative accounts of their journeys through Europe and descriptions of historic landmarks that are valid for the current traveler. Here are passages of literature that transcend the commonplace and capture the grandeur of great works of art, of cities and countryside.

For the most part descriptions have been chosen of places that have changed little. Victor Hugo's description of Notre Dame, Washington Irving's sketch of Westminster Abbey, Shelley's impressions of Rome, Henry James' comments on the byways of London, Somerset Maugham's reminiscences of Seville, Hemingway's recreation of the bullring in Madrid—all these are vivid canvases to stir the imagination today.

Patently, the perspectives of geniuses differ from those of the ordinary beholder. Thus, great writers, such as Shelley and Dickens, traveling in Italy may have rightly regarded themselves as peers of the great masters. One might even imagine Victor Hugo, a man noted for his vanity (who once proclaimed that the century would be called "the age of Hugo"), standing on a bridge over the Seine, surveying the great Cathedral of Notre Dame, and deciding that he would create a structure in language as monumental as the Cathedral itself.

Others had a different vantage point. Mark Twain found that differences in customs and manners were most striking, and reported with zest and humor on the traits of the "natives," and the reactions of an "innocent" American tourist. Yet, despite the changes wrought by modern communications, the characteristics he wrote of still exist.

Henry Adams' masterful piece on Mont-Saint-Michel belongs also in the domain of art history. It is, however, an invaluable guide to the appreciation of the Cathedral by the discerning traveler.

Occasionally, some of the prose of the earlier pieces bears the patina of another era. But, like the glow on illustrious antiques, it belongs there. For the most part the writings are fit to be inscribed on the places they depict, going beyond the concrete and the tangible to the aura and spirit that surround masterworks of man and nature.

Contents

I. GREAT BRITAIN

II. FRANCE

III. ITALY

IV. SPAIN

Part One:
Great Britain

Northwest View of Westminster Abbey

Washington Irving: Westminster Abbey

Washington Irving (1783-1859) was the first internationally known American writer. He was also a diplomat, serving first as secretary to the legation in London, and later as minister to Spain. Irving loved England, and his essay on Westminster Abbey is a minor masterpiece. Royalty is crowned in the Abbey; of Elizabeth's coronation there, Shakespeare wrote in "Henry VIII":

> ...the choir,
> With all the choicest music of the kingdom,
> Together sung Te Deum.

Historic personages of the artistic and political worlds are buried there. Since Irving's time, plaques have been mounted for world leaders, including Franklin Delano Roosevelt and Herbert Asquith. The abbey, however, remains eternally the same.

> When I behold, with deep astonishment,
> To famous Westminster how there resorte,
> Living in brasse or stony monument,
> The princes and the worthies of all sorte;
> Doe not I see reformde nobilitie,
> Without contempt, or pride, or ostentation,
> And looke upon offenseless majesty,

Naked of pomp or earthly domination?
And how a play-game of a painted stone
Contents the quiet now and silent sprites,
Whome all the world which late they stood upon,
Could not content nor quench their appetites.
    Life is a frost of cold felicitie,
    And death the thaw of all our vanitie.
                    Christolero's Epigrams, by T. B. 1598.

On one of those sober and rather melancholy days, in the
latter part of autumn, when the shadows of morning and
evening almost mingle together, and throw a gloom over the
decline of the year, I passed several hours in rambling about
Westminster Abbey. There was something congenial to the
season in the mournful magnificence of the old pile; and as I
passed its threshold, it seemed like stepping back into the
regions of antiquity, and losing myself among the shades of
former ages.

I entered from the inner court of Westminster school,
through a long, low, vaulted passage, that had an almost
subterranean look, being dimly lighted in one part by
circular perforations in the massive walls. Through this dark
avenue I had a distant view of the cloisters, with the figure of
an old verger, in his black gown, moving along their shadowy
vaults, and seeming like a spectre from one of the
neighbouring tombs.

The approach to the abbey through these gloomy monastic
remains, prepares the mind for its solemn contemplation.
The cloister still retains something of the quiet and seculsion
of former days. The gray walls are discoloured by damps, and
crumbling with age; a coat of hoary moss has gathered over
the inscriptions of the mural monuments, and obscured the
death's heads, and other funeral emblems. The sharp touches
of the chisel are gone from the rich tracery of the arches; the
roses which adorned the key-stones have lost their leafy
beauty; every thing bears marks of the gradual dilapidations
of time, which yet has something touching and pleasing in its
very decay.

The sun was pouring down a yellow autumnal ray into the
square of the cloisters; beaming upon a scanty plot of grass in

the centre, and lighting up an angle of the vaulted passage with a kind of dusty splendour. From between the arcades, the eye glanced up to a bit of blue sky, or a passing cloud; and beheld the sun-gilt pinnacles of the abbey towering into the azure heaven.

As I paced the cloisters, sometimes contemplating this mingled picture of glory and decay, and sometimes endeavouring to decipher the inscriptions on the tombstones, which formed the pavement beneath my feet, my eyes were attracted to three figures, rudely carved in relief, but nearly worn away by the footsteps of many generations. They were the effigies of three of the early abbots; the epitaphs were entirely effaced; the names alone remained, having no doubt been renewed in later times; (Vitalis. Abbas. 1082, and Gislebertus Crispinus. Abbas. 1114, and Laurentius. Abbas. 1176). I remained some little while, musing over these casual relics of antiquity, thus left like wrecks upon this distant shore of time, telling no tale but that such beings had been and had perished; teaching no moral but the futility of that pride which hopes still to exact homage in its ashes, and to live in an inscription. A little longer, and even these faint records will be obliterated, and the monument will cease to be a memorial. Whilst I was yet looking down upon the gravestones, I was roused by the sound of the abbey clock, reverberating from buttress to buttress, and echoing among the cloisters. It is almost startling to hear this warning of departed time sounding among the tombs, and telling the lapse of the hour, which, like a billow, has rolled us onward towards the grave.

I pursued my walk to an arched door opening to the interior of the abbey. On entering here, the magnitude of the building breaks fully upon the mind, contrasted with the vaults of the cloisters. The eye gazes with wonder at clustered columns of gigantic dimensions, with arches springing from them to such an amazing height; and man wandering about their bases, shrunk into insignificance in comparison with his own handy-work. The spaciousness and gloom of this vast edifice produce a profound and mysterious awe. We step cautiously and softly about, as if fearful of disturbing the hallowed silence of the tomb; while every footfall whispers along the walls, and chatters among the sepulchres, making us more sensible of the quiet we have interrupted.

It seems as if the awful nature of the place presses down upon the soul, and hushes the beholder into noiseless reverence. We feel that we are surrounded by the congregated bones of the great men of past times, who have filled history with their deeds, and the earth with their renown. And yet it almost provokes a smile at the vanity of human ambition, to see how they are crowded together, and justled in the dust; what parsimony is observed in doling out a scanty nook — a gloomy corner — a little portion of earth, to those whom, when alive, kingdoms could not satisfy: and how many shapes, and forms, and artifices, are devised to catch the casual notice of the passenger, and save from forgetfulness, for a few short years, a name which once aspired to occupy ages of the world's thought and admiration.

I passed some time in Poet's Corner, which occupies an end of one of the transepts or cross aisles of the abbey. The monuments are generally simple; for the lives of literary men afford no striking themes for the sculptor. Shakspeare and Addison have statues erected to their memories; but the greater part have busts, medallions, and sometimes mere inscriptions. Notwithstanding the simplicity of these memorials, I have always observed that the visiters to the abbey remain longest about them. A kinder and fonder feeling takes place of that cold curiosity or vague admiration with which they gaze on the splendid monuments of the great and the heroic. They linger about these as about the tombs of friends and companions; for indeed there is something of companionship between the author and the reader. Other men are known to posterity only through the medium of history, which is continually growing faint and obscure; but the intercourse between the author and his fellow men is ever new, active, and immediate. He has lived for them more than for himself; he has sacrificed surrounding enjoyments, and shut himself up from the delights of social life, that he might the more intimately commune with distant minds and distant ages. Well may the world cherish his renown; for it has been purchased, not by deeds of violence and blood, but by the diligent dispensation of pleasure. Well may posterity be grateful to his memory; for he has left it an inheritance, not of empty names and sounding actions, but whole treasures of wisdom, bright gems of thought, and golden veins of language.

From Poet's Corner I continued my stroll towards that part of the abbey which contains the sepulchres of the kings. I wandered among what once were chapels, but which are now occupied by the tombs and monuments of the great. At every turn, I met with some illustrious name, or the cognizance of some powerful house renowned in history. As the eye darts into these dusky chambers of death, it catches glimpses of quaint effigies: some kneeling in niches, as if in devotion; others stretched upon the tombs, with hands piously pressed together; warriors in armour, as if reposing after battle; prelates, with crosiers and mitres; and nobles in robes and coronets, lying as it were in state. In glancing over this scene, so strangely populous, yet where every form is so still and silent, it seems almost as if we were treading a mansion of that fabled city, where every being had been suddenly transmuted into stone.

I paused to contemplate a tomb on which lay the effigy of a knight in complete armour. A large buckler was on one arm; the hands were pressed together in supplication upon the breast; the face was almost covered by the morion; the legs were crossed in token of the warrior's having been engaged in the holy war. It was the tomb of a crusader; of one of those military enthusiasts, who so strangely mingled religion and romance, and whose exploits form the connecting link between fact and fiction — between the history and the fairy tale. There is something extremely picturesque in the tombs of these adventurers, decorated as they are with rude armorial bearings and Gothic sculpture. They comport with the antiquated chapels in which they are generally found; and in considering them, the imagination is apt to kindle with the legendary associations, the romantic fictions, the chivalrous pomp and pageantry, which poetry has spread over the wars for the Sepulchre of Christ. They are the relics of times utterly gone by; of beings passed from recollection; of customs and manners with which our's have no affinity. They are like objects from some strange and distant land, of which we have no certain knowledge, and about which all our conceptions are vague and visionary. There is something extremely solemn and awful in those effigies on Gothic tombs, extended as if in the sleep of death, or in the supplication of the dying hour. They have an effect infinitely more impressive on my feelings than the fanciful attitudes, the over-wrought conceits, and allegorical groups, which abound on modern monuments. I have been struck, also, with the superiority of many of the old sepulchral inscriptions. There was a noble way, in former times, of saying things simply, and yet saying them proudly: and I do not know an epitaph that breathes a loftier consciousness of family worth and honourable lineage, than one which affirms, of a noble house, that "all the brothers were brave, and all the sisters virtuous."

In the opposite transept to Poet's Corner, stands a monument which is among the most renowned achievements of modern art; but which, to me, appears horrible rather than sublime. It is the tomb of Mrs. Nightingale, by Roubillac. The bottom of the monument is represented as throwing open its marble doors, and a sheeted skeleton is starting forth. The shroud is falling from his fleshless frame as he lanches his dart at his victim. She is sinking into her affrighted husband's arms, who strives, with vain and frantic effort, to avert the blow. The whole is executed with terrible truth and spirit; we almost fancy we hear the gibbering yell of triumph, bursting from the distended jaws of the spectre. — But why should we thus seek to clothe death with unnecessary terrors, and to spread horrors round the tomb of those we love? The grave should be surrounded by everything that might inspire tenderness and veneration for the dead; or that might win the living to virtue. It is the place, not of disgust and dismay, but of sorrow and meditation.

While wandering about these gloomy vaults and silent aisles, studying the records of the dead, the sound of busy existence from without occasionally reaches the ear: — the rumbling of the passing equipage; the murmur of the multitude; or perhaps the light laugh of pleasure. The contrast is striking with the deathlike repose around; and it has a strange effect upon the feelings, thus to hear the surges of active life hurrying along and beating against the very walls of the sepulchre.

I continued in this way to move from tomb to tomb, and from chapel to chapel. The day was gradually wearing away; the distant tread of loiterers about the abbey grew less and less frequent; the sweet-tongued bell was summoning to evening prayers; and I saw at a distance the choristers, in their white surplices, crossing the aisle and entering the choir. I stood before the entrance to Henry the Seventh's chapel. A flight of steps leads up to it, through a deep and gloomy, but magnificent arch. Great gates of brass, richly and delicately wrought, turn heavily upon their hinges, as if proudly reluctant to admit the feet of common mortals into this most gorgeous of sepulchres.

On entering, the eye is astonished by the pomp of architecture, and the elaborate beauty of sculptured detail. The very walls are wrought into universal ornament, encrusted with tracery, and scooped into niches, crowded with the statues of saints and martyrs. Stone seems, by the cunning labour of the chisel, to have been robbed of its weight and density, suspended aloft, as if by magic, and the fretted roof achieved with the wonderful minuteness and airy security of a cobweb.

Along the sides of the chapel are the lofty stalls of the Knights of the Bath, richly carved of oak, though with the grotesque decorations of Gothic architecture. On the pinnacles of the stalls are affixed the helmets and crests of the knights, with their scarfs and swords; and above them are suspended their banners, emblazoned with armorial bearings, and contrasting the splendour of gold and purple and crimson, with the cold gray fretwork of the roof. In the midst of this grand mausoleum stands the sepulchre of its founder, — his effigy, with that of his queen, extended on a sumptuous tomb, and the whole surrounded by a superbly wrought brazen railing.

There is a sad dreariness in this magnificence; this strange mixture of tombs and trophies; these emblems of living and aspiring ambition, close beside mementos which show the dust and oblivion in which all must sooner or later terminate. Nothing impresses the mind with a deeper feeling of loneliness, than to tread the silent and deserted scene of former throng and pageant. On looking round on the vacant stalls of the knights and their esquires, and on the rows of dusty but gorgeous banners that were once borne before them, my imagination conjured up the scene when this hall was bright with the valour and beauty of the land; glittering with the splendour of jewelled rank and military array; alive with the tread of many feet, and the hum of an admiring multitude. All had passed away; the silence of death had settled again upon the place; interrupted only by the casual chirping of birds, which had found their way into the chapel, and built their nests among its friezes and pendants — sure signs of solitariness and desertion. When I read the names inscribed on the banners, they were those of men scattered far and wide about the world; some tossing upon distant seas; some under arms in distant lands; some mingling in the busy intrigues of courts and cabinets: all seeking to deserve one more distinction in this mansion of shadowy honours — the melancholy reward of a monument.

Two small aisles on each side of this chapel present a touching instance of the equality of the grave, which brings down the oppressor to a level with the oppressed, and mingles the dust of the bitterest enemies together. In one is the sepulchre of the haughty Elizabeth; in the other is that of her victim, the lovely and unfortunate Mary. Not an hour in the day, but some ejaculation of pity is uttered over the fate of the latter, mingled with indignation at her oppressor. The walls of Elizabeth's sepulchre continually echo with the sighs of sympathy heaved at the grave of her rival.

A peculiar melancholy reigns over the aisle where Mary lies buried. The light struggles dimly through windows darkened by dust. The greater part of the place is in deep shadow, and the walls are stained and tinted by time and weather. A marble figure of Mary is stretched upon the tomb, round which is an iron railing, much corroded, bearing her national emblem — the thistle. I was weary with wandering, and sat down to rest myself by the monument, revolving in my mind the chequered and disastrous story of poor Mary.

The sound of casual footsteps had ceased from the abbey. I could only hear, now and then, the distant voice of the priest repeating the evening service, and the faint responses of the choir; these paused for a time, and all was hushed. The stillness, the desertion and obscurity that were gradually prevailing around, gave a deeper and more solemn interest to the place:

> For in the silent grave no conversation,
> No joyful tread of friends, no voice of lovers,
> No careful father's counsel — nothing's heard,
> For nothing is, but all oblivion,
> Dust, and an endless darkness.

Suddenly the notes of the deep-labouring organ burst upon the ear, falling with doubled and redoubled intensity, and rolling, as it were, huge billows of sound. How well do their volume and grandeur accord with this mighty building! With what pomp do they swell through its vast vaults, and breathe their awful harmony through these caves of death, and make the silent sepulchre vocal! And now they rise in triumphant acclamation, heaving higher and higher their accordant notes, and piling sound on sound. — And now they pause, and the soft voices of the choir break out into sweet gushes of melody; they soar aloft, and warble along the roof, and seem to play about these lofty vaults like the pure airs of heaven. Again the pealing organ heaves its thrilling thunders, compressing air into music, and rolling it forth upon the soul. What long-drawn cadences! What solemn sweeping concords! It grows more and more dense and powerful — it fills the vast pile, and seems to jar the very walls — the ear is stunned — the senses are overwhelmed. And now it is winding up in full jubilee — it is rising from the earth to heaven — the very soul seems rapt away, and floated upwards on this swelling tide of harmony!

I sat for some time lost in that kind of reverie which a strain of music is apt sometimes to inspire: the shadows of evening were gradually thickening around me; the monuments began to cast deeper and deeper gloom; and the distant clock again gave token of the slowly waning day.

I rose, and prepared to leave the abbey. As I descended the flight of steps which lead into the body of the building, my eye was caught by the shrine of Edward the Confessor, and I ascended the small staircase that conducts to it, to take from thence a general survey of this wilderness of tombs. The shrine is elevated upon a kind of platform, and close around it are the sepulchres of various kings and queens. From this eminence the eye looks down between pillars and funeral trophies to the chapels and chambers below, crowded with tombs; where warriors, prelates, courtiers, and statesmen, lie mouldering in "their beds of darkness." Close by me stood the great chair of coronation, rudely carved of oak, in the barbarous taste of a remote and Gothic age. The scene seemed almost as if contrived, with theatrical artifice, to produce an effect upon the beholder. Here was a type of the beginning and the end of human pomp and power; here it was literally but a step from the throne to the sepulchre. Would not one think that these incongruous mementos had been gathered together as a lesson to living greatness?— to show it, even in the moment of its proudest exaltation, the neglect and dishonour to which it must soon arrive? how soon that crown which encircles its brow must pass away; and it must lie down in the dust and disgraces of the tomb, and be trampled upon by the feet of the meanest of the multitude? For, strange to tell, even the grave is here no longer a sanctuary. There is a shocking levity in some natures, which leads them to sport with awful and hallowed things; and there are base minds, which delight to revenge on the illustrious dead the abject homage and grovelling servility which they pay to the living. The coffin of Edward the Confessor has been broken open, and his remains despoiled of their funeral ornaments; the sceptre has been stolen from the hand of the imperious Elizabeth, and the effigy of Henry the Fifth lies headless. Not a royal monument but bears some proof how false and fugitive is the homage of mankind. Some are plundered; some mutilated; some covered with ribaldry and insult — all more or less outraged and dishonoured! The last beams of day were now faintly streaming through the painted windows in the high vaults above me: the lower parts of the abbey were already wrapped in the obscurity of twilight. The chapels and aisles grew darker and darker. The effigies of the kings faded into shadows; the marble figures of the monuments assumed strange shapes in the uncertain light; the evening breeze crept through the aisles like the cold breath of the grave; and even the distant footfall of a verger, traversing the Poet's Corner, had something strange and dreary in its sound. I slowly retraced my morning's walk, and as I passed out at the portal of the cloisters, the door, closing with a jarring noise behind me, filled the whole building with echoes.

I endeavoured to form some arrangement in my mind of the objects I had been contemplating, but found they were already falling into indistinctness and confusion. Names, inscriptions, trophies, had all become confounded in my recollection, though I had scarcely taken my foot from off the threshold. What, thought I, is this vast assemblage of sepulchres but a treasury of humiliation; a huge pile of re-iterated homilies on the emptiness of renown, and the certainty of oblivion? It is, indeed, the empire of Death; his great shadowy palace; where he sits in state, mocking at the relics of human glory, and spreading dust and forgetfulness on the monuments of princes. How idle a boast, after all, is the immortality of a name! Time is ever silently turning over his pages; we are too much engrossed by the story of the present, to think of the characters and anecdotes that gave interest to the past; and each age is a volume thrown aside to be speedily forgotten. The idol of to-day pushes the hero of yesterday out of our recollection; and will, in turn, be supplanted by his successor of to-morrow. "Our fathers," says Sir Thomas Brown, "find their graves in our short memories, and sadly tell us how we may be buried in our survivors'." History fades into fable; fact becomes clouded with doubt and controversy; the inscription moulders from the tablet; the statue falls from the pedestal. Columns, arches, pyramids, what are they but heaps of sand—and their epitaphs, but characters written in the dust? What is the security of the tomb, or the perpetuity of an embalmment? The remains of Alexander the Great have been scattered to the wind, and his empty sarcophagus is now the mere curiosity of a museum. "The Egyptian mummies, which Cambyses or time hath spared, avarice now consumeth; Mizraim cures wounds, and Pharaoh is sold for balsams."

What then is to insure this pile, which now towers above me, from sharing the fate of mightier mausoleums? The time must come when its gilded vaults, which now spring so loftily, shall lie in rubbish beneath the feet; when, instead of the sound of melody and praise, the wind shall whistle through the broken arches, and the owl hoot from the shattered tower—when the garish sunbeam shall break into these gloomy mansions of death; and the ivy twine round the fallen column; and the fox-glove hang its blossoms about the nameless urn, as if in mockery of the dead. Thus man passes away; his name perishes from record and recollection; his history is as a tale that is told, and his very monument becomes a ruin.

Oliver Goldsmith: St. Paul's

Oliver Goldsmith (1730-1774) wrote a series of essays printed in the Public Ledger as "Chinese Letters," gently satirizing English ways through the eyes of an imaginary Chinese gentleman writing home from London. The following essay is one of these letters. St. Paul's is one of the most famous landmarks in London. Prince Hal said of Falstaff, "This oily rascal is as well known as St. Paul's." Since Goldsmith's day, Paul's Cross, an open-air pulpit, has been added, and many other famous figures, such as Kitchener and T.E. Lawrence, have been buried here.

Some time since I sent thee, O holy disciple of Confucius, an account of the grand abbey, or mausoleum, of the kings and heroes of this nation. I have since been introduced to a temple not so ancient, but far superior in beauty and magnificence. In this, which is the most considerable of the empire, there are no pompous inscriptions, no flattery paid the dead, but all is elegant and awfully simple. There are, however, a few rags hung round the walls, which have, at a vast expense, been taken from the enemy in the present war. The silk of which they are composed, when new, might be valued at half a string of copper money in China; yet this wise people fitted out a fleet and an army in order to seize them, though now grown old, and scarcely capable of being patched up into a handkerchief. By this conquest the English are said to have gained, and the French to have lost, much honor. Is the honor of European nations placed only in tattered silk?

In this temple I was permitted to remain during the whole service; and were you not already acquainted with the religion of the English, you might from my description be inclined to believe them as grossly idolatrous as the disciples of Lao. The idol which they seem to address strides like a colossus over the door of the inner temple, which here, as with the Jews, is esteemed the most sacred part of the building. Its oracles are delivered in a hundred various tones, which seem to inspire the worshipers with enthusiasm and awe. An old woman, who appeared to be the priestess, was employed in various attitudes as she felt the inspiration. When it began to speak, all the people remained fixed in silent attention, nodding assent, looking approbation, appearing highly edified by those sounds which to a stranger might seem inarticulate and unmeaning.

When the idol had done speaking, and the priestess had locked up its lungs with a key, observing almost all the company leaving the temple, I concluded the service was over, and, taking my hat, was going to walk away with the crowd, when I was stopped by the Man in Black, who assured me that the ceremony had scarcely yet begun.

"What!" cried I. "Do I not see almost the whole body of worshipers leaving the church? Would you persuade me that such numbers who profess religion and mortality would, in this shameless manner, quit the temple before the service was concluded? You surely mistake; not even the Kalmouks would be guilty of such an indecency, though all the object of their worship was but a joint-stool."

My friend seemed to blush for his countrymen, assuring me that those whom I saw running away were only a parcel of musical blockheads, whose passion was merely for sounds, and whose heads were as empty as a fiddle-case. "Those who remain behind," says he, "are the true religious. They make use of music to warm their hearts, and to lift them to a proper pitch of rapture. Examine their behavior, and you will

St. Paul's Cathedral

confess there are some among us who practice true devotion."

I now looked round me as he directed, but saw nothing of that fervent devotion which he had promised. One of the worshipers appeared to be ogling the company through a glass. Another was fervent, not in addresses to heaven, but to his mistress; a third whispered; a fourth took snuff; and the priest himself, in a drowsy tone, read over the "duties" of the day.

"Bless my eyes!" cried I, as I happened to look toward the door, "what do I see? One of the worshipers fallen fast asleep, and actually sunk down on his cushion! He is now enjoying the benefit of a trance; or does he receive the influence of some mysterious vision ?"

"Alas! alas!" replied my companion. "No such thing. He has only had the misfortune of eating too hearty a dinner, and finds it impossible to keep his eyes open."

Turning to another part of the temple, I perceived a young lady just in the same circumstances and attitude. "Strange!" cried I. "Can she too have overeaten herself?"

"Oh, fie!" replied my friend, "You now grow censorious. She grow drowsey from eating too much! That would be profanation. She only sleeps now from having sat up all night at a brag party."

"Turn me where I will, then," says I, "I can perceive no single symptom of devotion among the worshipers, except from that old woman in the corner, who sits groaning behind the long sticks of a mourning fan. She indeed seems greatly edified with what she hears."

Ay," replied my friend, "I knew we should find some to catch you. I know her; that is the deaf lady who lives in the cloisters."

In short, the remissness of behavior in almost all the worshipers, and some even of the guardians, struck me with surprise. I had been taught to believe that none were ever promoted to offices in the temple but men remarkable for their superior sanctity, learning, and rectitude; that there was no such thing heard of as persons being introduced into the church merely to oblige a senator, or provide for the younger branch of a noble family. I expected, as their minds were continually set upon heavenly things, to see their eyes directed there also, and hoped from their behavior to perceive their inclinations corresponding with their duty. But I am since informed that some are appointed to preside over temples they never visit, and, while they receive all the money, are contented with letting others do all the good. — Adieu.

Max Beerbohm:
Madame Tussaud

Max Beerbohm (1872-1956) succeeded George Bernard
Shaw as drama critic of the Saturday Review (London). He
was a master of wit and a caricaturist of great flair. In a
"moment of boredom and a desire for diversion," he strayed
to Madame Tussaud's waxworks on Marylebone Road. The
waxworks were brought to England in 1802 by a Swiss woman
who had been imprisoned during the French Revolution.
New figures of celebrities are added constantly to the exhibit
which has become a London landmark. The waxwork's
Chamber of Horrors has supplied grist to many a
scriptwriter's mill; but only on the screen does a wax figure
move an eyeball at midnight.

To plume one's self on a negative virtue, is surely the
cheapest form of self-righteousness, and I am not puffed up
when I declare that I never was "one of those miserable
males" who are ever seeking "sensations" and "experiences."
Indeed, I have often suspected that these seekers are but the
figment of certain philosophic brains. We all, naturally, have
moments of boredom and the desire for diversion. In such a
moment, lately, I myself did stray beyond the portal of a
scarlet edifice in the Marylebone Road and did wander
among wax-works. My visit may have been a "sensation" or
an "experience"or both, but it was not at all nice. In future I
shall stick to ennui.

Max Beerbohm

What is it that pervades this congress of barren effigies? Why is their atmosphere so sinister, so subtly exhaustive? For all creatures, it is said, life ebbs lowest and death's meridian is in those chill, still intervals before the sun's relapse or resurrection. I can well imagine that no invalid, laid in either interval among these wax-works, could survive for many minutes. They frightened me, I remember, when I was a little child and was taken to see them as a treat. In a sense, they frightened me again, yesterday. But my fear, when I came among them, did not arise from any notion that they were real men and women, bewitched into an awful calm. I could have cried to be taken home. Nay, I could not tear myself from their company. Powerless of escape, as in a dream, I must needs wander on, pausing before each one of those cadaverous and ignoble dolls, hating the tallowy faces and glass eyes that stared back at me; the rusty clothes; the smooth, nailless, little hands. I wished to Heaven I had never come into the place, yet must I needs stay there. The orchestra, playing lively tunes, did but intensify the gloom and horror of the exhibition. One would prefer no music in a sarcophagus. Why were they ranged here, these dolls? What fascination had they? They were not life-like. They gave me no illusion.

I remembered how Ouida, in one of her earlier books, had told us of one who came to the dim hall of some Florentine villa, gazing round at the pagan statues that were there, had fancied himself in the presence of the immortal gods, and had abased himself before them. Could any man, I wondered, entering Madame Tussaud's initial chamber, fancy that the old Kings and Queens of England had come to life? Mrs. Markham being his sole authority for most of their faces, he would not be hampered by any positive conceptions. For aught one knows, Richard Coeur de Lion may have had some such face as yonder person on the dais, and King Stephen's image may be the image of King Stephen. But oh, what stiff and inadequate absurdities! That fatuous puppet, called Mr. Gladstone, in the next room, is scarcely less convincing. And even when the familiar features of some man or woman have been moulded correctly, how little one cares how futile it all seems! The figures are animated with no

Street, walk briskly through the forecourt — pigeon-haunted, as Mr. Muirhead observes — and dive under the allegorical sculptures, feeling as certain as Westmacott himself of the Progress of Humanity; and as I go, I tell myself that this time there shall be no shirking, no incurious idling about and then a sudden bolt for tea and tobacco; I will be a good Museum man, a visitor inspired by a little of that Muirhead spirit. (After all, I possess his *Guide to London*. A man left it in my rooms at Cambridge and I have kept it ever since.) In the old novels, the hero frequently took the heroine round the museums and galleries, and astonished her by the extent of his knowledge and the power he had of making everything live. "Look at this," he would say, pointing to half a Grecian foot, a Roman hand, the bottom of an Egyptian vase, or the remains of a Babylonian water-jug; and then he would sketch lightly the whole background of the civilization, the remote and enchanting past, from which this object came. That is the kind of man I should like to be when I visit one of these places. And I never pass beneath that colonnaded main façade without telling myself very firmly that this time there must be no nonsense.

If there was a little room somewhere in the British Museum that contained only about twenty exhibits and good lighting, easy chairs, and a notice imploring you to smoke, I believe I should become a museum man. I should have time to look at something properly, to meditate over it. As it is, however, I wander from room to room, floor to floor, in a kind of uneasy dream. I begin to feel like a ghost as I flit past those rows of gilded coffins, down those long aisles flanked by colossal-winged lions and man-headed bulls. I do not say that this is altogether unpleasant. Perhaps extreme old age is something like this, when you drift like a dead leaf through the winter of your years, and your very grandchildren and the younger members of the club seem as remote and fantastic as winged lions and man-headed bulls. Perhaps when we die, we slip quietly into this museum atmosphere, into regions equally quiet and shadowy, warm but sunless, where things out of Nineveh loom gigantically and gems from ancient Crete glitter faintly in the dusk, and it is all one, a dream of life in which Apollo and Aphrodite are stony, dumb—until at last a bell rings and we rush out to tea and Great Russell Street, or find ourselves kicking and mewing on another planet.

Sometimes in the British Museum I entertain myself with a fancy that I have been projected into some Socialistic and Utopian State of the future. The very air, which appears to have been warmed and disinfected in the basement, sustains this fancy. There is Utopia in your nostrils. Then the officials, the uniformed attendants, all help. The visitors as a whole do nothing to destroy the illusion. Different as they are in appearance and manner, they all have the look, intelligent but docile, of good citizens, men and women who would fit snugly into a Socialistic State. Frequently their hair is wild, but all else about them is tame enough. You have a feeling that most of them are quietly pleased to have left behind them the roaring chaos of Tottenham Court Road and New Oxford Street. Their faces light up with a faint gleam of pleasure and interest the moment they catch sight of these ordered rooms, in which everything is so neatly ticketed and so nicely dead. They happily tiptoe forward, safe in a little world where nothing has escaped the officials and the catalogue. With a sober pleasure they follow the elderly lecturer, who talks of Pericles and Pheidias and points to a tiny Parthenon in a glass case, a Parthenon that will never be disturbed by a wind whistling over from the Ægean, by the shouts of enraged citizens, by the glitter of foreign shields and ships. Even the children here are all dressed alike, subdued and earnest, and have to march forward two by two, under the eye of a schoolmistress. And shouting, singing, fighting, drinking, and making love seem to be strange antics of long, long ago, early habits of mankind that may be discovered from a study of the specimens and are duly noted in the catalogue. Reproductions of such specimens may be obtained, you feel, by students engaged in genuine research by application to the proper authorities. And so the fanciful evidence accumulates, though as none of us happens to know what the well-drilled Socialistic and Utopian State will be like, obviously such evidence is not worth much. A fancy, that is all.

I was there the other day, and drifted about as idly and
foolishly as ever, acquiring no information of any kind. No,
that is not strictly true. I made one discovery, relating to the
age of the official type, the born Civil Service man. How long
has this type existed? I do not know, but now I can go back
with confidence to 3300 B.C. He was alive then, because
there is a solid and unmistakable image of him in the British
Museum, labelled "Sumerian official 1st Dynasty of Ur."
There he is to the life, looking as if at any moment he will
slowly open those large grey heavy-lidded eyes, stare at us
solemnly for a minute, and then declare that "really he hasn't
the least idea." His forehead is small and slopes back sharply;
there is no mistaking the supercilious cut of the large
eye-socket; his eyebrows must have been thin and always
slightly raised, and the eyes themselves must have been of
that bulging stupid kind, his nose juts forward well, a perky
triangle; and his mouth and chin are small and mean. His
arms are folded at ease, and he presents a figure of repose.
He is waiting there until somebody has filled in the proper
form. That somebody has been dead these five thousand
years, but he does not know it, and even if he knew he would
not care. He is very happy here in the Museum. And nobody
will persuade me that I do not know that man, though few
people can know less about the 1st Dynasty of Ur than I do.
But I am convinced that that Dynasty had its Oxford
somewhere and that this man went there and sneaked off
with a First and a piffling essay prize, and then hurried into
the Civil Service and after that never hurried again. If I had
stayed another minute in front of him, he would have
referred me to another department. Undoubtedly he likes the
Museum, but he would be happier still in Whitehall. One day
he will hear about Whitehall, and will then calmly get down
from his pedestal and go there. I shall not be very surprised
if, one day, I catch sight of him lunching at one of the more
exclusive clubs.

After leaving the Sumerian official, I only halted for
another minute, and that was on the landing of the mosaic
staircase, which offered me a most curious spectacle. A
number of little schoolgirls, in blue coats and red-ribboned

hats, filed past me on this landing, and I saw them against
the background of that colossal head of Rameses the Second,
which stands against the wall facing this landing. The head
was illuminated from below, and its vast spread of features
looked as if they had been newly transported from one of the
wilder Arabian Nights. Cutting across the lower half of this
nightmare face was a bobbing procession of little red-
ribboned straw hats. I knew at once that I should see nothing
more fantastic than that if I stayed for hours (unless, of
course, I remained all night, and then I do not know what
one might see), so off I went. As I stood for a moment at the
entrance, meeting the cold air as if for the first time, I
happened to glance to the left, and there I encountered the
level dark gaze of Hoa-Haka-Nana-Ia, from Easter Island,
that remotest and most mysterious of all islands. I asked him
who he was and what he was doing, standing quietly there in
the very heart of Bloomsbury, but he made no reply. He
merely looked at me — sardonically. I have a feeling that at
certain odd times, perhaps about two in the morning, he stirs
a little and quietly chuckles.

Henry James: London

As a young man, Henry James (1843-1916) made several trips to Europe. He settled in England permanently in 1876, became a British subject in 1915, and was awarded the Order of Merit a month before he died. In addition to his many novels he wrote several books of travels: Transatlantic Sketches, *1875;* Portrait of Places, *1883;* English Hours, *1905;* Italian Hours, *1909. His impressions reveal a spirit that examines and looks upon the world around with keen intelligence and a cultivated eye rather than with emotion, and a mind that seeks out the basic, unchanging aspects of a country and its people. The following section, called* London, *was published in* Century Magazine *in December, 1888.*

There is a certain evening that I count as virtually a first impression, —the end of a wet, black Sunday, twenty years ago, about the first of March. There had been an earlier vision, but it had turned to grey, like faded ink, and the occasion I speak of was a fresh beginning. No doubt I had mystic prescience of how fond of the murky modern Babylon I was one day to become; certain it is that as I look back I find every small circumstance of these hours of approach and arrival still as vivid as if the solemnity of an opening era had breathed upon it. The sense of approach was already almost intolerably strong at Liverpool, where, as I remember, the perception of the English character of everything was as acute as a surprise, though it could only be a surprise without a

Henry James

shock. It was expectation exquisitely gratified, super-
abundantly confirmed. There was a find of wonder indeed
that England should be as English as, for my entertainment,
she took the trouble to be; but the wonder would have been
greater, and all the pleasure absent, if the sensation had not
been violent. It seems to sit there again like a visiting
presence, as it sat opposite to me at breakfast at a small table
in a window of the old coffee-room of the Adelphi Hotel — the
unextended (as it then was), the unimproved, the unblush-
ingly local Adelphi. Liverpool is not a romantic city, but that
smoky Saturday returns to me as a supreme success, measured
by its association with the kind of emotion in the hope of
which, for the most part, we betake ourselves to far countries.

It assumed this character at an early hour — or rather,
indeed, twenty-four hours before — with the sight, as one
looked across the wintry ocean, of the strange, dark, lonely
freshness of the coast of Ireland. Better still, before we could
come up to the city, were the black steamers knocking about
in the yellow Mersey, under a sky so low that they seemed to
touch it with their funnels, and in the thickest, windiest light.
Spring was already in the air, in the town; there was no rain,
but there was still less sun — one wondered what had become,
on this side of the world, of the big white splotch in the
heavens; and the grey mildness, shading away into black at
every pretext, appeared in itself a promise. This was how it
hung about me, between the window and the fire, in the
coffee-room of the hotel — late in the morning for breakfast,
as we had been long disembarking. The other passengers had
dispersed, knowingly catching trains for London (we had
only been a handful); I had the place to myself, and I felt as
if I had an exclusive property in the impression. I prolonged
it, I sacrificed to it, and it is perfectly recoverable now, with
the very taste of the national muffin, the creak of the waiter's
shoes as he came and went (could anything be so English as
this intensely professional back? it revealed a country of
tradition), and the rustle of the newspaper I was too excited
to read.

I continued to sacrifice for the rest of the day; it didn't
seem to me a sentient thing, as yet, to enquire into the means

of getting away. My curiosity must indeed have languished, for I found myself on the morrow in the slowest of Sunday trains, pottering up to London with an interruptedness which might have been tedious without the conversation of an old gentleman who shared the carriage with me and to whom my alien as well as comparatively youthful character had betrayed itself. He instructed me as to the sights of London and impressed upon me that nothing was more worthy of my attention than the great cathedral of St. Paul. "Have you seen St. Peter's in Rome? St. Peter's is more highly embellished, you know; but you may depend upon it that St. Paul's is the better building of the two." The impression I began with speaking of was, strictly, that of the drive from Euston, after dark, to Morley's Hotel in Trafalgar Square. It was not lovely — it was in fact rather horrible; but as I move again through dusky, tortuous miles, in the greasy four-wheeler to which my luggage had compelled me to commit myself, I recognise the first step in an initiation of which the subsequent stages were to abound in pleasant things. It is a kind of humiliation in the great city not to know where you are going, and Morley's Hotel was then, to my imagination, only a vague ruddy spot in the general immensity. The immensity was the great fact, and that was a charm; the miles of housetops and viaducts, the complication of junctions and signals through which the train made its way to the station had already given me the scale. The weather had turned to wet, and we went deeper and deeper into the Sunday night. The sheep in the fields, on the way from Liverpool, had shown in their demeanour a certain consciousness of the day; but this momentous cab-drive was an introduction to the rigidities of custom. The low black houses were inanimate as so many rows of coal-scuttles, save where at frequent corners, from a gin-shop, there was a flare of light more brutal still than the darkness. The custom of gin — that was equally rigid, and in this first impression the public-houses counted for much.

Morley's Hotel proved indeed to be a ruddy spot; brilliant, in my recollection, is the coffee-room fire, the hospitable mohogany, the sense that in the stupendous city this, at any rate for the hour, was a shelter and a point of view. My remembrance of the rest of the evening — I was probably very tired — is mainly a remembrance of a vast four-poster. My little bedroom-candle, set in its deep basin, caused this monument to project a huge shadow and to make me think, I scarce knew why, of *The Ingoldsby Legends*. If at a tolerably early hour the next day I found myself approaching St. Paul's, it was not wholly in obedience to the old gentleman in the railway-carriage; I had an errand in the City, and the City was doubtless prodigious. But what I mainly recall is the romantic consciousness of passing under the Temple Bar, and the way two lines of *Henry Esmond* repeated themselves in my mind as I drew near the masterpiece of Sir Christopher Wren. "The stout, red-faced woman" whom Esmond had seen tearing after the stag-hounds over the slopes at Windsor was not a bit like the effigy "which turns its stony back upon St. Paul's and faces the coaches struggling up Ludgate Hill." As I looked at Queen Anne over the apron of my hansom — she struck me as very small and dirty, and the vehicle ascended the mild incline without an effort — it was a thrilling thought that the statue had been familiar to the hero of the imcomparable novel. All history appeared to live again, and the continuity of things to vibrate through my mind.

To this hour, as I pass along the Strand, I take again the walk I took there that afternoon. I love the place to-day, and that was the commencement of my passion. It appeared to me to present phenomena, and to contain objects of every kind, of an inexhaustible interest, in particular it struck me as desirable and even indispensable that I should purchase most of the articles in most of the shops. My eyes rest with a certain tenderness on the places where I resisted and on those where I succumbed. The fragrance of Mr. Rimmel's establishment is again in my nostrils; I see the slim young lady (I hear her pronunciation) who waited upon me there. Sacred to me to-day is the particular aroma of the hair-wash that I bought of her. I pause before the granite portico of Exeter Hall (it was unexpectedly narrow and wedge-like), and it evokes a cloud of associations which are none the less impressive because they are vague; coming from I don't know where — from *Punch,* from Thackeray, from volumes of the *Illustrated London News* turned over in childhood; seeming connected with Mrs. Beecher Stowe and *Uncle Tom's Cabin.* Memorable is a rush I made into a glover's at Charing Cross — the one you pass, going eastward, just before you turn into the station; that, however, now that I think of it, must have been in the morning, as soon as I issued from the hotel. Keen within me was a sense of the importance of deflowering, of despoiling the shop.

A day or two later, in the afternoon, I found myself staring at my fire, in a lodging of which I had taken possession on foreseeing that I should spend some weeks in London. I had just come in, and, having attended to the distribution of my luggage, sat down to consider my habitation. It was on the ground floor, and the fading daylight reached it in a sadly damaged condition. It struck me as stuffy and unsocial, with its mouldy smell and its decoration of lithographs and wax-flowers — an impersonal black hole in the huge general blackness. The uproar of Piccadilly hummed away at the end of the street, and the rattle of a heartless hansom passed close to my ears. A sudden horror of the whole place came over me, like a tiger-pounce of homesickness which had been watching its moment. London was hideous, vicious, cruel, and above all overwhelming; whether or no she was "careful of the type," she was as indifferent as Nature herself to the single life. In the course of an hour I should have to go out to dinner, which was not supplied on the premises, and that effort assumed the form of a desperate and dangerous quest. It appeared to me that I would rather remain dinnerless, would rather even starve, than sally forth into the infernal town, where the natural fate of an obscure stranger would be to be trampled to death in Piccadilly and have his carcass thrown into the Thames. I did not starve, however, and I eventually attached myself by a hundred human links to the dreadful, delightful city. That momentary vision of its smeared face and stony heart has remained memorable to me, but I am happy to say that I can easily summon up others.

II

It is, no doubt, not the taste of every one, but for the real London-lover the mere immensity of the place is a large part of its savour. A small London would be an abomination, as it fortunately is an impossibility, for the idea and the name are beyond everything an expression of extent and number. Practically, of course, one lives in a quarter, in a plot; but in imagination and by a constant mental act of reference the accommodated haunter enjoys the whole — and it is only of him that I deem it worth while to speak. He fancies himself, as they say, for being a particle in so unequalled an aggregation; and its immeasurable circumference, even though unvisited and lost in smoke, gives him the sense of a social, an intellectual margin. There is a luxury in the knowledge that he may come and go without being noticed, even when his comings and goings have no nefarious end. I don't mean by this that the tongue of London would indeed be worthy of a chapter by itself. But the eyes which at least in some measure feed its activity are fortunately for the common advantage solicited at any moment by a thousand different objects. If the place is big, everything it contains is certainly not so; but this may at least be said — that if small questions play a part there, they play it without illusions about its importance. There are too many quesitons, small or great; and each day, as it arrives, leads its children, like a kind of mendicant mother, by the hand. Therefore perhaps the most general characteristic is the absence of insistence. Habits and inclinations flourish and fall, but intensity is never one of them. The spirit of the great city is not analytic, and, as they come up, subjects rarely receive at its hands a treatment drearily earnest or tastelessly thorough. There are not many — of those of which London disposes with the assurance begotten of its large experience — that wouldn't lend themselves to a tenderer manipulation elsewhere. It takes a very great affair, a turn of the Irish screw or a divorce case lasting many days, to be fully threshed out. The mind of Mayfair, when it aspires to show what it really can do, lives in the hopes of a new divorce case, and an indulgent providence — London is positively in certain ways the spoiled child of the world — abundantly recognises this particular aptitude and humours the whim.

The compensation is that material does arise; that there is a great variety, if not morbid subtlety; and that the whole of the procession of events and topics passes across your stage. For the moment I am speaking of the inspiration there may be in the sense of far frontiers; the London-lover loses himself in the swelling consciousness, delights in the idea that the town which encloses him is after all only a paved country, a state by itself. This is his condition of mind quite as much if he be an adoptive as if he be a matter-of-course son. I am by no means sure even that he need be of Anglo-Saxon race and have inherited the birthright of English speech; though, on the other hand, I make no doubt that these advantages minister greatly to closeness of allegiance. The great city spreads her dusky mantle over innumerable races and creeds, and I believe there is scarcely a known form of worship that has not some temple there (have I not attended at the Church of Humanity, in Lamb's Conduit, in company with an American lady, a vague old gentleman, and several seamstresses?) or any communion of men that has not some club or guild. London is indeed an epitome of the round world, and just as it is a commonplace to say that there is nothing one can't "get" there, so it is equally true that there is nothing one may not study at first hand.

One doesn't test these truths every day, but they form part of the air one breathes (and welcome, says the London-hater, — for there be such perverse reasoners, — to the pestilent compound). They colour the thick, dim distances which in my opinion are the most romantic town-vistas in the world; they mingle with the troubled light to which the straight, ungarnished aperture in one's dull, undistinctive house-front affords a passage and which makes an interior of friendly corners, mysterious tones, and unbetrayed ingenuities, as well as with the low, magnificent medium of the sky, where the smoke and fog and the weather in general, the strangely undefined hour of the day and season of the year, the emanations of industries and the reflection of furnaces, the red gleams and blurs that may or may not be of sunset — as

you never see any *source* of radiance, you can't in the least
tell — all hang together in a confusion, a complication, a
shifting but irremoveable canopy. They form the undertone
of the deep, perpetual voice of the place. One remembers
them when one's loyalty is on the defensive; when it is a
question of introducing as many striking features as possible
into the list of fine reasons one has sometimes to draw up,
that eloquent catalogue with which one confronts the hostile
indictment — the array of *other* reasons which may easily be as
long as one's arm. According to these other reasons it
plausibly and conclusively stands that, as a place to be happy
in, London will never do. I don't say it is necessary to meet so
absurd an allegation except for one's personal complacency.
If indifference, in so gorged an organism, is still livelier than
curiosity, you may avail yourself of your own share in it
simply to feel that since such and such a person doesn't care
for real richness, so much the worse for such a such a person.
But once in a while the best believer recognises the impulse to
set his religion in order, to sweep the temple of his thoughts
and trim the sacred lamp. It is at such hours as this that he
reflects with elation that the British capital is the particular
spot in the world which communicates the greatest sense of
life.

III

The reader will perceive that I do not shrink even from the
extreme concession of speaking of our capital as British, and
this in a shameless connnection with the question of loyalty
on the part of an adoptive son. For I hasten to explain that if
half the source of one's interest in it comes from feeling that
it is the property and even the home of the human
race, — Hawthorne, that best of Americans, says so somewhere, and places it in this sense side by side with
Rome, — one's appreciation of it is really a large sympathy, a
comprehensive love of humanity. For the sake of such a
charity as this one may stretch one's allegiance; and the most
alien of the cockneyfied, though he may bristle with every
protest at the intimation that England has set its stamp upon

him, is free to admit with conscious pride that he had
submitted to Londonisation. It is a real stroke of luck for a
particular country that the capital of the human race
happens to be British. Surely every other people would have it
theirs if they could. Whether the English deserve to hold it
any longer might be an interesting field of enquiry; but -as
they have not yet let it slip, the writer of these lines professes
without scruple that the arrangement is to his personal taste.
For, after all, if the sense of life is greatest there, it is a sense
of the life of people of our consecrated English speech. It is
the headquarters of that strangely elastic tongue; and I make
this remark with a full sense of the terrible way in which the
idiom is misused by the populace in general, than whom it
has been given to few races to impart to conversation less of
the charm of tone. For a man of letters who endeavours to
cultivate, however modestly, the medium of Shakespeare and
Milton, of Hawthorne and Emerson, who cherishes the notion
of what it has achieved and what it may even yet achieve,
London must ever have a great illustrative and suggestive
value, and indeed a kind of sanctity. It is the single place in
which most readers, most possible lovers, are gathered
together; it is the most inclusive public and the largest social
incarnation of the language, of the tradition. Such a
personage may well let it go for this, and leave the German
and the Greek to speak for themselves, to express the grounds
of *their* predilection, presumably very different.

When a social product is so vast and various, it may be
approached on a thousand different sides, and liked and
disliked for a thousand different reasons. The reasons of
Piccadilly are not those of Camden Town, nor are the
curiosities and discouragements of Kilburn the same as those
of Westminster and Lambeth. The reasons of Piccadilly — I
mean the friendly ones — are those of which, as a general
thing, the rooted visitor remains most conscious; but it must
be confessed that even these, for the most part, do not lie
upon the surface. The absence of style, or rather of the
intention of style, is certainly the most general characteristic
of the face of London. To cross to Paris under this impression
is to find one's self surrounded with far other standards.
There everything reminds you that the idea of beautiful

and stately arrangement has never been out of fashion, that the art of composition has always been at work or at play. Avenues and squares, gardens and quays, have been distributed for effect, and to-day the splendid city reaps the accumulation of all this ingenuity. The result is not in every quarter interesting, and there is a tiresome monotony of the "fine" and the symmetrical, above all, of the deathly passion for making things "to match." On the other hand the whole air of the place is architectural. On the banks of the Thames it is a tremendous chapter of accidents — the London-lover has to confess to the existence of miles upon miles of the dreariest, stodgiest commonness. Thousands of acres are covered by low black houses of the cheapest construction, without ornament, without grace, without character or even identity. In fact there are many, even in the best quarters, in all the region of Mayfair and Belgravia, of so paltry and inconvenient, especially of so diminutive a type (those that are let in lodgings — such poor lodgings as they make — may serve as an example), that you wonder what peculiarly limited domestic need they are constructed to meet. The great misfortune of London to the eye (it is true that this remark applies much less to the City), is the want of elevation. There is no architectural impression without a certain degree of height, and the London street-vista has none of that sort of pride.

All the same, if there be not the intention, there is at least the accident, of style, which, if one looks at it in a friendly way, appears to proceed from three sources. One of these is simply the general greatness, and the manner in which that makes a difference for the better in any particular spot; so that, though you may often perceive yourself to be in a shabby corner, it never occurs to you that this is the end of it. Another is the atmosphere, with its magnificent mystifications, which flatters and superfuses, makes everything brown, rich, dim, vague, magnifies distances and minimises details, confirms the inference of vastness by suggesting that, as the great city makes everything, it makes its own system of weather and its own optical laws. The last is the congregation of the parks, which constitute an ornament not esewhere to be matched, and give the place a superiority that none of its uglinesses overcome. They spread themselves with such a luxury of space in the centre of the town that they form a part of the impression of any walk, of almost any view, and, with an audacity altogether their own, make a pastoral landscape under the smoky sky. There is no mood of the rich London climate that is not becoming to them — I have seen them look delightfully romamtic, like parks in novels, in the wettest winter — and there is scarcely a mood of the appreciative resident to which they have not something to say. The high things of London, which here and there peep over them, only make the spaces vaster by reminding you that you are, after all, not in Kent or Yorkshire; and these things, whatever they be — rows of "eligible" dwellings, towers of churches, domes of institutions — take such an effective grey-blue tint that a clever water-colourist would seem to have put them in for pictorial reasons.

The view from the bridge over the Serpentine has an extraordinary nobleness, and it has often seemed to me that the Londerer, twitted with his low standard, may point to it with every confidence. In all the town-scenery of Europe there can be few things so fine; the only reproach it is open to is that it begs the question by seeming — in spite of its being the pride of five millions of people — not to belong to a town at all. The towers of Notre Dame, as they rise in Paris from the island that divides the Seine, present themselves no more impressively than those of Westminster as you see them looking doubly far beyond the shining stretch of Hyde Park water. Equally delectable is the large river-like manner in which the Serpentine opens away between its wooded shores. Just after you have crossed the bridge (whose very banisters, old and ornamental, of yellowish-brown stone, I am particularly fond of), you enjoy on your left, through the gate of Kensington Gardens as you go towards Bayswater, an altogether enchanting vista — a foot-path over the grass, which loses itself beneath the scattered oaks and elms exactly as if the place were a "chase." There could be nothing less like London in general than this particular morsel, and yet it takes London, of all cities, to give you such an impression of the country.

IV

It takes London to put you in the way of a purely rustic walk from Notting Hill to Whitehall. You may traverse this immense distance — a most comprehensive diagonal — altogether on soft, fine turf, amid the song of birds, the bleat of lambs, the ripple of ponds, the rustle of admirable trees. Frequently have I wished that, for the sake of such a daily luxury and of exercise made romantic, I were a Government clerk living, in snug domestic conditions, in a Pembridge villa, — let me suppose, — and having my matutinal desk in Westminster. I should turn into Kensington Gardens at their northwest limit, and I should have my choice of a hundred pleasant paths to the gates of Hyde Park. In Hyde Park I should follow the water-side, or the Row, or any other fancy of the occasion; liking best, perhaps, after all, the Row in its morning mood, with the mist hanging over the dark-red course, and the scattered early riders taking an identity as the soundless gallop brings them nearer. I am free to admit that in the Season, at the conventional hours, the Row becomes a weariness (save perhaps just for a glimpse once a year, to remind one's self how much it is like Du Maurier); the preoccupied citizen eschews it and leaves it for the most part to the gaping barbarian. I speak of it now from the point of view of the pedestrian; but for the rider as well it is at its best when he passes either too early or too late. Then, if he be not bent on comparing it to its disadvantage with the bluer and the boskier alleys of the Bois de Boulogne, it will not be spoiled by the fact that, with its surface that looks like tan, its barriers like those of the ring on which the clown stands to hold up the hoop to the young lady, its empty benches and chairs, its occasional orange-peel, its mounted policemen patrolling at intervals like expectant supernumeraries, it offers points of real contact with a circus whose lamps are out. The sky that bends over it is frequently not a bad imitation of the dingy tent of such an establishment. The ghosts of past cavalcades seem to haunt the foggy arena, and somehow they are better company than the mashers and elongated beauties of current seasons. It is not without

interest to remember that most of the salient figures of
English society during the present century—and English
society means, or rather has hitherto meant, in a large
degree, English history—have bobbed in the saddle between
Apsley House and Queen's Gate. You may call the roll if you
care to, and the air will be thick with dumb voices and dead
names, like that of some Roman amphitheatre.

It is doubtless a signal proof of being a London-lover
quand même that one should undertake an apology for so
bungled an attempt at a great public place as Hyde Park
Corner. It is certain that the improvements and embellish-
ments recently enacted there have only served to call further
attention to the poverty of the elements and to the fact that
this poverty is terribly illustrative of general conditions. The
place is the beating heart of the great West End, yet its main
features are a shabby, stuccoed hospital, the low park-gates,
in their neat but unimposing frame, the drawing-room
windows of Apsley House and of the commonplace frontages
on the little terrace beside it; to which must be added, of
course, the only item in the whole prospect that is in the least
monumental—the arch spanning the private road beside the
gardens of Buckingham Palace. This structure is now
bereaved of the rueful effigy which used to surmount it—the
Iron Duke in the guise of a tin soldier—and has not been
enriched by the transaction as much as might have been
expected. There is a fine view of Piccadilly and Knights-
bridge, and of the noble mansions, as the house-agents call
them, of Grosvenor Place, together with a sense of generous
space beyond the vulgar little railing of the Green Park; but,
except for the impression that there would be room for
something better, there is nothing in all this that speaks to
the imagination: almost as much as the grimy desert of
Trafalgar Square the prospect conveys the idea of an
opportunity wasted.

None the less has it on a fine day in spring an
expressiveness of which I shall not pretend to explain the
source further than by saying that the flood of life and luxury
is immeasurably great there. The edifices are mean, but the
social stream itself is monumental, and to an observer not

purely stolid there is more excitement and suggestion than I can give a reason for in the long, distributed waves of traffic, with the steady policemen making their rhythm, which roll together and apart for so many hours. Then the great, dim city becomes bright and kind, the pall of smoke turns into a veil of haze carelessly worn, the air is coloured and almost scented by the presence of the biggest society in the world, and most of the things that meet the eye—or perhaps I should say more of them, for the most in London is, no doubt, ever the realm of the dingy—present themselves as "well appointed." Everything shines more or less, from the window-panes to the dog-collars. So it all looks, with its myriad variations and qualifications, to one who surveys it over the apron of a hansom, while that vehicle of vantage, better than any box at the opera, spurts and slackens with the current.

It is not in a hansom, however, that we have figured our punctual young man, whom we must not desert as he fares to the southeast, and who has only to cross Hyde Park Corner to find his way all grassy again. I have a weakness for the convenient, familiar, treeless, or almost treeless, expanse of the Green Park and the friendly part it plays as a kind of encouragement to Piccadilly. I am so fond of Piccadilly that I am grateful to any one or anything that does it a service, and nothing is more worthy of appreciation than the southward look it is permitted to enjoy just after it passes Devonshire House—a sweep of horizon which it would be difficult to match among other haunts of men, and thanks to which, of a summer's day, you may spy, beyond the browsed pastures of the foreground and middle distance, beyond the cold chimneys of Buckingham Palace and the towers of Westminster and the swarming river-side and all the southern parishes, the hard modern twinkle of the roof of the Crystal Palace.

If the Green Park is familiar, there is still less of the exclusive in its pendant, as one may call it,—for it literally hangs from the other, down the hill,—the remnant of the former garden of the queer, shabby old palace whose black, inelegant face stares up St. James's Street. This popular resort

has a great deal of character, but I am free to confess that
much of its character comes from its nearness to the
Westminster slums. It is a park of intimacy, and perhaps the
most democratic corner of London, in spite of its being in the
royal and military quarter and close to all kinds of stateliness.
There are few hours of the day when a thousand smutty
children are not sprawling over it, and the unemployed lie
thick on the grass and cover the benches with a brotherhood
of greasy corduroys. If the London parks are the
drawing-rooms and clubs of the poor, — that is of those poor
(I admit it cuts down the number) who live near enough to
them to reach them, — these particular grass-plots and alleys
may be said to constitute the very *salon* of the slums.

I know not why, being such a region of greatness, — great
towers, great names, great memories; at the foot of the
Abbey, the Parliament, the fine fragment of Whitehall, with
the quarters of the sovereign right and left, — but the edge of
Westminster evokes as many associations of misery as of
empire. The neighbourhood has been much purified of late,
but it still contains a collection of specimens — though it is far
from unique in this — of the low, black element. The air
always seems to me heavy and thick, and here more than
elsewhere one hears old England — the panting, smoke-stained
Titan of Matthew Arnold's fine poem — draw her deep breath
with effort. In fact one is nearer to her heroic lungs, if those
organs are figured by the great pinnacled and fretted
talking-house on the edge of the river. But this same dense
and conscious air plays such everlasting tricks to the eye that
the Foreign Office, as you see it from the bridge, often looks
romantic, and the sheet of water it overhangs poetic —
suggests an Indian palace bathing its feet in the Ganges. If
our pedestrian achieves such a comparison as this he has
nothing left but to go on to his work — which he will find close
at hand. He will have come the whole way from the far
northwest on the green — which is what was to be
demonstrated.

V

I feel as if I were taking a tone almost of boastfulness, and
no doubt the best way to consider the matter is simply to
say — without going into the treachery of reasons — that, for

one's self, one likes this part or the other. Yet this course
would not be unattended with danger, inasmuch as at the
end of a few such professions we might find ourselves
committed to a tolerance of much that is deplorable. London
is so clumsy and so brutal, and has gathered together so many
of the darkest sides of life, that it is almost ridiculous to talk
of her as a lover talks of his mistress, and almost frivolous to
appear to ignore her disfigurements and cruelties. She is like
a mighty ogress who devours human flesh; but to me it is a
mitigating circumstance — that the ogress herself is human. It
is not in wantonness that she fills her maw, but to keep
herself alive and do her tremendous work. She has no time
for fine discriminations, but after all she is as good-natured
as she is huge, and the more you stand up to her, as the
phrase is, the better she takes the joke of it. It is mainly when
you fall on your face before her that she gobbles you up. She
heeds little what she takes, so long as she has her stint, and
the smallest push to the right or the left will divert her
wavering bulk from one form of prey to another. It is not to
be denied that the heart tends to grow hard in her company;
but she is a capital antidote to the morbid, and to live with
her successfully is an education of the temper, a consecration
of one's private philosophy. She gives one a surface for which
in a rough world one can never to be too thankful. She may
take away reputations, but she forms character. She teaches
her victims not to "mind," and the great danger for them is
perhaps that they shall learn the lesson too well....

Robert Louis Stevenson: Edinburgh

It is natural that Stevenson (1850-1894) should write of Edinburgh, as he was born there and studied to be an engineer at the university. He gave up engineering for the law, the law for writing. In describing Edinburgh, Stevenson conveys the quality of the city, but his condemnation of the climate must be considered in relation to his lifelong struggle against tuberculosis. Since his account, kilts, bagpipes, tartans, and flannel petticoats have largely given way to modern attire. In his lifelong search for health, he traveled extensively; these voyages resulted in many travel books, such as Travels with a Donkey in the Cévennes. *The writer ultimately reached America, his first trip by steerage, and in 1879, on a visit to California, he married.* Treasure Island *made him famous. Stevenson later (1889) sailed to the South Seas and became a planter in Samoa.*

The ancient and famous metropolis of the North sits overlooking a windy estuary from the slope and summit of three hills. No situation could be more commanding for the head city of a kingdom; none better chosen for noble prospects. From her tall precipice and terraced gardens she looks far and wide on the sea and broad champaigns. To the east you may catch at sunset the spark of the May light-house, where the Firth expands into the German Ocean; and away to the west, over all the carse of Stirling, you can see the first snows upon Ben Ledi.

But Edinburgh pays cruelly for her high seat in one of the vilest climates under heaven. She is liable to be beaten upon by all the winds that blow, to be drenched with rain, to be buried in cold sea fogs out of the east, and powdered with the snow as it comes flying southward from the Highland hills. The weather is raw and boisterous in winter, shifty and ungenial in summer, and a downright meteorological purgatory in the spring. The delicate die early, and I, as a survivor, among bleak winds and plumping rain, have been sometimes tempted to envy them their fate. For all who love shelter and the blessings of the sun, who hate dark weather and perpetual tilting against squalls, there could scarcely be found a more unhomely and harassing place of residence. Many such aspire angrily after that Somewhere-else of the imagination, where all troubles are supposed to end. They lean over the great bridge which joins the New Town with the Old—that windiest spot, or high altar, in this northern temple of the winds and watch the trains smoking out from under them and vanishing into the tunnel on a voyage to brighter skies. Happy the passengers who shake off the dust of Edinburgh, and have heard for the last time the cry of the east wind among her chimney-tops! And yet the place establishes an interest in people's hearts; go where they will, they find no city of the same distinction; go where they will, they take a pride in their old home.

Venice, it has been said, differs from all other cities in the sentiment which she inspires. The rest may have admirers; she only, a famous fair one, counts lovers in her train. And, indeed, even by her kindest friends, Edinburgh is not considered in a similar sense. These like her for many reasons, not any one of which is satisfactory in itself. They like her whimsically, if you will, and somewhat as a virtuoso dotes upon his cabinet. Her attraction is romantic in the narrowest meaning of the term. Beautiful as she is, she is not so much beautiful as interesting. She is pre-eminently Gothic, and all the more so since she has set herself off with some Greek airs, and erected classic temples on her crags. In a word, and above all, she is a curiosity. The Palace of Holyrood has been left aside in the growth of Edinburgh, and stands grey and silent in a workman's quarter and among breweries and gas works. It is a house of many memories.

Great people of yore, kings and queens, buffoons and grave ambassadors, played their stately farce for centuries in Holyrood. Wars have been plotted, dancing has lasted deep into the night, murder has been done in its chambers. There Prince Charlie held his phantom levées, and in a very gallant manner represented a fallen dynasty for some hours. Now, all these things of clay are mingled with the dust, the king's crown itself is shown for sixpence to the vulgar; but the stone palace has outlived these changes. For fifty weeks together, it is no more than a show for tourists and a museum of old furniture; but on the fifty-first, behold the palace rewakened and mimicking its past. The Lord Commissioner, a kind of stage sovereign, sits among stage courtiers; a coach and six and clattering escort come and go before the gate; at night, the windows are lighted up, and its near neighbours, the workmen, may dance in their own houses to the palace music. And in this the palace is typical. There is a spark among the embers; from time to time the old volcano smokes. Edinburgh has but partly abdicated, and still wears, in parody, her metropolitan trappings. Half a capital and half a country town, the whole city leads a double existence; it has long traces of the one and flashes of the other; like the king of the Black Isles, it is half alive and half a monumental marble. There are armed men and cannon in the citadel overhead; you may see the troops marshalled on the high parade; and at night after the early winter even-fall, and in the morning before the laggard winter dawn, the wind carries abroad over Edinburgh the sound of drums and bugles. Grave judges sit bewigged in what was once the scene of imperial deliberations. Close by in the High Street perhaps the trumpets may sound about the stroke of noon; and you see a troop of citizens in tawdry masquerade; tabard above, heather-mixture trowser below, and the men themselves trudging in the mud among unsympathetic bystanders. The grooms of a well-appointed circus tread the streets with a better presence. And yet these are the Heralds and Pursuivants of Scotland, who are about to proclaim a new law of the United Kingdom before two-score boys, and

thieves, and hackney-coachmen. Meanwhile, every hour the
bell of the University rings out over the hum of the streets,
and every hour a double tide of students, coming and going,
fills the deep archways. And lastly, one night in the
spring-time — or say one morning rather, at the peep of
day — late folk may hear the voices of many men singing a
psalm in unison from a church on one side of the old High
Street; and a little after, or perhaps a little before, the sound
of many men singing a psalm in unison from another church
on the opposite side of the way. There will be something in
the words about the dew of Hermon, and how goodly it is to
see brethren dwelling together in unity. And late folk will tell
themselves that all this singing denotes the conclusion of two
yearly ecclesiastical parliaments — the parliaments of
Churches which are brothers in many admirable virtues, but
not specially like brothers in this particular of a tolerant and
peaceful life.

Again, meditative people will find a charm in a certain
consonancy between the aspects of the city and its odd and
stirring history. Few places, if any, offer a more barbaric
display of contrasts to the eye. In the very midst stands one of
the most satisfactory crags in nature — a Bass Rock upon dry
land, rooted in a garden shaken by passing trains, carrying a
crown of battlements and turrets, and describing its warlike
shadow over the liveliest and brightest thoroughfare of the
New Town. From their smoky beehives, ten stories high, the
unwashed look down upon the open squares and gardens of
the wealthy; and gay people sunning themselves along Princes
Street, with its mile of commercial palaces all beflagged upon
some great occasion, see, across a gardened valley set with
statues, where the washings of the Old Town flutter in the
breeze at its high windows. And then, upon all sides, what a
clashing of architecture! In this one valley, where the life of
the town goes most busily forward, there may be seen, shown
one above and behind another by the accidents of the
ground, buildings in almost every style upon the globe.
Egyptian and Greek temples, Venetian palaces and Gothic
spires, are huddled one over another in a most admired

Robert Louis Stevenson

Edinburgh

disorder; while, above all, the brute mass of the Castle and the summit of Arthur's Seat look down upon these imitations with a becoming dignity, as the works of Nature may look down upon the monuments of Art. But Nature is a more indiscriminate patroness than we imagine, and in no way frightened of a strong effect. The birds roost as willingly among the Corinthian capitals as in the crannies of the crag; the same atmosphere and daylight clothe the eternal rock and yesterday's imitation portico; and as the soft northern sunshine throws out everything into a glorified distinctness — or easterly mists, coming up with the blue evening, fuse all these incongruous features into one, and the lamps begin to glitter along the street, and faint lights to burn in the high windows across the valley — the feeling grows upon you that this also is a piece of nature in the most intimate sense; that this profusion of eccentricities, this dream in masonry and living rock, is not a drop-scene in a theatre, but a city in the world of everyday reality, connected by railway and telegraph-wire with all the capitals of Europe, and inhabited by citizens of the familiar type, who keep ledgers, and attend church, and have sold their immortal portion to a daily paper. By all the canons of romance, the place demands to be half deserted and leaning towards decay; birds we might admit in profusion, the play of the sun and winds, and a few gipsies encamped in the chief thoroughfare; but these citizens, with their cabs and tramways, their trains and posters, are altogether out of key. Chartered tourists, they make free with historic localities, and rear their young among the most picturesque sites with a grand human indifference. To see them thronging by, in their neat clothes and conscious moral rectitude, and with a little air of possession that verges on the absurd, is not the least striking feature of the place.

And the story of the town is as eccentric as its appearance. For centuries it was a capital thatched with heather, and more than once, in the evil days of English invasion, it has gone up in flame to heaven, a beacon to ships at sea. It was the jousting-ground of jealous nobles, not only on greenside, or by the King's Stables, where set tournaments were fought

three years he kept falling — grease coming and buttons going from the square-skirted coat, the face puffing and pimpling, the shoulders growing bowed, the hair falling scant and grey upon his head; and the last that ever I saw of him, he was standing at the mouth of an entry with several men in moleskin, three parts drunk, and his old black raiment daubed with mud. I fancy that I still can hear him laugh. There was something heart-breaking in his gradual declension at so advanced an age; you would have thought a man of sixty out of the reach of these calamities; you would have thought that he was niched by that time into a safe place in life, whence he could pass quietly and honourably into the grave.

One of the earliest marks of these *dégringolades* is, that the victim begins to disappear from the New Town thoroughfares, and takes to the High Street, like a wounded animal to the woods. And such an one is the type of the quarter. It also has fallen socially. A scutcheon over the door somewhat jars in sentiment where there is a washing at every window. The old man, when I saw him last, wore the coat in which he had played the gentlemen three years before; and that was just what gave him so pre-eminent an air of wretchedness.

It is true that the over-population was at least as dense in the epoch of lords and ladies, and that nowadays some customs which made Edinburgh notorious of yore have been fortunately pretermitted. But an aggregation of comfort is not distasteful like an aggregation of the reverse. Nobody cares how many lords and ladies, and divines and lawyers, may have been crowded into these houses in the past — perhaps the more the merrier. The glasses clink around the china punch-bowl, some one touches the virginals, there are peacocks' feathers on the chimney, and the tapers burn clear and pale in the red firelight. That is not an ugly picture in itself, nor will it become ugly upon repetition. All the better if the like were going on in every second room; the land would only look the more inviting. Times are changed. In one house, perhaps two-score families herd together; and, perhaps, not one of them is wholly out of reach of want. The great hotel is given over to discomfort from the foundation to the chimney-tops; everywhere a pinching, narrow habit, scanty meals, and an air of sluttishness and dirt. In the first room there is a birth, in another a death, in a third a sordid drinking-bout, and the detective and the Bible-reader cross upon the stairs. High words are audible from dwelling to dwelling, and children have a strange experience from the first; only a robust soul, you would think, could grow up in such conditions without hurt. And even if God tempers His dispensations to the young, and all the ill does not arise that our apprehensions may forecast, the sight of such a way of living is disquieting to people who are more happily circumstanced. Social inequality is nowhere more ostentatious than in Edinburgh. I have mentioned already how, to the stroller along Princes Street, the High Street callously exhibits its back garrets. It is true, there is a garden between. And although nothing could be more glaring by way of contrast, sometimes the opposition is more immediate; sometimes the thing lies in a nutshell, and there is not so much as a blade of grass between the rich and poor. To look over the South Bridge and see the Cowgate below full of crying hawkers, is to view one rank of society from another in the twinkling of an eye.

One night I went along the Cowgate after everyone was abed but the policeman, and stopped by hazard before a tall *land*. The moon touched upon its chimneys, and shone blankly on the upper windows; there was no light anywhere in the great bulk of building; but as I stood there it seemed to me that I could hear quite a body of quiet sounds from the interior; doubtless there were many clocks ticking, and people snoring on their backs. And thus, as I fancied, the dense life within made itself faintly audible in my ears, family after family contributing its quota to the general hum, and the whole pile beating in tune to its timepieces, like a great disordered heart. Perhaps it was little more than a fancy altogether, but it was strangely impressive at the time, and gave me an imaginative measure of the disproportion between the quantity of living flesh and the trifling walls that separated and contained it.

There was nothing fanciful, at least, but every circumstance of terror and reality, in the fall of the *land* in the High
Street. The building had grown rotten to the core; the entry
underneath had suddenly closed up so that the scavenger's
barrow could not pass; cracks and reverberations sounded
through the house at night; the inhabitants of the huge old
human beehive discussed their peril when they encountered
on the stair; some had even left their dwellings in a panic of
fear, and returned to them again in a fit of economy or
self-respect; when, in the black hours of a Sunday morning,
the whole structure ran together with a hideous uproar and
tumbled story upon story to the ground. The physical shock
was felt far and near; and the moral shock travelled with the
morning milkmaid into all the suburbs. The church bells
never sounded more dismally over Edinburgh than that grey
forenoon. Death had made a brave harvest, and, like
Samson, by pulling down one roof, destroyed many a home.
None who saw it can have forgotten the aspect of the gable;
here it was plastered, there papered, according to the rooms;
here the kettle still stood on the hob, high overhead; and
there a cheap picture of the Queen was pasted over the
chimney. So, by this disaster, you had a glimpse into the life
of thirty families, all suddenly cut off from the revolving
years. The *land* had fallen; and with the *land* how much! Far
in the country, people saw a gap in the city ranks, and the
sun looked through between the chimneys in an unwonted
place. And all over the world, in London, in Canada, in New
Zealand, fancy what a multitude of people could explain with
truth: "The house that I was born in fell last night!"

Part Two:
France

Victor Hugo: Notre Dame and Paris View

Victor Hugo (1802-1885) dominated French literature of his era. The following passage is taken from Notre Dame de Paris, known later in English translation as The Hunchback of Notre Dame. The cathedral is on the Île de la Cité, a small island on which the city of Paris was first built. Recently, the government began to dig down in the great square in front of the Cathedral of Notre Dame to build an underground garage; the work was halted when workmen unearthed the remnants of an earlier church. In Hugo's day, as now, there was bustle about the cathedral; miniatures of the Virgin and religious carvings were hawked to the devoted. The cathedral, however, remains as it has stood for centuries, the supreme symbol of creativity in the Middle Ages (construction was started in 1163).

Assuredly the Cathedral of Notre-Dame at Paris is, to this day, a majestic and sublime edifice. But noble as it has remained while growing old, one cannot but regret, cannot but feel indignant at the innumerable degradations and mutilations inflicted on the venerable pile, both by the action of time and the hand of man, regardless alike of Charlemagne, who laid the first stone, and Philip Augustus, who laid the last.

On the face of this ancient queen of our cathedrals, beside

each wrinkle one invariably finds a scar. *"Tempus edax, homo edacior,"* which I would be inclined to translate: "Time is blind, but man is senseless."

Had we, with the reader, the leisure to examine, one by one, the traces of the destruction wrought on this ancient church, we should have to impute the smallest share to Time, the largest to men, and more especially to those whom we must perforce call *artists,* since, during the last two centuries, there have been individuals among them who assumed the title of architect.

And first of all, to cite only a few prominent examples, there are surely few such wonderful pages in the book of Architecture as the facades of the Cathedral. Here unfold themselves to the eye, successively and at one glance, the three deep Gothic doorways; the richly traced and sculptured band of twenty-eight royal niches; the immense central rose-window, flanked by its two lateral windows, like a priest by the deacon and subdeacon; the lofty and fragile gallery of trifoliated arches supporting a heavy platform on its slender columns; finally, the two dark and massive towers with their projecting slate roofs — harmonious parts of one magnificent whole, rising one above another in five gigantic storeys, massed yet unconfused, their innumerable details of statuary, sculpture, and carving boldly allied to the impassive grandeur of the whole. A vast symphony in stone, as it were; the colossal achievement of a man and a nation — one and yet complex — like the Iliades and the Romances to which it is sister — prodigious result of the union of all the resources of an epoch, where on every stone is displayed in a hundred variations the fancy of the craftsman controlled by the genius of the artist; in a word, a sort of human Creation, mighty and prolific, like the divine Creation, of which it seems to have caught the double characteristics — variety and eternity.

And what we say here of the facade applies to the entire church; and what we say of the Cathedral of Paris may be said of all the ministers of Christendom in the Middle Ages.

Everything stands in its proper relation in that self-evolved art, is logical, well-proportioned. By measuring one toe you can estimate the height of the giant.

To return to the facade of Notre-Dame, as we see it to-day,

when we stand lost in pious admiration of the mighty and awe-inspiring Cathedral, which, according to the chroniclers, strikes the beholder with terror — *quæ mole sua terrorem incutit spectantibus.*

Three important things are now missing in that facade: the flight of eleven steps which raised it above the level of the ground; the lower row of statues occupying the niches of the three doorways; and the upper series of twenty-eight, which filled the gallery of the first story and represented the earliest Kings of France, from Childebert to Philip Augustus, each holding in his hand the "imperial orb."

The disappearance of the steps is due to Time, which by slow and irresistible degrees has raised the level of the soil of the city. But Time, though permitting these eleven steps, which added to the stately elevation of the pile, to be swallowed by the rising tide of the Paris pavement, has given to the Cathedral more perhaps than he took away; for it was the hand of Time that steeped its facade in those rich and sombre tints by which the old age of monuments becomes their period of beauty.

But who has overthrown the two rows of statues? Who has left the niches empty? Who has scooped out, in the very middle of the central door, that new and bastard-pointed arch? Who has dared to hang in it, cheek by jowl with Biscornette's arabesques, that tasteless and clumsy wooden door with Louis XV carvings? Man — the architects — the artists of our own day!

And, if we enter the interior of the edifice, who has overthrown the colossal St. Christopher, proverbial among statues as the Grande Salle of the Palais among Halls, as the spire of Strasbourg Cathedral among steeples? And the countless figures kneeling, standing, equestrian, men, women, children, kings, bishops, knights, of stone, marble, gold, silver, brass, even wax — which peopled all the spaces between the columns of the nave and the choir — what brutal hand has swept them away? Not that of Time.

And who replaced the ancient Gothic altar, splendidly charged with shrines and reliquaries, by that ponderous marble sarcophagus with its stone clouds and cherubs' heads, which looks like an odd piece out of the Val de Grâce or of the Invalides? And who was so besotted as to fix this lumbering stone anachronism into the Carlovingian pavement of Hercandus? Was it not Louis XIV, in fulfilment of the vow of Louis XIII?

And who put cold white glass in the place of those "richly coloured" panes which caused the dazzled eyes of our forefathers to wander undecided from the rose-window over the great doorway to the pointed ones of the chancel and back again? And what would a priest of the sixteenth century say to the fine yellow wash with which the vandal Archbishops have smeared the walls of their Cathedral? He would recollect that this was the colour the hangman painted over houses of evil-fame; he would recall the Hôtel de Petit-Bourbon plastered all over with yellow because of the treason of its owner, the Connétable — "a yellow of so permanent a dye," says Sauval, "and so well laid on, that the passage of more than a century has not succeeded in dimming its colour." He would think that the Holy Place had become infamous and would flee from it.

And if we ascend the Cathedral, passing over a thousand barbarisms of every description — what has become of the charming little belfry, fretted, slender, pointed, sonorous, which rose from the point of intersection of the transept, and every whit as delicate and as bold as its neighbour the spire (likewise destroyed) of the Sainte-Chapelle, soared into the blue, farther even than the towers. An architect "of taste" (1787) had it amputated, and deemed it sufficient reparation to hide the wound under the great lead plaster which looks like the lid of a sauce-pan.

Thus has the marvellous art of the Middle Ages been treated in almost every country, but especially in France. In its ruin three distinct factors can be traced, causing wounds of varying depths. First of all, Time, which has gradually made breaches here and there and gnawed its whole surface; next, religious and political revolutions, which, in the blind fury natural to them, wreaked their tempestuous passions upon it, rent its rich garment of sculpture and carving, burst in its rose-windows, broke its necklets of arabesques and figurines, tore down its statues, one time for their mitres, another time for their crowns; and finally, the various fashions, growing ever more grotesque and senseless, which, from the anarchical yet splendid deviations of the Renaissance onwards, have succeeded one another in the inevitable decadence of Architecture. Fashion has committed more crimes than revolution. It has cut to the quick, it has attacked the very bone and framework of the art; has mangled, pared, dislocated, destroyed the edifice—in its form as in its symbolism, in its coherence as in its beauty. This achieved, it set about renewing—a thing which Time and Revolution, at least, never had the presumption to do. With unblushing effrontery, "in the interests of good taste," it has plastered over the wounds of Gothic architecture with its trumpery knick-knacks, its marble ribbons and knots, its metal rosettes—a perfect eruption of ovolos, scrolls, and scallops; of draperies, garlands, fringes; of marble flames and brazen clouds; of blowzy cupids and inflated cherubs, which began by devouring the face of art in the oratory of Catherine de Medicis, and ended by causing it to expire, tortured and grimacing, two centuries later, in the boudoir of Mme. Dubarry.

Thus, to sum up the points we have just discussed, the ravages that now disfigure Gothic architecture are of three distinct kinds. furrows and blotches wrought by the hand of Time; practical violence—brutalities, bruises, fractures—the outcome of revolution, from Luther down to Mirabeau; mutilations, amputations, dislocation of members, restorations, the result of the labours—Greek, Roman, and barbarian—of the professors following out the rules of Vitruvius and Vignola. That magnificent art which the Goths created has been murdered by the Academies.

To the devastations of Time and Revolutions—carried out at least with impartiality and grandeur—have been added those of a swarm of school-trained architects, duly licensed and incorporated, degrading their art deliberately and, with all the discernment of bad taste, substituting the Louis XV fussiness for Gothic simplicity, and all to the greater glory of the Parthenon. This is the kick of the ass to the dying lion; it is the ancient oak, dead already above, gnawed at the roots by worms and vermin.

How remote is this from the time when Robert Cenalis,

Victor Hugo

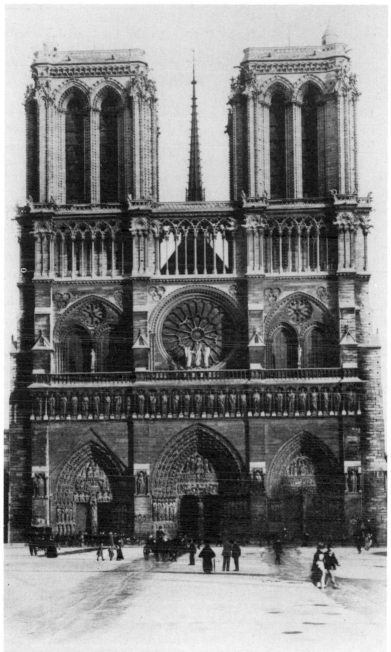

The Cathedral of Notre Dame

comparing Notre-Dame at Paris with the far-famed Temple
of Diana at Ephesus, "so much vaunted by the ancient
pagans," which immortalized Erostratus, considered the
Gallican Cathedral "more excellent in length, breadth,
height, and structure."

For the rest, Notre-Dame cannot, from the architectural
point of view, be called complete, definite, classified. It is not
a Roman church, neither is it a Gothic church. It is not
typical of any style of architecture. Notre-Dame has not, like
the Abbey of Tournus, the grave and massive squareness, the
round, wide, vaulted roof, the fridgid nudity, the majestic
simplicity of the edifices which have their origin in the
Roman arch. Nor is it like the Cathedral of Bourges, the
splendid, airy, multiform, foliated, pinnacled, efflorescent
product of the Gothic arch. Impossible, either, to rank it
among that antique family of churches—sombre, mysterious,
low-pitched, cowering, as it were, under the weight of the
round arch; half Egyptian, wholly hieroglyphical, wholly
sacerdotal, wholly symbolical; as regards ornament, rather
overloaded with lozenges and zigzags than with flowers, with
flowers than animals, with animals than human figures; less
the work of the architect than the Bishop, the first
transformation of the art still deeply imbued with theocratic
and military discipline, having its root in the Byzantine
Empire, and stopping short at William the Conqueror. Nor,
again, can the Cathedral be ranked with that other order of
lofty, aerial churches, with their wealth of painted windows
and sculptured work, with their sharp pinnacles and bold
outlines; communal and citizen—regarded as political
symbols; free, capricious, untrammelled—regarded as works
of art. This is the second transformation of architecture—no
longer cryptic, sacerdotal, inevitable, but artistic,progressive,
popular—beginning with the return from the Crusades and
ending with Louis XI.

Notre-Dame is neither pure Roman, like the first, nor pure
Gothic, like the second; it is an edifice of the transition
period. The Saxon architect had just finished erecting the
first pillars of the nave when the pointed arch, brought back
by the Crusaders, arrived and planted itself victorious on the

broad Roman capitals which were intended only to support round arches. Master, henceforth, of the situation, the pointed arch determined the construction of the rest of the building. Inexperienced and timid at its commencement, it remains wide and low, restraining itself, as it were, not daring to soar up into the arrows and lancets of the marvellous cathedrals of the later period. It would almost seem that it was affected by the proximity of the heavy Roman pillars.

Not that these edifices showing the transition from Roman to Gothic are less worthy of study than the pure models. They express a gradation of the art which would else be lost. It is the grafting of the pointed arch on to the circular arch.

Notre-Dame de Paris, in particular, is a curious specimen of this variety. Every surface, every stone of this venerable pile, is a page of the history not only of the country, but of science and of art. Thus — to mention here only a few of the chief details — whereas the small Porte Rouge almost touches the limits of fifteenth century Gothic delicacy, the pillars of the nave, by their massiveness and great girth, reach back to the Carlovingian Abbey of Saint-Germain-des-Prés. One would imagine that six centuries lay between that door and those pillars. Not even the Hermetics fail to find in the symbols of the grand doorway a satisfactory compendium of their science, of which the Church of Saint-Jacques-de-la-Boucherie was so complete a hieroglyph. This the Roman Abbey — the Church of the Mystics — Gothic art — Saxon art — the ponderous round pillar reminiscent of Gregory VII, the alchemistic symbolism by which Nicolas Flamel paved the way for Luther — papal   unity — schism — Saint-Germain-des-Prés — Saint-Jacques-de-la-Boucherie — all are blended, combined, amalgamated in Notre-Dame. This generative Mother-Church is, among the other ancient churches of Paris, a sort of Chimera: she has the head of one, the limbs of another, the body of a third — something of all.

These hybrid edifices are, we repeat, by no means the least interesting to the artist, the antiquary, and the historian. They let us realize to how great a degree architecture is a primitive matter, in that they demonstrate, as do the

Cyclopean remains, the Pyramids of Egypt, the gigantic
Hindu pagodas, that the greatest productions of architecture
are not so much the work of individuals as of a
community;are rather the offspring of a nation's labour than
the outcome of individual genius; the deposit of a whole
people; the heaped-up treasure of centuries; the residuum
left by the successive evaporations of human society; in a
word, a species of formations. Each wave of time leaves its
coating of alluvium, each race deposits its layer on the
monuments, each individual contributes his stone to it. Thus
do the beavers work, thus the bees, thus man. Babel, that
great symbol of architecture, is a bee-hive.

Great edifices, like the great mountains, are the work of
ages. Often art undergoes a transformation while they are
waiting pending completion — *pendent opera interrupta* —
they then proceed imperturbably in conformity with the new
order of things. The new art takes possession of the monument at the point at which it finds it, absorbs itself into it,
develops it after its own idea, and completes it if it can. The
matter is accomplished without disturbance, without effort,
without reaction, in obedience to an undeviating, peaceful
law of nature — a shoot is grafted on, the sap circulates, a
fresh vegetation is in progress. Truly, there is matter for
mighty volumes; often, indeed, for a universal history of
mankind, in these successive layers of different periods of art,
on different levels of the same edifice. The man, the artist,
the individual, are lost sight of in these massive piles that
have no record of authorship; they are an epitome, a
totalization of human intelligence. Time is the architect — a
nation is the builder.

Reviewing here only Christo-European architecture, that
younger sister of the great Masonic movements of the East, it
presents the aspect of a huge formation divided into three
sharply defined superincumbent zones: the Roman, the
Greek, and that of the Renaissance, which we would prefer to
call the Creco-Romanesque. The Roman stratum, the oldest
and lowest of the three, is occupied by the circular arch,
which reappears, supported by the Greek column, in the
modern and upper stratum of the Renaissance. Between the

two comes the pointed arch. The edifices which belong exclusively to one or other of these three strata are perfectly distinct, uniform, and complete in themselves. The Abbey of Jumièges is one, the Cathedral of Reims another, the Sainte-Croix of Orleans is a third. But the three zones mingle and overlap one another at the edges, like the colours of the solar spectrum; hence these complex buildings, these edifices of the gradational, transitional period. One of them will be Roman as to its feet, Greek as to its body, and Greco-Romanesque as to its head. That happens when it has taken six hundred years in the building. But that variety is rare: the castle-keep of Étampes is a specimen. Edifices of two styles are more frequent. Such is Notre-Dame of Paris, a Gothic structure, rooted by its earliest pillars in the Roman zone which the portal of Saint-Denis and the nave of Saint-Germain-des-Prés are entirely sunk. Such again is the semi-Gothic Chapter Hall of Bocherville, in which the Roman layer reaches half-way up. Such is the Cathedral at Rouen, which would be wholly Gothic had not the point of its central spire reached up into the Renaissance.

For the rest, all these gradations, these differences, do but affect the surface of the building. Art has changed its skin, but the actual conformation of the Christian Church has remained untouched. It has ever the same internal structure, the same logical disposition of the parts. Be the sculptured and decorated envelope of a cathedral as it will, underneath, at least, as germ or rudiment, we invariably find the Roman basilica. It develops itself unswervingly on this foundation and following the same rules. There are invariably two naves crossing each other at right angles, the upper end of which, rounded off in a half circle, forms the choir; there are always two lower-pitched side-aisles for the processions—the chapels—sort of lateral passages communicating with the nave by its intercolumnar spaces. These conditions once fulfilled, the number of chapels, doorways steeples, spires, may be varied to infinity, according to the fancy of the age, the nation, or the art. The proper observances of worship once provided for and insured, architecture is free to do as she pleases. Statues, stained glass, rose-windows, arabesques, flutings, capitals, bas-reliefs — all these flowers of fancy she distributes as best suits her particular scheme of the moment. Hence the prodigious variety in the exterior of these edifices, in the underlying structure of which there rules so much order and uniformity. The trunk of the tree is unchanging; its vegetation only is variable.

A Bird's-Eye View of Paris

We have endeavoured to restore for the reader this admirable Cathedral of Notre-Dame. We have briefly enumerated most of the beauties it possessed in the fifteenth century, though lost to it now; but we have omitted the chief one — the view of Paris as it then appeared from the summits of the towers.

When, after long gropings up the dark perpendicular stair-case which pierces the thick walls of the steeple towers, one emerged at last unexpectedly on to one of the two high platforms inundated with light and air, it was in truth a marvellous picture spread out before you on every side; a spectacle *sui generis* of which those of our readers can best form an idea who have had the good fortune to see a purely Gothic city, complete and homogeneous, of which there are still a few remaining, such as Nuremberg in Bavaria, Vittoria in Spain, or even smaller specimens, provided they are well-preserved, like Vitré in Brittany and Nordhausen in Prussia.

The Paris of that day, the Paris of the fifteenth century, was already a giant city. We Parisians in general are mistaken as to the amount of ground we imagine we have gained since then. Paris, since the time of Louis XI, has not increased by much more than a third; and, truth to tell, has lost far more in beauty than ever it has gained in size.

Paris first saw the light on that ancient island in the Seine, the Cité, which has, in fact, the form of a cradle. The strand of this island was its first enclosure, the Seine its first moat.

For several centuries Paris remained an island, with two bridges, one north, the other south, and two bridge heads, which were at once its gates and fortresses: the Grand-Chatelet on the right bank, the Petit-Châtelet on the left. Then, after the kings of the first generation, Paris, finding itself too cramped on its island home, where it no longer had room to turn round, crossed the river; whereupon, beyond each of the bridge-fortresses, a first circle of walls and towers began to enclose pieces of land on either side of the Seine. Of this ancient wall some vestiges were still standing in the last century; to-day, nothing is left but the memory, and here and there a tradition, such as the Baudets or Baudoyer Gate — *porta bagauda.*

By degrees the flood of dwellings, constantly pressing forward from the heart of the city, overflows, saps, eats away, and finally swallows up this enclosure. Philip Augustus makes a fresh line of circumvallation, and immures Paris within a chain of massive and lofty towers. For upward of a century the houses press upon one another, accumulate, and rise in this basin like water in a reservoir. They begin to burrow deeper in the ground, they pile storey upon storey, they climb one upon another, they shoot up in height like all compressed growth, and each strives to raise its head above its neighbour for a breath of air. The streets grow ever deeper and narrower, every open space fills up and disappears, till, finally, the houses overleap the wall of Philip Augustus, and spread themselves joyfully over the country like escaped prisoners, without plan or system, gathering themselves together in knots, cutting slices out of the surrounding fields for gardens, taking plenty of elbow-room.

By 1367, the town has made such inroads on the suburb that a new enclosure has become necessary, especially on the right bank, and is accordingly built by Charles V. But a town like Paris is in a state of perpetual growth — it is only such cities that become capitals. They are the reservoirs into which are directed all the streams — geographical, political, moral, intellectual — of a country, all the natural tendencies of the people; wells of civilization, so to speak — but also outlets where commerce, manufacture, intelligence, population, all that there is of vital fluid, of life, of soul, in a people, filters through and collects incessantly, drop by drop, century by

ART-STUDENTS AND COPYISTS IN THE LOUVRE GALLERY, PARIS.—Drawn by Winslow Homer.—[See Page 20.]

Paris vers 1530

Plan dit " d'Arnoullet "

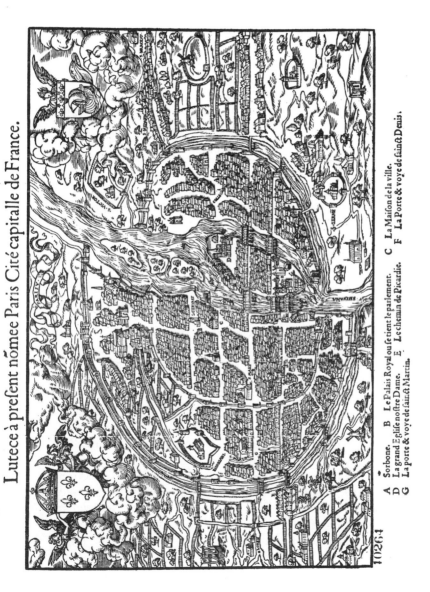

Lutece à preſent nõmee Paris Cité capitalle de France.

A　Sorbone.　B　Le Palais Royal ou ſe tient le parlement.　C　La Maiſon de la ville.
D　La grand Egliſe noſtre Dame.　E　Le chemin de Picardie.　F　La Porte & voye de ſainct Denis.
G　La porte & voye de ſainct Martin.

10264

century. The wall of Charles V, however, endures the same
fate as that of Philip Augustus. By the beginning of the fifteenth century it, too, is overstepped, left behind, the new
suburb hurries on, and in the sixteenth century it seems visibly
to recede farther and farther into the depths of the old city, so
dense has the new town become outside it.

Thus, by the fifteenth century — to go no farther — Paris had
already consumed the three concentric circles of wall,
which, in the time of Julian the Apostate, were in embryo, so
to speak, in the Grand-Châtelet and the Petit-Châtelet. The
mighty city had successively burst its four girdles of wall like a
child grown out of last year's garments. Under Louis XI,
clusters of ruined towers belonging to the old fortified walls
were still visible, rising out of the sea of houses like hilltops
out of an inundation — the archipelagoes of the old Paris,
submerged beneath the new.

Since then, unfortunately for us, Paris has changed again;
but it has broken through one more enclosure, that of Louis
XV, a wretched wall of mud and rubbish, well worthy of the
King who built it and of the poet who sang of it:

"Le mur murant Paris rend Paris murmurant."

In the fifteenth century Paris was still divided into three
towns, perfectly distinct and separate, having each its
peculiar features, speciality, manners, customs, privileges,
and history: the City, the University, the Town. The City,
which occupied the island, was the oldest and the smallest of
the trio — the mother of the other two — looking, if we may be
allowed the comparison, like a little old woman between two
tall and blooming daughters. The University covered the left
bank of the Seine from the Tournelle to the Tour de
Nesle — points corresponding in the Paris of to-day to the
Halles-aux-Vins and the Mint, its circular wall taking in a
pretty large portion of that ground on which Julian had built
his baths. It also included the Hill of Sainte-Geneviève. The
outermost point of the curving wall was the Papal Gate; that
is to say, just about the site of the Pantheon. The Town, the
largest of the three divisions of Paris, occupied the right

bank. Its quay, interrupted at several points, stretched along
the Seine from the Tour de Billy to the Tour du Bois; that is,
from the spot where the Grenier d'Abondance now stands to
that occupied by the Tuileries. These four points at which the
Seine cut through the circumference of the capital — la
Tournelle and the Tour de Nesle on the left, the Tour de
Billy and the Tour de Bois on the right bank — were called
par excellence "the four towers of Paris." The Town
encroached more deeply into the surrounding country than
did the University. The farthest point of its enclosing wall
(the one built by Charles V) was at the gates of Saint-Denis
and Saint-Martin, the situation of which has not changed.

As we have already stated, each of these three great
divisions of Paris was a town — but a town too specialized to
be complete, a town which could not dispense with the other
two. So, too, each had its peculiarly characteristic aspect. In
the City, churches were the prevailing feature; in the Town,
Palaces; in the University, colleges. Setting aside the less
important originalities of Paris and the capricious legal
intricacies of the right of way, and taking note only of the
collective and important masses in the chaos of communal
jurisdictions, we may say that, broadly speaking, the island
belonged to the Bishop, the right bank to the Provost of the
Merchants' Guild, and the left bank to the Rector of the
University. The Provost of Paris — a royal, not a municipal
office — had authority over all. The City boasted Notre
Dame; the Town, the Louvre and the Hôtel-de-Ville; the
University, the Sorbonne. Again, the Town had the Halles,
the City the Hôtel-Dieu, the University the Pré aux Clercs.
Crimes committed by the students on the right bank, were
tried on the island in the Palais de Justice, and punished on
the right bank at Montfaucon, unless the Rector, feeling the
University to be strong and the King weak, thought fit to
intervene; for the scholars enjoyed the privilege of being
hanged on their own premises.

Most of these privileges (we may remark in passing), and
there were some of even greater value than this, had been
extorted from the kings by mutiny and revolts. It is the
immemorial course: *Le roi ne lâche que quand le peuple*

arrache — the King only gives up what the people wrest from him. There is an old French charter which defines this popular loyalty with great simplicity: *Civibus fidelitas in reges, quœ tamen aliquoties seditionibus interrupta, multa peperit privilegia.*

In the fifteenth century the Seine embraced five islands within the purlieus of Paris:the Louvre, on which trees then grew; the Île-aux-Vaches and the Île Notre-Dame, both uninhabited except for one poor hovel, both fiefs of the Bishop (in the seventeenth century these two islands were made into one and built upon, now known as the Îls Saint-Louis); finally the City, having at its western extremity the islet of the Passeur-aux-Vaches — the cattle ferry — now buried under the foundations of the Pont Neuf. The City had, in those days, five bridges — three on the right: the Pont Notre-Dame and the Pont-au-Change being stone, and the Pont-aux-Meuniers of wood; and two on the left: the Petit-Pont of stone, and the Pont Saint-Michel of wood — all lined with houses. The University had six gates built by Philip Augustus, namely — starting from the Tournelle — the Porte Saint-Victor, the Porte Bordelle, the Porte Papale, the Porte Saint-Jacques, the Port Saint-Michel and the Porte Saint Germain. The town also had six gates, built by Charles V, namely — starting from the Tour de Billy — the Porte Saint-Antoine, the Porte du Temple, the Porte Saint-Martin, the Porte Saint-Denis, the Porte Montmartre and the Porte Saint-Honoré. All these gates were strong, and at the same time handsome — which is no detriment to strength. A wide and deep fosse, filled during the winter months with a swift stream supplied by the Seine, washed the foot of the walls all round Paris. At night the gates were shut, the river was barred at the two extremities of the town by the massive iron chains, and Paris slept in peace.

From a bird's-eye view, these three great divisions — the City, the University, and the Town — presented each an inextricably tangled network of streets to the eye. Nevertheless, one recognised at a glance that the three fragments formed together a single body. You at once distinguished two long, parallel streets running, without a break or deviation, almost in a straight line through all these towns from end to end, from south to north, at right angles with the Seine; connecting, mingling, transfusing them, incessantly pouring the inhabitants of one into the walls of the other, blending the three into one. One of these two streets ran from the Porte Saint-Jacques to the Porte Saint-Martin, and was called Rue Saint-Jacques in the University, Rue de la Juiverie (Jewry) in the City, and Rue Saint-Martin in the Town, crossing the river twice, as the Petit-Pont and the Pont Notre-Dame. The second — which was called Rue de la Harpe on the left bank, Rue de la Barillerie on the island, Rue Saint-Denis on the right bank, Pont Saint-Michel on one arm of the Seine, Pont-au-Change on the other — ran from the Porte Saint-Michel in the University to the Porte Saint-Denis in the Town. For the rest, under however many names, they were still only the two streets, the two thoroughfares, the two mother-streets, the main arteries of Paris, from which all the other ducts of the triple city started, or into which they flowed.

Independently of these two principal streets, cutting diametrically through the breadth of Paris and common to the entire capital, the Town and the University had each its own main street running in the direction of their length, parallel to the Seine, and intersecting the two "arterial" streets at right angles. Thus, in the Town you descended in a straight line from the Porte Saint-Antoine to the Porte Saint-Victor to the Porte Saint-Germain. These two great thoroughfares, crossing the first two mentioned, formed the frame on to which was woven the knotted, tortuous network of the streets of Paris. In the inextricable tangle of this network, however, on closer inspection, two sheaf-like clusters of streets could be distinguished, one in the University, one in the Town, spreading out from the bridges to the gates. Something of the same geometrical plan still exists.

Now, what aspect did this present when viewed from the top of the towers of Notre-Dame in 1482?

That is what we will endeavor to describe.

To the spectator, arrived breathless on this summit, the first glance revealed only a bewildering jumble of roofs,

chimneys, streets, bridges, squares, spires, and steeples.
Everything burst upon the eye at once — the carved gable, the
high, pointed roof, the turret clinging to the corner wall, the
stone pyramid of the eleventh century, the slate obelisk of the
fifteenth, the round, stark tower of the donjon-keep, the
square and elaborately decorated tower of the church, the
large, the small, the massive, the airy. The gaze was lost for
long and completely in this maze, where there was nothing
that had not its own originality, its reason, its touch of
genius, its beauty; where everything breathed of art, from
the humblest house with its painted and carved front, its
visible timber framework, its low-browed doorway and
projecting storeys, to the kingly Louvre itself, which, in those
days, boasted a colonnade of towers. But here are the most
important points which struck the eye when it became
somewhat accustomed to this throng of edifices.

To begin with, the City. "The island of the City," as Sauval
observes — who, with all his pompous verbosity, sometimes
hits upon these happy turns of phrase — "the island of the City
is shaped like a great ship sunk into the mud and run
aground lengthwise, about mid-stream of the Seine." As we
have already shown, in the fifteenth century this ship was
moored to the two banks of the Seine by five bridges. This
likeness to a ship had also struck the fancy of the heraldic
scribes; for, according to Favyn and Pasquier, it was from
this circumstance, and not from the siege by the Normans,
that is derived the ship emblazoned in the arms of Paris. To
him who can decipher it, heraldry is an algebra, a complete
language. The whole history of the later half of the Middle
Ages is written in heraldry, as is that of the first half in the
symbolism of the Roman churches — the hieroglyphics of
feudalism succeeding those of theocracy.

The City, then, first presented itself to the view, with its
stern to the east and its prow to the west. Facing towards the
prow there stretched an endless line of old roofs, above which
rose, broad and domed, the lead-roofed transept of the
Sainte-Chapelle, like an elephant with its tower, except that
here the tower was the boldest, airiest, most elaborate and
serrated spire that ever showed the sky through its fretted

cone. Just in front of Notre-Dame three streets opened into
the Cathedral close — a fine square of old houses. On the
south side of this glowered the furrowed, beetling front of the
Hôtel-Dieu, with its roof as if covered with boils and warts.
Then, on every side, right, left, east, and west, all within the
narrow circuit of the City, rose the steeples of its twenty-one
churches, of all dates, shapes, and sizes, from the low, worm-
eaten Roman belfry of Saint-Denis du Pas (*carcer Glaucini*)
to the slender, tapering spires of Saint-Pierre aux Bœufs and
Saint-Landry. Behind Notre-Dame northward, stretched the
cloister with its Gothic galleries; southward, the semi-Roman
palace of the Bishop, and eastward, an uncultivated piece of
ground, the *terrain*, at the point of the island. Furthermore,
in this sea of houses, the eye could distinguish, by the high,
perforated mitres of stone which at that period capped even
its topmost attic windows, the palace presented by the town,
in the reign of Charles VI, to Jovénal des Ursins; a little
farther on, the black-barred roofs of the market-shed in the
Marché Palus; farther off still, the new chancel of
Saint-Germain le Vieux, lengthened in 1458 by taking in a
piece of the Rue aux Febves, with here and there a glimpse of
cause-way, crowded with people, some pillory at a corner of
the street, some fine piece of the pavement of Philip
Augustus — magnificent flagging, furrowed in the middle for
the benefit of the horses, and so badly replaced in the middle
of the sixteenth century by the wretched cobblestones called
"*pavé de la Ligue*"; some solitary court-yard with one of those
diaphanous wrought-iron stair-case turrets they were so fond
of in the fifteenth century, one of which is still to be seen in
the Rue des Bourdonnais. Lastly, to the right of the
Sainte-Chapelle, westward, the Palais de Justice displayed its
group of towers by the water's edge. The trees of the royal
gardens, which occupied the western point of the island, hid
the ferry-man's islet from view. As for the water, it was hardly
visible on either side of the City from the towers of
Notre-Dame: the Seine disappeared under the bridges, and
the bridges under the houses.

And when one looked beyond these bridges, on which the
house-roofs glimmered green — moss-grown before their time

from the mists of the river — and turned one's gaze to the left towards the University, the first building which caught the eye was a low, extensive cluster of towers, the Petit-Châtelet, whose yawning gateway swallowed up the end of the Petit-Pont. Then, if you ran your eye along the river bank from east to west, from the Tournelle to the Tour de Nesle, it was one long line of houses with sculptured beams, coloured windows, overhanging storeys jutting out over the roadway — an interminable zigzag of gabled houses broken frequently by the opening of some street, now and then by the frontage or corner of some grand mansion with its gardens and its court-yards, its wings and outbuildings; standing proudly there in the midst of this crowding, hustling throng of houses, like a grand seigneur among a mob of rustics. There were five or six of these palaces along the quay, from the Logis de Lorraine, which shared with the Bernardines the great neighbouring enclosure of the Tournelle, to the Tour de Nesle, the chief tower of which formed the boundary of Paris, and whose pointed gables were accustomed, for three months of the year, to cut with their black triangles the scarlet disk of the setting sun.

Altogether, this side of the Seine was the least mercantile of the two: there was more noise and crowding of scholars than artisans, and there was no quay, properly speaking, except between the Pont Saint-Michel and the Tour de Nesle. The rest of the river bank was either a bare strand, like that beyond the Bernardine Monastery, or a row of houses with their feet in the water, as between the two bridges. This was the domain of the washerwomen; here they called to one another, chattered, laughed, and sang, from morning till night along the river side, while they beat the linen vigorously — as they do to this day, contributing not a little to the gaiety of Paris.

The University itself appeared as one block forming from end to end a compact and homogeneous whole. Seen from above, this multitude of closely packed, angular, clinging roofs, built, for the most part, on one geometrical principle, gave the impression of the crystallization of one substance. Here the capricious cleavage of the streets did not cut up the

mass into such disproportionate slices. The forty-two colleges
were distributed pretty equally over the whole, and were in
evidence on all sides. The varied and charming rooflines of
these beautiful buildings originated in the same art which
produced the simple roofs they overtopped, being practically
nothing more than a repetition, in the square or cube, of the
same geometrical figure. Consequently, they lent variety to
the whole without confusing it, completed without overload-
ing it — for geometry is another form of harmony. Several
palatial residences lifted their heads sumptuously here and
there above the picturesque roofs of the left bank: the Logis
de Nevers, the Logis de Rome, the Logis de Reims, which
have disappeared; also the Hôtel de Cluny, which for the
consolation of the artist still exists, but the tower of which was
so stupidly shortened a few years ago. Near the Hôtel Cluny
stood the Baths of Julian, a fine Roman palace with circular
arches. There was, besides, a number of abbeys, more
religious in style, of graver aspect than the secular residences,
but not inferior either in beauty or in extent. The most
striking of these were the Bernardines' Abbey with its three
steeples; Sainte-Geneviève, the square tower of which still
exists to make us more deeply regret the rest; the Sorbonne,
part college, part monastery, of which so admirable a nave
still survives; the beautiful quadrilateral Monastery of the
Mathurins; adjacent to it the Benedictine Monastery, within
the wall of which they managed to knock up a theatre
between the issue of the seventh and eighth editions of this
book; the Abbey of the Cordeliers, with its three enormous
gables in a row; that of the Augustines, the tapering spire of
which was, after the Tour de Nesle, the second pinnacle at
this side of Paris, counting from the west. The colleges, the
connecting link between the cloister and the world, held
architecturally the mean between the great mansions and the
abbeys, more severe in their elegance, more massive in their
sculpture than the palaces, less serious in their style of
architecture than the religious houses. Unfortunately,
scarcely anything remains of these buildings, in which
Gothic art held so admirable a balance between the
sumptuous and the simple. The churches (and they were

numerous and splendid in the University quarter, illustrating every architectural era, from the Roman arches of Saint-Julien to the Gothic arches of Saint-Severin)—the churches dominated the whole, and as one harmony more in that sea of harmonies they pierced in quick succession the waving, fretted outline of the gabled roofs with their boldly cut spires, their steeples, their tapering pinnacles, themselves but a magnificent exaggeration of the sharp angles of the roofs.

The ground of the University quarter was hilly, swelling in the southeast to the vast mound of the Montagne Sainte-Geneviève. It was curious to note, from the heights of Notre-Dame, the multitude of narrow and tortuous streets (now the *Quartier Latin*), the clusters of houses, spreading helter-skelter in every direction down the steep sides of this hill to the water-edge, some apparently rushing down, others climbing up, and all clinging one to the other.

The inhabitants thronging the streets looked, from that height and at that distance, like a swarm of ants perpetually passing and repassing each other, and added greatly to the animation of the scene.

And here and there, in the spaces between the roofs, the steeples, the innumerable projections which so fantastically bent and twisted and notched the outermost line of the quarter, you caught a glimpse of a moss-grown wall, a thickset round tower, an embattled, fortress-like gateway— the wall of Philip Augustus. Beyond this stretched the verdant meadows, ran the great high-roads with a few houses straggling along their sides, growing fewer the farther they were removed from the protecting barrier. Some of these suburbs were considerable. There was first—taking the Tournelle as the point of departure—the market-town of Saint-Victor, with its one-arched bridge spanning the Bièvre; its Abbey, where the epitaph of King Louis the Fat— *epitaphium Ludovici Grossi*—was to be seen; and its church with an octagonal spire, flanked by four belfry towers of the eleventh century (there is a similar one still to be seen at Étampes). Then there was Saint-Marceau, which already boasted three churches and a convent; then, leaving on the left the mill of the Gobelins with its white wall of enclosure, you came to the Faubourg Saint-Jacques with its beautifully carved stone cross at the cross-roads; the Church of Saint-Jacques du Haut-Pas, then a charming Gothic structure; Saint-Magloire, with a beautiful nave of the fourteenth century, which Napoleon turned into a hayloft; and Notre-Dame-des-Champs, which contained some Byzantine mosaics. Finally, after leaving in the open fields the Chartreux Monastery, a sumptuous edifice contemporary to the Palais de Justice with its garden divided off into compartments, and the deserted ruins of Vauvert, the eye turned westward and fell upon the three Roman spires of Saint-Germain-des-Prés, in the rear of which the market-town of Saint-Germain, already quite a large parish, formed fifteen or twenty streets, the sharp steeple of Saint-Sulpice marking one of the corners of the town boundary. Close by was the square enclosure of the Foire Saint-Germain, where the fairs were held—the present market-place. Then came the abbot's pillory, a charming little round tower, capped by a cone of lead; farther on were the tile-fields and the Rue du Four, leading to the manorial bakehouse; then the mill on its raised mound; finally, the Lazarette, a small, isolated building scarcely discernible in the distance.

But what especially attracted the eye and held it long was the Abbey itself. Undoubtedly this monastery, in high repute both as a religious house and as a manor, this abbey-palace, wherein the Bishop of Paris esteemed it a privilege to pass one night; with a refectory which the architect had endowed with the aspect, the beauty, and the splendid rose-window of a cathedral; its elegant Lady Chapel; its monumental dormitories, its spacious gardens, its portcullis, its drawbridge, its belt of crenated wall, which seemed to stamp its crested outline on the meadow beyond, its court-yards where the glint of armour mingled with the shimmer of gold-embroidered vestments — the whole grouped and marshalled round the three high Roman towers firmly planted on a Gothic transept — all this, I say, produced a magnificent effect against the horizon.

When at length, after long contemplating the University,
you turned towards the right bank — the Town — the scene
changed its character abruptly. Much larger than the
University quarter, the Town was much less of a united
whole. The first glance showed it to be divided into several
singularly distinct areas. First, on the east, in that part of the
Town which still takes its name from the "marais" — the
morass into which Camulogènes led Caesar — there was a
great group of palaces extending to the water's edge. Four
huge mansions, almost contiguous — the Hôtels Jouy, Sens,
Barbeau, and the Logis de la Reine mirrored in the Seine
their slated roofs and slender turrets. These four edifices
filled the space between the Rue des Nonaindières to the
Celestine Abbey, the spire of which formed a graceful relief
to their line of gables and battlements. Some squalid,
moss-grown hovels overhanging the water in front of these
splendid buildings were not sufficient to conceal from view
the beautifully ornamented corners of their facades, their
great square stone casements, their Gothic porticoes
surmounted by statues, the bold, clear-cut parapets of their
walls, and all those charming architectural surprises which
give Gothic art the appearance of forming her combinations
afresh for each new structure. Behind these palaces ran in
every direction, now cleft, palisaded, and embattled like a
citadel, now veiled by great trees like a Carthusian
monastery, the vast and multiform encircling wall of that
marvellous Hôtel Saint-Pol, where the King of France had
room to lodge superbly twenty-two princes of the rank of the
Dauphin and the Duke of Burgundy with their retinues and
their servants, not to mention the great barons, and the
Emperor when he came to visit Paris, and the lions, who had
a palace for themselves within the royal palace. And we must
observe here that a prince's lodging comprised in those days
not less than eleven apartments, from the state chamber to
the oratory, besides all the galleries, the baths, the "sweating-
rooms," and other "superfluous places" with which each suite
of apartments was provided — not to mention the gardens
specially allotted to each guest of the King, nor the kitchens,
store-rooms, pantries, and general refectories of the house-

hold; the inner court-yards in which were situated twenty-two general offices, from the bake-house to the royal cellarage; the grounds for every sort and description of game—mall, tennis, tilting at the ring, etc.; aviaries, fish-ponds, menageries, stables, cattle-sheds, libraries, armouries, and foundries. Such was, at that day, a King's palace—a Louvre, an Hôtel Saint-Pol—a city within a city.

From the tower on which we have taken up our stand, one obtained of the Hôtel Saint-Pol, though half-hidden by the four great mansions we spoke of, a very considerable and wonderful view. You could clearly distinguish in it, though skilfully welded to the main building by windowed and pillared galleries, the three mansions which Charles V had absorbed into his palace: the Hôtel du Petit-Muce with the fretted parapet that gracefully bordered its roof; the Hôtel of the Abbot of Saint-Maur, having all the appearance of a fortress, with its massive tower, its machicolations, loopholes, iron bulwarks, and over the great Saxon gate, between the two grooves for the drawbridge, the escutcheon of the Abbot; the Hôtel of the Comte d'Étampes, of which the keep, ruined at its summit, was arched and notched like a cock's-comb; here and there, three or four ancient oaks grouped together in one great bushy clump; a glimpse of swans floating on clear pools, all flecked with light and shadow; picturesque corners of innumerable court-yards; the Lion house, with its low Gothic arches on short Roman pillars, its iron bars and continuous roaring; cutting right through this picture the scaly spire of the Ave-Maria Chapel; on the left, the Mansion of the Provost of Paris, flanked by four delicately perforated turrets; and, in the centre of it all, the Hôtel Saint-Pol itself, with its multiplicity of facades, its successive enrichments since the time of Charles V, the heterogeneous excrescences with which the fancy of the architects had loaded it during two centuries, with all the roofs of its chapels, all its gables, its galleries, a thousand weather-cocks turning to the four winds of heaven, and its two lofty, contiguous towers with conical roofs surrounded by battlements at the base, looking like peaked hats with the brim turned up.

Continuing to mount the steps of this amphitheatre of

palaces, rising tier upon tier in the distance, having crossed
the deep fissure in the roofs of the Town which marked the
course of the Rue Saint-Antoine, the eye travelled on to the
Logis d'Angoulême, a vast structure of several periods, parts
of which were glaringly new and white, blending with the rest
about as well as a crimson patch on a blue doublet.
Nevertheless, the peculiarly sharp and high-pitched roof of
the modern palace — bristling with sculptured gargoyles, and
covered with sheets of lead, over which ran sparkling
incrustations of gilded copper in a thousand fantastic
arabesques — this curiously damascened roof rose gracefully
out of the brown ruins of the ancient edifice, whose massive
old towers, bulging cask-like with age, sinking into themselves
with decrepitude, and rent from top to bottom, looked like
great unbuttoned waistcoats. Behind rose the forest of spires
of the Palais des Tournelles. No show-place in the world — not
even Chambord or the Alhambra — could afford a more
magical, more ethereal, more enchanting spectacle than this
grove of spires, bell-towers, chimneys, weather-cocks, spiral
stair-cases; of airy lantern towers that seemed to have been
worked with a chisel; of pavilions; of spindle-shaped turrets,
all diverse in shape, height, and position. It might have been
a gigantic chess-board in stone.

That sheaf of enormous black towers to the right of the
inky Tournelles, pressing one against the other, and bound
together, as it were, by a circular moat; that donjon-keep,
pierced far more numerously with shot-holes than with
windows, its drawbridge always raised, its portcullis always
lowered — that is the Bastile. Those objects like black beaks
projecting from the embrasures of the battlements, and
which, from a distance, you might take for rain-spouts, are
cannon. Within their range, at the foot of the formidable
pile, is the Porte Saint-Antoine, crouching between its two
towers.

Beyond the Tournelles, reaching to the wall of Charles V,
stretched in rich diversity of lawns and flower-beds a velvet
carpet of gardens and royal parks, in the heart of which,
conspicuous by its maze of trees and winding paths, one
recognised the famous labyrinthine garden presented by

Louis XI to Coictier. The great physician's observatory rose out of the maze like a massive, isolated column with a tiny house for its capital. Many a terrible astrological crime was perpetrated in the laboratory. This is now the Place Royale.

As we have said, the Palace quarter, of which we have endeavoured to convey some idea to the reader, though merely pointing out the chief features, filled the angle formed by the Seine and the wall of Charles V on the east. The centre of the Town was occupied by a congeries of dwelling-houses. For it was here that the three bridges of the City on the right bank discharged their streams of passengers; and bridges lead to the building of houses before palaces. This collection of middle-class dwellings, closely packed together like the cells of a honeycomb, was, however, by no means devoid of beauty. The sea of roofs of a great city has much of the grandeur of the ocean about it. To begin with, the streets in their crossings and windings cut up the mass into a hundred charming figures, streaming out from the Halles like the rays of a star. The streets of Saint-Denis and Saint-Martin, with their innumerable ramifications, went up side by side like two great trees intertwining their branches; while such streets as the Rue de la Plâterie, Rue de la Verrerie, Rue de la Tixeranderie, etc., wound in tortuous lines through the whole. Some handsome edifices, too, thrust up their heads through the petrified waves of this sea of gables. For instance, at the head of the Pont-aux-Changeurs, behind which you could see the Seine foaming under the mill-wheels of the Pont-aux-Meuniers, there was the Châtelet, no longer a Roman keep, as under Julian the Apostate, but a feudal tower of the thirteenth century, and built of stone so hard that three hours' work with the pick did not remove more than the size of a man's fist. Then there was the square steeple of Saint-Jacques-de-la-Boucherie, with its richly sculptured corners, most worthy of admiration even then, though it was not completed in the fifteenth century; it lacked in particular the four monsters which, still perched on the four corners of its roof, look like sphinxes offering to modern Paris the enigma of the old to unriddle. Rault, the sculptor, did not put them up till 1526, and received twenty francs for his trouble. There was the Maison-aux-Piliers, facing the Place de Grève, of which we have already given the reader some idea; there was Saint-Gervais, since spoilt by a doorway "in good taste"; Saint-Méry, of which the primitive pointed arches were scarcely more than circular; Saint-Jean, whose magnificent spire was proverbial; and twenty other edifices which disdained not to hide their wonders in that chaos of deep, dark, narrow streets. Add to these the carved stone crosses, more numerous at the crossways than even the gibbets; the cemetery of the Innocents, of whose enclosing wall you caught a glimpse in the distance; the pillory of the Halles, just visible between two chimneys of the Rue de la Cossonnerie; the gibbet of the Croix du Trahoir at the corner of the ever-busy thoroughfare; the round stalls of the Corn Market; fragments of the old wall of Philip Augustus, distinguishable here and there, buried among the houses; mouldering, ivy-clad towers, ruined gateways, bits of crumbling walls; the quay with its myriad booths and gory skinning yards; the Seine, swarming with boats from the Port au Foin or hay wharf to the For-l'Evêque, and you will be able to form some adequate idea of what the great irregular quadrangle of the Town looked like in 1482.

Besides these two quarters—the one of palaces, the other of houses—the Town contributed a third element to the view: that of a long belt of abbeys which bordered almost its entire circumference from east to west; and, lying just inside the fortified wall which encircled Paris, furnished a second internal rampart of cloisters and chapels. Thus, immediately adjoining the park of the Tournelles, between the Rue Saint-Antoine and the old Rue du Temple, stood the old convent of Sainte-Catherine, with its immense grounds, bounded only by the city wall. Between the old and the new Rue du Temple was the Temple itself, a grim sheaf of lofty towers, standing haughty and alone, surrounded by a vast, embattled wall. Between the Rue Neuve du Temple and the Rue Saint-Martin, in the midst of gardens, stood the Abbey of Saint-Martin, a superb fortified church, whose girdle of towers and crown of steeples were second only to Saint-Germain-Des-Prés in strength and splendour.

Between the two streets of Saint-Martin and Saint-Denis stretched the convent enclosure of the Trinité, and between the Rue Saint-Denis and the Rue Montorgueil that of Filles-Dieu. Close by, one caught a glimpse of the mouldering roofs and broken wall of the Cour des Miracles, the only profane link in that pious chain.

Lastly, the fourth area, standing out distinctly in the conglomeration of roofs on the right bank, and occupying the eastern angle formed by the city wall and the river wall, was a fresh knot of palaces and mansions clustered round the foot of the Louvre. The old Louvre of Philip Augustus, that stupendous pile whose enormous middle tower mustered round it twenty-three major towers, irrespective of the smaller ones, appeared from the distance as if encased within the Gothic roof-lines of the Hôtel d'Alençon and the Petit-Bourbon. This hydra of towers, this guardian monster of Paris, with its twenty-four heads ever erect, the tremendous ridge of its roof sheathed in lead or scales of slate and glistening in metallic lustre, furnished an unexpected close to the western configuration of the Town.

This, then, was the town of Paris in the fifteenth century— an immense mass—what the Romans called *insula*—of burgher dwelling-houses, flanked on either side by two blocks of palaces, terminated the one by the Louvre, the other by the Tournelles, bordered on the north by a long chain of abbeys and walled gardens all blended and mingling in one harmonious whole; above these thousand buildings with their fantastic outline of tiled and slated roofs, the steeples— fretted, fluted, honeycombed—of the forty-four churches on the right bank; myriads of streets cutting through it; as boundary: on one side a circuit of lofty walls with square towers (those of the University wall were round); on the other, the Seine, intersected by bridges and carrying numberless boats.

Beyond the walls a few suburbs hugged the protection of the gates, but they were less numerous and more scattered than on the side of the University. In the rear of the Bastile about twenty squalid cottages huddled round the curious stonework of the Croix-Faubin, and the abutments of the

Abbey of Saint-Antoine des Champs; then came Popincourt, buried in cornfields; then La Courtille, a blithe village of taverns; the market-town of Saint-Laurent with its church steeple appearing in the distance as if one of the pointed towers of the Porte Saint-Martin; the suburb of Saint-Denis with the vast enclosure of Saint-Ladre; outside the Porte-Montmartre, the Grange-Bâtelière encircled by white walls; behind that again, with its chalky slopes, Montmartre, which then had almost as many churches as wind-mills, but has only retained the wind-mills, for the world is now merely concerned for bread for the body. Finally, beyond the Louvre, among the meadows, stretched the Faubourg Saint-Honoré, already a considerable suburb, and the verdant pastures of Petite-Bretagne and the Marché-aux-Porceaux or pig-market, in the middle of which stood the horrible furnace where they seethed the false coiners.

On the top of a hill, rising out of the solitary plain between La Courtille and Saint-Laurent, you will have remarked a sort of building, presenting the appearance, in the distance, of a ruined colonnade with its foundation laid bare. But this was neither a Pantheon nor a Temple of Jupiter; it was Montfaucon.

Now, if the enumeration of so many edifices, brief as we have done our best to make it, has not shattered in the reader's mind the image of old Paris as fast as we have built it up, we will recapitulate in a few words. In the centre, the island of the City like an immense tortoise, stretching out its tiled bridges like scaly paws from under its gray shell of roofs. On the left, the dense, bristling, square block of the University; on the right, the high semicircle of the Town, showing many more gardens and isolated edifices than the other two. The three areas, City, University, and Town, are veined with streets innumerable. Athwart the whole runs the Seine — "the fostering Seine," as Peter du Breul calls it — encumbered with islands, bridges, and boats. All around, a vast plain checkered with a thousand forms of cultivation and dotted with fair villages; to the left, Issy, Vanvres, Vaugirarde, Montrouge, Gentilly, with its round and its square tower, etc.; to the right, a score of others from

Conflans to Ville-l'Evêque; on the horizon, a border of hills ranged in a circle, the rim of the basin, as it were. Finally, far to the east, Vincennes with its seven square towers; southward, Bicêtre and its sharp-pointed turrets; northward, Saint-Denis with it spire; and in the west, Saint-Cloud and its castle-keep. Such was the Paris which the ravens of 1482 looked down upon from the heights of Notre-Dame.

And yet this was the city of which Voltaire said that "before the time of Louis XIV it only possessed four handsome examples of architecture"—the dome of the Sorbonne, the Val-de-Grâce, the modern Louvre, and I forget the fourth—the Luxembourg, perhaps. Fortunately, Voltaire was none the less the author of *Candide*; and none the less the man of all others in the long line of humanity who possessed in highest perfection the *rire diabolique*—the sardonic smile. It proves, besides, that one may be a brilliant genius, and yet know nothing of an art one has not studied. Did not Molière think to greatly honour Raphael and Michael Angelo by calling them "the Mignads of their age"?

But to return to Paris and the fifteenth century.

It was in those days not only a beautiful city; it was a homogeneous city, a direct product—architectural and historical—of the Middle Ages, a chronicle in stone. It was a city composed of two architectural strata only—the Roman-esque and the Gothic—for the primitive Roman layer had long since disappeared excepting in the Baths of Julian, where it still pierced through the thick overlying crust of the Middle Ages. As for the Celtic stratum, no trace of it was dis-coverable even when sinking wells.

Fifty years later, when the Renaissance came, and with that unity of style, so severe and yet so varied, associated its dazzling wealth of fantasy and design, its riot of Roman arches, Doric columns and Gothic vaults, its delicate and ideal sculpture, its own peculiar tastes in arabesques and capitals, its architectural paganism contemporary with Luther, Paris was perhaps more beautiful still though less harmonious to the eye and the strictly artistic sense. But that splendid period was of short duration. The Renaissance was not impartial; it was not content only to erect, it must also pull down; to be sure, it required space. Gothic Paris was complete but for a moment. Scarcely was Saint-Jacques-de-la-Boucherie finished when the demolition of the old Louvre began.

Since then the great city has gone on losing her beauty day by day. The Gothic Paris, which was effacing the Roman-esque, has been effaced in its turn. But what name shall be given to the Paris which has replaced it?

We have the Paris of Catherine de Medicis in the Tuileries; the Paris of Henri II in the Hôtel-de-Ville, both edifices in the grand style; the Place Royale shows us the Paris of Henri IV — brick fronts, stone copings, and slate roofs — tricolour houses; the Val-de-Grâce is the Paris of Louis XIII — low and broad in style, with basket-handle arches and something indefinably pot-bellied about its pillars and humpbacked about its domes. We see the Paris of Louis XIV in the Invalides — stately, rich, gilded, cold; the Paris of Louis XV at Saint-Sulpice — scrolls and love-knots and clouds, vermicelli and chicory leaves — all in stone; the Paris of Louis XVI in the Panthéon, a bad copy of Saint Peter's at Rome (the building has settled rather crookedly, which has not tended to improve its lines); the Paris of the Republic at the School of Medicine — a spurious hash of Greek and Roman, with about as much relation to the Coliseum or the Pantheon as the constitution of the year III has to the laws of Minos — a style known in architecture as "the Messidor"; the Paris of Napoleon in the Place Vendome — a sublime idea, a bronze column made of cannons; the Paris of the Restoration at the Bourse — an abnormally white colonnade supporting an abnormally smooth frieze — it is perfectly square and cost twenty million francs.

To each of these characteristic buildings there belongs, in virtue of a similarity of style, of form, and of disposition, a certain number of houses scattered about the various districts easily recognised and assigned to their respective dates by the eye of the connoisseur. To the seeing eye, the spirit of a period and the features of a King are traceable even in the knocker of a door.

The Paris of to-day has, therefore, no typical characteristic physiognomy. It is a collection of samples of several periods, of which the finest have disappeared. The capital is increasing in houses only, and what houses! At this rate, there will be a new Paris every fifty years. The historic significance, too, of its architecture is lessened day by day. The great edifices are becoming fewer and fewer, are being swallowed up before our eyes by the flood of houses. Our fathers had a Paris of stone; our sons will have a Paris of stucco.

As for the modern structures of this new Paris, we would much prefer not to dilate upon them. Not that we fail to give them their due. The Sainte-Geneviève of M. Soufflot is certainly the finest tea-cake that ever was made of stone. The palace of the Légion d'Honneur is also a most distinguished piece of confectionery. The dome of the Corn Market is a jockey-cap set on the top of a high ladder. The towers of Saint-Sulpice are two great clarinets — a shape which is as good as any other — and the grinning zigzag of the telegraph agreeably breaks the monotony of their roofs. Saint-Roch possesses a door that can only be matched in magnificence by that of Saint Thomas Aquinas; also it owns a Calvary in alto-relievo down in a cellar, and a monstrance of gilded wood — real marvels these, one must admit. The lantern tower in the maze at the Botanical Gardens is also vastly ingenious. As regards the Bourse, which is Greek as to its colonnade, Roman as to the round arches of its windows and doors, and Renaissance as to its broad, low, vaulted roof, it is indubitably in purest and most correct style; in proof of which we need only state that it is crowned by an attic story such as was never seen in Athens — a beautiful straight line, gracefully intersected at intervals by chimney pots. And, admitting that it be a rule in architecture that a building should be so adapted to its purpose that that purpose should at once be discernible in the aspect of the edifice, no praise is too high for a structure which might, from its appearance, be indifferently a royal palace, a chamber of deputies, a town hall, a college, a riding-school, an academy, a warehouse, a court of justic, a museum, a barracks, a mausoleum, a temple, or a theatre — and all the time it is an Exchange. Again, a building should be appropriate to the climate. This one is obviously constructed for our cold and rainy skies. It has an almost flat roof, as they obtain in the East, so that in winter, when it snows, that roof has to be swept, and, of course, we all know that roofs are intended to be swept. And as regards the purpose of which we spoke just now, the building fulfils it to admiration: it is a Bourse in France as it would have been a Temple in Greece. It is true that the architect has been at great pains to conceal the face of the clock, which would have spoilt the pure lines of the facade; but in return, we have the colonnade running round the entire building, under which, on high-days and holidays, the imposing procession of stock-brokers and exchange-agents can display itself in all its glory.

These now are undoubtedly very superior buildings. Add to them a number of such handsome, interesting, and varied streets as the Rue de Rivoli, and I do not despair of Paris offering one day to the view, if seen from a balloon, that wealth of outline, that opulence of detail, that diversity of aspect, that indescribable air of grandeur in its simplicity, of the unexpected in its beauty, which characterizes — a draught-board.

Nevertheless, admirable as the Paris of to-day may seem to you, conjure up the Paris of the fifteenth century; rebuild it in imagination; look through that amazing forest of spires, towers, and steeples; pour through the middle of the immense city the Seine, with its broad green and yellow pools that make it iridescent as a serpent's skin; divide it at the island points, send it swirling round the piers of the bridges; project sharply against an azure horizon the Gothic profile of old Paris; let its outline float in a wintry mist clinging round its numerous chimneys; plunge it in deepest night, and watch the fantastic play of light and shadow in that sombre labyrinth of edifices; cast into it a ray of moonlight, showing it vague and uncertain, with its towers rearing their massive heads above the mists; or go back to the night scene, touch up the thousand points of the spires and gables with shadow, let it stand out more ridged and jagged than a shark's jaw against a coppery sunset sky — and then compare.

And if you would receive from the old city an impression

the modern one is incapable of giving, go at dawn on some
great festival — Easter or Whitsuntide — and mount to some
elevated point, whence the eye commands the entire capital,
and be present at the awakening of the bells. Watch, at a
signal from heaven — for it is the sun that gives — those
thousand churches starting from their sleep. First comes
scattered notes passing from church to church, as when
musicians signal to one another that the concert is to begin.
Then, suddenly behold — for there are moments when the
ear, too, seems to have sight — behold, how, at the same
moment, from every steeple there rises a column of sound, a
cloud of harmony. At first the vibration of each bell mounts
up straight, pure, isolated from the rest, into the resplendent
sky of morn; then, by degrees, as the waves spread out, they
mingle, blend, unite one with the other, and melt into one
magnificent concert. Now it is one unbroken stream of
sonorous sound poured incessantly from the innumerable
steeples — floating, undulating, leaping, eddying over the city,
the deafening circle of its vibration extending far beyond the
horizon. Yet this scene of harmony is no chaos. Wide and
deep though it be, it never loses its limpid clearness; you can
follow the windings of each separate group of notes that
detaches itself from the peal; you can catch the dialogue,
deep and shrill by turns, between the *bourdon* and the
crecelle; you hear the octaves leap from steeple to steeple,
darting winged, airy, strident from the bell of silver,
dropping halt and broken from the bell of wood. You listen
delightedly to the rich gamut, incessantly ascending and
descending, of the seven bells of Saint-Eustache; clear and
rapid notes flash across the whole in luminous zigzags, and
then vanish like lightning. That shrill, cracked voice over
there comes from the Abbey of Saint-Martin; here the hoarse
and sinister growl of the Bastile; at the other end the boom
of the great tower of the Louvre. The royal carillon of the
Palais scatters its glittering trills on every side, and on them,
at regular intervals, falls the heavy clang of the great bell of
Notre-Dame, striking flashes from them as the hammer from
the anvil. At intervals, sounds of every shape pass by, coming
from the triple peal of Saint-Germain-des-Prés. Then, ever

and anon, the mass of sublime sound opens and gives passage
to the *stretto* of the Ave-Maria chapel, flashing through like a
shower of meteors. Down below, in the very depths of the
chorus, you can just catch the chanting inside the churches,
exhaled faintly through the pores of their vibrating domes.
Here, in truth, is an opera worth listening to. In general, the
murmur that rises up from Paris during the daytime is the
city talking; at night it is the city breathing; but this is the
city singing. Lend your ear, then, to this *tutti* of the bells;
diffuse over the *ensemble* the murmur of half a million of
human beings, the eternal plaint of the river, the ceaseless
rushing of the wind, the solemn and distant quartet of the
four forests set upon the hills, round the horizon, like so
many enormous organ-cases; muffle in this, as in a sort of
twilight, all of the great central peal that might otherwise be
too hoarse or too shrill, and then say whether you know of
anything in the world more rich, more blithe, more golden,
more dazzling, than this tumult of bells and chimes — this
furnace of music, these ten thousand brazen voices singing at
once in flutes of stone, three hundred feet high — this city
which is now but one vast orchestra — this symphony with the
mighty uproar of a tempest.

Henry James: Chartres

In the following letter to the Tribune, *Henry James describes a trip to Chartres. It is best to see Chartres when the light is soft, for the cathedral has moods which are at times severe. The cathedral, built in the Middle Ages, is considered a perfect work of architecture, the high point of French Gothic.*

Chartres

Paris, April 9. — The spring in Paris, since it has fairly begun, has been enchanting. The sun and the moon have been blazing in emulation, and the difference between the blue sky of day and of night has been as slight as possible. There are no clouds in the sky, but there are little thin green clouds, little puffs of raw, tender verdure, caught and suspended upon the branches of the trees. All the world is in the streets; the chairs and tables which have stood empty all winter before the cafe doors are at a premium; the theaters have become intolerably close — the puppet shows in the Champs Élysées are the only form of dramatic entertainment which seems consistent with the season. By the way of doing honor, at a small cost, to this ethereal mildness, I went out the other day to the ancient town of Chartres, where I spent several hours of the purest felicity. Pure felicity, in this hard world, always deserves to be recorded, and I cannot deny myself the pleasure of commemorating my admiration of one of the most beautiful churches in France. If one has not been traveling for a long time, there is, to an appreciative mind, a sort of intoxication in the mere fact of changing his place, and if one does so on a lovely spring day, under picturesque circumstances, the satisfaction is at its highest. To this perhaps rather frivolous emotion I must confess myself extremely susceptible, and the effect of it was to send me down to Chartres in a shamelessly optimistic state of mind. I was so prepared to be entertained and pleased with everything that it is only a mercy that the Cathedral happens to be a really fine building. If it had not been, I should still have admired it inordinately and rendered myself guilty of heaven knows what unpardonable aesthetic error. But I am almost ashamed to say how soon my entertainment began. It began, I think, with my hailing a little open carriage on the boulevard and causing myself to be driven to the Western Railway station — away across the river, up the Rue Bonaparte, of art-student memories, and along the big, straight Rue de Rennes to the Boulevard Montparnasse. Of course, at this rate, by the time I reached Chartres — the journey is of a couple of hours — I had almost drained the cup of pleasure. But it was replenished at the station, at the buffet, from the very good bottle of wine I drank with my breakfast. Here, by the way, is another excellent excuse for being enchanted with any day's excursion in France — wherever you are, you may breakfast well. There may, indeed, if the station is very small, be no buffet; but if there is a buffet, you may be sure that civilization — in the persons of a sympathetic young woman in a well-made black dress, and a rapid, zealous, grateful waiter — presides at it. It was quite the least, as the French say, that after my breakfast I should have thought the Cathedral, as I saw it from the foot of the steep hill on which the town stands, rising high above the clustered houses, and seeming to make of their red-roofed agglomeration a mere pedestal for its immense beauty, promised remarkably well. You see it so as you emerge from the station, and then, as you climb slowly into town, you lose sight of it. You perceive Chartres to be a rather shabby little *ville de province,* with a few sunny, empty open places, and crooked, shady streets, in which two or three times you lose your way, until at last, after more than once catching a glimpse, high above some slit between the houses, of the clear gray towers shining against the blue sky, you push forward again, risk another short cut, turn another interposing corner, and stand before you the goal of your pilgrimage.

I spent a long time looking at Chartres Cathedral; I revolved around it, like a moth around a candle; I went away and I came back; I chose twenty different standpoints; I observed it during the different hours of the day, and saw it in the moonlight as well as the sunshine. I gained, in a word, a certain sense of familiarity with it; and yet I despair of giving any very coherent account of it. Like most French cathedrals, it rises straight out of the street, and it is without that setting of turf and trees and deaneries and canonries which contribute so largely to the impressiveness of the great English churches. Thirty years ago a row of old houses was glued to its base and made their back walls of its sculptured sides. These have been plucked away, and, relatively speaking, the church is fairly isolated. But the little square that surrounds it is regretfully narrow, and you flatten your back against the opposite houses in the vain attempt to stand off and survey the towers. The proper way to look at the towers would be to go up in a balloon and hang poised, face to face with them, in the blue air. There is, however, perhaps an advantage in being forced to stand so directly under them, for this position gives you an overwhelming impression of their height. I have seen, I suppose, churches as beautiful as this one, but I do not remember ever to have been so touched and fascinated by architectural beauty. The endless upward reach of the great west front, the clear, silvery tone of its surface, the way a few magnificent features are made to occupy its vast, serene expanse, its simplicity, majesty, and dignity—these things crowd upon one's sense with an eloquence that one must not attempt to translate into words. The impressions produced by architecture lend themselves as little to interpretation by another medium as those produced by music. Certainly there is something of the beauty of music in the sublime proportions of the façade of Chartres.

The doors are rather low, as those of the English cathedrals are apt to be, but (standing three together) are set in a deep

framework of sculpture — rows of arching grooves, filled with
admirable little images, standing with their heels on each
other's heads. The church as it now exists, except the
northern tower, dates from the middle of the thirteenth
century, and these closely packed figures are full of the
grotesqueness of the period. Above the triple portals is a vast
round-topped window, in three divisions, of the grandest
dimensions and the stateliest effect. Above this window is a
circular window of immense circumference, with a double
row of sculptured spokes radiating from its center and
looking on its great lofty field of stone, as expansive and sym-
bolic as if it were the wheel of Time itself. Higher still is a
beautiful cornice and stretching across the front from tower
to tower; and above this is a range of niched statues of kings —
fifteen, I believe, in number. Above the statues is a gable,
with an image of the Virgin and Child on its front, and
another of Christ on its apex. In the relation of all these parts
there is such a spaciousness and harmony that while on the
one side the eye rests on a great many broad stretches of
naked stone, there is no approach on the other to overpro-
fusion of detail. The little gallery that I have spoken of,
beneath the statues of the kings, had for me a peculiar
charm. Unavailable, at its tremendous altitude, for other
purposes, it seemed fantastically intended for the little images
to step down and walk about upon. When the great façade
begins to glow in the late afternoon light, you can imagine
them strolling up and down their long balcony in couples,
pausing with their elbows on the balustrade, resting their
stony chins in their hands, and looking out, with their little
blank eyes, on the great view of the old French monarchy
they once ruled, and which now has passed away. The two
great towers of the Cathedral are among the noblest of their
kind. They rise in solid simplicity to about as great a height as
the eye often troubles itself to travel and then, suddenly, they
begin to execute a magnificent series of feats in architectural
gymnastics. This is especially true of the northern spire,
which is a late creation, dating from the sixteenth century.
The other is relatively quiet; but its companion is a sort of
tapering bouquet of sculptured stone. Statues and buttresses,

gargoyles, arabesques, and crockets pile themselves in successive stages, until the eye loses the sense of everything but a sort of architectural lacework. The pride of Chartres, after its front, is the two portals of its transepts — great dusky porches, in three divisions, covered with more images than I have space to talk about. Wherever you look, along the sides of the church, a time-worn image is niched or perched. The face of each flying buttress is garnished with one, with the features quite melted away.

The inside of the Cathedral corresponds in vastness and grandeur to the outside — it is the perfection of Gothic in its prime. But I looked at it rapidly, the place was so intolerably cold. It seemed to answer one's query of what becomes of the winter when the spring chases it away. The winter hereabouts has sought an asylum in Chartres Cathedral, where it has found plenty of room and may reside in a state of excellent preservation until it can safely venture abroad again. I thought I had been in cold churches before, but the thought had been an injustice to the temperature of Chartres. The nave was full of little padded chairs of the Chartres *bourgeoisie,* whose faith, I hope for their comfort, is of the good old red-hot complexion. In a higher temperature I should have done more justice to the magnificent old glass of the windows — which glowed through the icy dusk like the purple and orange of a winter sunset — and to the immense sculptured external casing of the choir. This latter is an extraordinary piece of work. It is a high Gothic screen, shutting in the choir, and covered with elaborate bas-reliefs of the sixteenth and seventeenth centuries, representing scenes from the life of Christ and of the Virgin. Some of the figures are admirable, and the effect of the whole great semi-circular wall, chiseled like a silver bowl, is superb. There is also a crypt of high antiquity and, I believe, great interest, to be seen; but my teeth chattered a respectful negative to the sacristan who offered to guide me to it. It was so agreeable to stand in the warm outer air again, that I spent the rest of the day in it.

Although, besides its cathedral, Chartres has no very rare architectural treasures, the place is picturesque, in a shabby, third-rate, poverty-stricken sort of fashion, and my observations were not unremunerative. There is a little church of Saint Aignan, of the sixteenth century, with an elegant, decayed façade, and a small tower beside it, lower than its own roof, to which it is joined, in quaint, Siamese-twin fashion, by a single long buttress. Standing there with its crumbling Renaissance doorway in a kind of grass-grown alcove, it reminded me of what the tourist encounters in small Italian towns. Most of the streets of Chartres are crooked lanes, winding over the face of the steep hill, the summit of the hill being occupied by half-a-dozen little open squares, which seem like reservoirs of the dullness and stillness that flow through the town. In the midst of one of them rises an old dirty brick obelisk, commemorating the glories of the young General Marceau of the First Republic — "soldier at sixteen, general at twenty-three, he died at twenty-seven." Chartres gives us an impression of extreme antiquity, but it is an antiquity that has gone down in the world. I saw very few of those stately little *hôtels,* with pilastered fronts, which look so well in the silent streets of provincial towns. The houses are mostly low, small, and of sordid aspect, and though many of them have overhanging upper stories, and steep, battered gables, there is nothing very exquisite in their quaintness.

I was struck, as an American always is in small French and English towns, with the immense number of shops, and their brilliant appearance, which seems so out of proportion to any visible body of consumers. At Chartres the shopkeepers must all feed upon each other, for, whoever buys, the whole population sells. The population in the streets appears to consist of several hundred brown old peasant women, between seventy and eighty years of age, with their faces cross-hatched with wrinkles and their quaint white coifs drawn tightly over their weather-blasted eyebrows. Labor-stricken grandams, all the world over, are the reverse of lovely, for the toil that wrestles for its daily bread, morsel by morsel, is not beautifying; but I thought I had never seen the possibilities of female ugliness so variously embodied as in the crones of Chartres. Some of them were leading small children

by the hand — little red-cheeked girls, in the close black caps
and black pinafores of humble French infancy — a costume
which makes French children always look like orphans. Those
who feel very "strongly" on the subject of these little people
being put out to nurse, as they generally are, may maintain
that there is truth in the symbol. Others of the old women
were guiding along the flinty lanes the steps of small donkeys,
some of them fastened into little carts, others with well-laden
backs. These were the only quadrupeds I perceived at
Chartres. Neither horse nor carriage did I behold, save at the
station the omnibuses of the rival inns — the Grand Monarque
and the Duc de Chartres — which glare at each other across
the Grande Place. A friend of mine told me that a few years
ago, passing through Chartres, he went by night to call upon
a gentleman who lived there. During his visit it came on to
rain violently, and when the hour for his departure arrived
the rain had made the streets impassable. There was no
vehicle to be had, and my friend was resigning himself to a
soaking. "You can be taken of course in the sedan chair,"
said his host with dignity. The sedan chair was produced, a
couple of servingmen grasped the handles, my friend stepped
into it, and went swinging back — through the last century —
to the Grand Monarque. This little anecdote, I imagine, still
paints Chartres socially.

Before dinner I took a walk on the planted promenade
which encircles the town — the Tour-de-ville it is called —
much of which is extremely picturesque. Chartres has lost her
walls as a whole, but here and there they survive, and play a
desultory part in holding the town together. In one place the
rampart is really magnificent — smooth, strong, and lofty,
curtained with ivy, and supporting on its summit an old
convent and its garden. Only one of the city gates remains — a
narrow arch of the fourteenth century, flanked by two
admirable round towers, and preceded by a fosse. If you
stoop a little, as you stand outside, the arch of this hoary old
gate makes a most picturesque setting for the picture of the
interior of the town, and on the inner hilltop against the sky
the large gray mass of the Cathedral. The ditch is full, and to
right and to left it flows along the base of the moldering wall,

through which the shabby backs of houses extrude, and which is garnished with little wooded galleries, lavatories of the town's soiled linen. These little galleries are filled with washerwomen, who crane over and dip their many-colored rags into the yellow stream. The old patched and interrupted wall, the ditch with its weedy edges, the spots of color, the white-capped laundresses in their little wooden cages — one lingers to look at it all. To wind up the day I dined at the table d'hôte at the Grand Monarque, in a company of *voyageurs de commerce,* where I continued my observations. The dinner costs three francs fifty centimes; the landlord sits at the table and carves the meats, now and then manipulating a recalcitrant joint rather freely; the guests empty the dregs of their glasses on the floor, and clean their knives and forks, between the courses, with bread crumbs. But even among these circumstances the classic French art of conversation is by no means lost, and in paying my three francs fifty centimes I felt that I was paying for something more than my material dinner.

Henry Adams: Mont-Saint-Michel

Henry Adams (1838-1918), grandson of the sixth president of the United States, was a historian who sought for some unifying force that would help explain the confusions of his changing world. He opposed the optimistic thinkers of his day, finding his unifying factor in the laws of energy, and claiming that the second law of thermodynamics that implies a universal tendency to dissipate energy, applies as well to human life. As his lifework, he sought to prove his theories of history by contrasting two historical periods: one, "the point in history when man held the highest idea of himself as a unit in a unified universe" and two, the divided universe of "twentieth-century multiplicity." An expression of the latter can be found in his great autobiography, The Education of Henry Adams; *for the former, he chose the thirteenth century, as embodied in the great complex of Benedictine Abbey buildings, churches and cathedrals of* Mont-Saint-Michel and Chartres, *from which study the following extract is taken. The small houses built into the rock enfolded in the great Abbey of Mont-Saint-Michel stand high on a seaside peak in Normandy.*

The Archangel loved heights. Standing on the summit of the tower that crowned his church, wings upspread, sword uplifted, the devil crawling beneath, and the cock, symbol of eternal vigilance, perched on his mailed foot, Saint Michael held a place of his own in heaven and on earth which seems, in the eleventh century, to leave hardly room for the Virgin of the Crypt at Chartres, still less for the Beau Christ of the thirteenth century at Amiens. The Archangel stands for Church and State, and both militant. He is the conqueror of Satan, the mightiest of all created spirits, the nearest to God. His place was where the danger was greatest; therefore you find him here. For the same reason he was, while the pagan danger lasted, the patron saint of France. So the Normans, when they were converted to Christianity, put themselves under his powerful protection. So he stood for centuries on his Mount in Peril of the Sea, watching across the tremor of the immense ocean, — *immensi tremor oceani,* — as Louis XI, inspired for once to poetry, inscribed on the collar of the Order of Saint Michael which he created. So soldiers, nobles, and monarchs went on pilgrimage to his shrine; so the common people followed, and still follow, like ourselves.

The church stands high on the summit of this granite rock, and on its west front is the platform, to which the tourist ought first to climb. From the edge of this platform, the eye plunges down, two hundred and thirty-five feet, to the wide sands or the wider ocean, as the tides recede or advance, under an infinite sky, over a restless sea, which even we tourists can understand and feel without books or guides; but when we turn from the western view, and look at the church door, thirty or forty yards from the parapet where we stand, one needs to be eight centuries old to know what this mass of encrusted architecture meant to its builders, and even then one must still learn to feel it. The man who wanders into the twelfth century is lost, unless he can grow prematurely young.

One can do it, as one can play with children. Wordsworth, whose practical sense equalled his intuitive genius, carefully limited us to "a season of calm weather," which is certainly best; but granting a fair frame of mind, one can still "have sight of that immortal sea" which brought us hither from the twelfth century; one can even travel thither and see the children sporting on the shore. Our sense is partially atrophied from disuse, but it is still alive, at least in old people, who alone, as a class, have the time to be young.

One needs only to be old enough in order to be as young as

one will. From the top of this Abbey Church one looks across the bay to Avranches, and towards Coutances and the Cotentin, — the *Constantinus pagus,* — whose shore, facing us, recalls the coast of New England. The relation between the granite of one coast and that of the other may be fanciful, but the relation between the people who live on each is as hard and practical a fact as the granite itself. When one enters the church, one notes first the four great triumphal piers or columns, at the intersection of the nave and transepts, and on looking into M. Corroyer's architectural study which is the chief source of all one's acquaintance with the Mount, one learns that these piers were constructed in 1058. Four out of five American tourists will instantly recall the only date of mediæval history they ever knew, the date of the Norman Conquest. Eight years after these piers were built, in 1066, Duke William of Normandy raised an army of forty thousand men in these parts, and in northern France, whom he took to England, where they mostly stayed. For a hundred and fifty years, until 1204, Normandy and England were united; the Norman peasant went freely to England with his lord, spiritual or temporal; the Norman woman, a very capable person, followed her husband or her parents; Normans held nearly all the English fiefs; filled the English Church; crowded the English Court; created the English law; and we know that French was still currently spoken in England as late as 1400, or therabouts, "After the scole of Stratford atte bowe." The aristocratic Norman names still survive in part, and if we look up their origin here we shall generally find them in villages so remote and insignificant that their place can hardly be found on any ordinary map; but the common people had no surnames, and cannot be traced, although for every noble whose name or blood survived in England or in Normandy, we must reckon hundreds of peasants. Since the generation which followed William to England in 1066, we can reckon twenty-eight or thirty from father to son, and, if you care to figure up the sum, you will find that you had about two hundred and fifty million arithmetical ancestors living in the middle of the eleventh century. The whole population of England and

northern France may then have numbered five million, but if
it were fifty it would not much affect the certainly that, if you
have any English blood at all, you have also Norman. If we
could go back and live again in all our two hundred and fifty
million arithmetical ancestors of the eleventh century, we
should find ourselves doing many surprising things, but
among the rest we should pretty certainly be ploughing most
of the fields of the Cotentin and Calvados; going to mass in
every parish church in Normandy; rendering military service
to every lord, spiritual or temporal, in all this region; and
helping to build the Abbey Church at Mont-Saint-Michel.
From the roof of the Cathedral of Coutances over yonder, one
may look away over the hills and woods, the farms and fields
of Normandy, and so familiar, so homelike are they, one can
almost take oath that in this, or the other, or in all, one knew
life once and has never so fully known it since.

Never so fully known it since! For we of the eleventh
century, hard-headed, close-fisted, grasping, shrewd, as we
were, and as Normans are still said to be, stood more fully in
the centre of the world's movement than our English
descendants ever did. We were a part, and a great part, of
the Church, of France, and of Europe. The Leos and
Gregories of the tenth and eleventh centuries leaned on us in
their great struggle for reform. Our Duke Richard-Sans-
Peur, in 966, turned the old canons out of the Mount in
order to bring here the highest influence of the time, the
Benedictine monks of Monte Cassino. Richard II, grandfather of William the Conqueror, began this Abbey Church
in 1020, and helped Abbot Hildebert to build it. When
William the Conqueror in 1066 set out to conquer England,
Pope Alexander II stood behind him and blessed his banner.
From that moment our Norman Dukes cast the Kings of
France into the shade. Our activity was not limited to
northern Europe, or even confined by Anjou and Gascony.
When we stop at Coutances, we will drive out to Hauteville to
see where Tancred came from, whose sons Robert and Roger
were conquering Naples and Sicily at the time when the
Abbey Church was building on the Mount. Normans were
everywhere in 1066, and everywhere in the lead of their age.

We were a serious race. If you want other proof of it, besides our record in war and in politics, you have only to look at our art. Religious art is the measure of human depth and sincerity; any triviality, any weakness, cries aloud. If this church on the Mount is not proof enough of Norman character, we will stop at Coutances for a wider view. Then we will go to Caen and Bayeux. From there, it would almost be worth our while to leap at once to Palermo. It was in the year 1131 or thereabouts that Roger began the Cathedral at Cefalu and the Chapel Royal at Palermo; it was about the year 1174 that his grandson William began the Cathedral of Monreale. No ari—either Greek or Byzantine, Italian or Arab—has ever created two religious types so beautiful, so serious, so impressive, and yet so different, as Mont-Saint-Michel watching over its northern ocean, and Monreale, looking down over its forests of orange and lemon, on Palermo and the Sicilian seas.

Down nearly to the end of the twelfth century the Norman was fairly master of the world in architecture as in arms, although the thirteenth century belonged to France, and we must look for its glories on the Seine and Marne and Loire; but for the present we are in the eleventh century,—tenants of the Duke or of the Church or of small feudal lords who take their names from the neighbourhood,—Beaumont, Carteret, Gréville, Percy, Pierpont,—who, at the Duke's bidding, will each call out his tenants, perhaps ten men-at-arms with their attendants, to fight in Brittany, or in the Vexin toward Paris, or on the great campaign for the conquest of England which is to come within ten years,—the greatest military effort that has been made in western Europe since Charlemagne and Roland were defeated at Roncesvalles three hundred years ago. For the moment, we are helping to quarry granite for the Abbey Church, and to haul it to the Mount, or load it on our boat. We never fail to make our annual pilgrimage to the Mount on the Archangel's Day, October 16. We expect to be called out for a new campaign which Duke William threatens against Brittany, and we hear stories that Harold the Saxon, the powerful Earl of Wessex in England, is a guest, or, as some say, a prisoner or a hostage, at the Duke's Court, and will go with us on the campaign. The year is 1058.

All this time we have been standing on the *parvis,* looking out over the sea and sands which are as good eleventh-century landscape as they ever were; or turning at times towards the church door which is the *pons seclorum,* the bridge of ages, between us and our ancestors. Now that we have made an attempt, such as it is, to get our minds into a condition to cross the bridge without breaking down in the effort, we enter the church and stand face to face with eleventh-century architecture; a ground-plan which dates from 1020; a central tower, or its piers, dating from 1058; and a church completed in 1135. France can offer few buildings of this importance equally old, with dates so exact. Perhaps the closest parallel to Mont-Saint-Michel is Saint-Benoît-Sur-Loire, above Orléans, which seems to have been a shrine almost as popular as the Mount, at the same time. Chartres was also a famous shrine, but of the Virgin, and the west porch of Chartres, which is to be our peculiar pilgrimage, was a hundred years later than the ground-plan of Mont-Saint-Michel, although Chartres porch is the usual starting-point of northern French art. Queen Matilda's Abbaye-aux-Dames, now the Church of the Trinity, at Caen, dates from 1066. Saint Sernin at Toulouse, the porch of the Abbey Church at Moissac, Notre-Dame-du-Port at Clermont, the Abbey Church at Vezelay, are all said to be twelfth-century. Even San Marco at Venice was new in 1020.

Yet in 1020 Norman art was already too ambitious. Certainly nine hundred years leave their traces on granite as well as on other material, but the granite of Abbot Hildebert would have stood securely enough, if the Abbot had not asked too much from it. Perhaps he asked too much from the Archangel, for the thought of the Archangel's superiority was clearly the inspiration of his plan. The apex of the granite rock rose like a sugar-loaf two hundred and forty feet (73.6 metres) above mean sea-level. Instead of cutting the summit away to give his church a secure rock foundation, which would have sacrificed about thirty feet of height, the Abbot took the apex of the rock for his level, and on all sides built

out foundations of masonry, to support the walls of his
church. The apex of the rock is the floor of the *croisée,* the
intersection of nave and transept. On this solid foundation
the Abbot rested the chief weight of the church, which was
the central tower, supported by the four great piers which
still stand; but from the croisée in the centre westward to the
parapet of the platform, the Abbot filled the whole space
with masonry, and his successors built out still farther, until
some two hundred feet of stonework ends now in a
perpendicular wall of eighty feet or more. In this space are
several ranges of chambers, but the structure might perhaps
have proved strong enough to support the light Romanesque
front which was usual in the eleventh century, had not
fashions in architecture changed in the great epoch of
building, a hundred and fifty years later, when Abbot Robert
de Torigny thought proper to reconstruct the west front, and
build out two towers on its flanks. The towers were no doubt
beautiful, if one may judge from the towers of Bayeux and
Coutances, but their weight broke down the vaulting
beneath, and one of them fell in 1300. In 1618 the whole
façade began to give way, and in 1776 not only the façade
but also three of the seven spans of the nave were pulled
down. Of Abbot Hildebert's nave, only four arches remain.

Still, the overmastering strength of the eleventh century is
stamped on a great scale here, not only in the four spans of
the nave, and in the transepts, but chiefly in the triumphal
columns of the croisée. No one is likely to forget what
Norman architecture was, who takes the trouble to pass once
through this fragment of its earliest bloom. The dimensions
are not great, though greater than safe construction
warranted. Abbot Hildebert's whole church did not exceed
two hundred and thirty feet in length in the interior, and the
span of the triumphal arch was only about twenty three feet,
if the books can be trusted. The nave of the Abbaye-aux-
Dames appears to have about the same width, and probably
neither of them was meant to be vaulted. The roof was of
timber, and about sixty-three feet high at its apex. Compared
with the great churches of the thirteenth century, this
building is modest, but its size is not what matters to us. Its

style is the starting-point of all our future travels. Here is your first eleventh-century church! How does it affect you?

Serious and simple to excess! is it not? Young people rarely enjoy it. They prefer the Gothic, even as you see it here, looking at us from the choir, through the great Norman arch. No doubt they are right, since they are young: but men and women who have lived long and are tired, — who want rest, — who have done with aspirations and ambition, — whose life has been a broken arch, — feel this repose and self-restraint as they feel nothing else. The quiet strength of these curved lines, the solid support of these heavy columns, the moderate proportions, even the modified lights, the absence of display, of effort, of self-consciousness, satisfy them as no other art does. They come back to it to rest, after a long circle of pilgrimage, — the cradle of rest from which their ancestors started. Even here they find the repose none too deep.

Indeed, when you look longer at it, you begin to doubt whether there is any repose in it at all, — whether it is not the most unreposeful thought ever put into architectural form. Perched on the extreme point of this abrupt rock, the Church Militant with its aspirant Archangel stands high above the world, and seems to threaten heaven itself. The idea is the stronger and more restless because the Church of Saint Michael is surrounded and protected by the world and the society over which it rises, as Duke William rested on his barons and their men. Neither the Saint nor the Duke was troubled by doubts about his mission. Church and State, Soul and Body, God and Man, are all one at Mont-Saint-Michel, and the business of all is to fight, each in his own way, or to stand guard for each other. Neither Church nor State is intellectual, or learned, or even strict in dogma. Here we do not feel the Trinity at all; the Virgin but little; Christ hardly more; we feel only the Archangel and the Unity of God. We have little logic here, and simple faith, but we have energy. We cannot do many things which are done in the centre of civilization, at Byzantium, but we can fight, and we can build a church. No doubt we think first of the church, and next of our temporal lord; only in the last instance do we think of our private affairs, and our private affairs sometimes suffer for it; but we reckon the affairs of Church and State to be ours, too, and we carry this idea very far. Our church on the Mount is ambitious, restless, striving for effect; our conquest of England, with which the Duke is infatuated, is more ambitious still; but all this is a trifle to the outburst which is coming in the next generation; and Saint Michael on his Mount expresses it all.

Taking architecture as an expression of energy, we can some day compare Mont-Saint-Michel with Beauvais, and draw from the comparison whatever moral suits our frame of mind; but you should first note that here, in the eleventh century, the Church, however simple-minded or unschooled, was not cheap. Its self-respect is worth noticing, because it was short-lived in its art. Mont-Saint-Michel, throughout, even up to the delicate and intricate stonework of its cloisters, is built of granite. The crypts and substructures are as well constructed as the surfaces most exposed to view. When we get to Chartres, which is largely a twelfth-century work, you will see that the cathedral there, too, is superbly built, of the hardest and heaviest stone within reach, which has nowhere settled or given way; while, beneath, you will find a crypt that rivals the church above. The thirteenth century did not build so. The great cathedrals after 1200 show economy, and sometimes worse. The world grew cheap, as worlds must.

You may like it all the better for being less serious, less heroic, less militant, and more what the French call *bourgeois,* just as you may like the style of Louis XV better than that of Louis XIV, — Madame du Barry better than Madame de Montespan, — for taste is free, and all styles are good which amuse; but since we are now beginning with the earliest, in order to step down gracefully to the stage, whatever it is, where you prefer to stop, we must try to understand a little of the kind of energy which Norman art expressed, or would have expressed if it had thought in our modes. The only word which describes the Norman style is the French word *naïf.* Littre says that *naïf* comes from *natif,* as *vulgar* comes from *vulgus,* as though native traits must be simple, and commonness must be vulgar. Both these derivative meanings were strange to the eleventh century.

Naïveté was simply natural and vulgarity was merely coarse.
Norman naïveté was not different in kind from the naïveté of
Burgundy or Gascony or Lombardy, but it was slightly
different in expression, as you will see when you travel south.
Here at Mont-Saint-Michel we have only a mutilated trunk of
an eleventh-century church to judge by. We have not even a
façade and shall have to stop at some Norman village — at
Thaon or Ouistreham — to find a west front which might suit
the Abbey here, but wherever we find it we shall find
something a little more serious, more military, and more
practical than you will meet in other Romanesque work,
farther south. So, too, the central tower or lantern — the most
striking feature of Norman churches — has fallen here at
Mont-Saint-Michel, and we shall have to replace it from
Cérisy-la-Forêt, and Lessay, and Falaise. We shall find much
to say about the value of the lantern on a Norman church,
and the singular power it expresses. We shall have still more
to say of the towers which flank the west front of Norman
churches, but these are mostly twelfth-century, and will lead
us far beyond Coutances and Bayeux, from *flèche* to *flèche,*
till we come to the flèche of all flèches, at Chartres.

We shall have a whole chapter of study, too, over the
eleventh-century apse, but here at Mont-Saint-Michel, Abbot
Hildebert's choir went the way of his nave and tower. He
built out even more boldly to the east than to the west, and
although the choir stood for some four hundred years, which
is a sufficient life for most architecture, the foundations gave
way at last, and it fell in 1421, in the midst of the English
wars, and remained a ruin until 1450. Then it was rebuilt, a
monument of the last days of the Gothic, so that now,
standing at the western door, you can look down the church,
and see the two limits of mediaeval architecture married
together, — the earliest Norman and the latest French.
Through the Romanesque arches of 1058, you look into the
exuberant choir of latest Gothic, finished in 1521. Although
the two structures are some five hundred years apart, they
live pleasantly together. The Gothic died gracefully in
France. The choir is charming, — far more charming than the
nave, as the beautiful woman is more charming than the
elderly man. One need not quarrel about styles of beauty, as

long as the man and woman are evidently satisfied and love
and admire each other still, with all the solidity of faith to
hold them up; but, at least, one cannot help seeing, as one
looks from the older to the younger style, that whatever the
woman's sixteenth-century charm may be, it is not the man's
eleventh-century trait of naïveté; — far from it! The simple,
serious, silent dignity and energy of the eleventh century have
gone. Something more complicated stands in their place;
graceful, self-conscious, rhetorical, and beautiful as perfect
rhetoric, with its clearness, light, and line, and the wealth of
tracery that verges on the florid.

The crypt of the same period, beneath, is almost finer still,
and even in seriousness stands up boldly by the side of the
Romanesque; but we have no time to run off into the
sixteenth century: we have still to learn the alphabet of art in
France. One must live deep into the eleventh century in
order to understand the twelfth, and even after passing years
in the twelfth, we shall find the thirteenth in many ways a
world of its own, with a beauty not always inherited, and
sometimes not bequeathed. At the Mount we can go no
farther into the eleventh as far as concerns architecture. We
shall have to follow the Romanesque to Caen and so up the
Seine to the Île de France, and across to the Loire and the
Rhone, far to the South where its home lay. All the other
eleventh-century work has been destroyed here or built over,
except at one point, on the level of the splendid crypt we just
turned from, called the Gros Piliers, beneath the choir.

There, according to M. Corroyer, in a corner between
great constructions of the twelfth century and the vast
Merveille of the thirteenth, the old refectory of the eleventh
was left as a passage from one group of buildings to the
other. Below it is the kitchen of Hildebert. Above, on the
level of the church, was the dormitory. These eleventh-
century abbatial buildings faced north and west, and are
close to the present parvis, opposite the last arch of the nave.
The lower levels of Hildebert's plan served as supports or
buttresses to the church above, and must therefore be older
than the nave; probably older than the triumphal piers of
1058.

Hildebert planned them in 1020, and died after carrying

his plans out so far that they could be completed by Abbot
Ralph de Beaumont, who was especially selected by Duke
William in 1048, "more for his high birth than for his
merits." Ralph de Beaumont died in 1060, and was
succeeded by Abbot Ranulph, an especial favourite of
Duchess Matilda, and held in high esteem by Duke William.
The list of names shows how much social importance was
attributed to the place. The Abbot's duties included that of
entertainment on a great scale. The Mount was one of the
most famous shrines of northern Europe. We are free to take
for granted that all the great people of Normandy slept at the
Mount and, supposing M. Corroyer to be right, that they
dined in this room, between 1050, when the building must
have been in use, down to 1122 when the new abbatial
quarters were built.

How far the monastic rules restricted social habits is a
matter for antiquaries to settle if they can, and how far those
rules were observed in the case of great secular princes; but
the eleventh century was not very strict, and the rule of the
Benedictines was always mild, until the Cistercians and Saint
Bernard stiffened its discipline toward 1120. Even then the
Church showed strong leanings toward secular poetry and
popular tastes. The drama belonged to it almost exclusively,
and the Mysteries and Miracle plays which were acted under
its patronage often contained nothing of religion except the
miracle. The greatest poem of the eleventh century was the
"Chanson de Roland," and of that the Church took a sort of
possession. At Chartres we shall find Charlemagne and
Roland dear to the Virgin, and at about the same time, as far
away as at Assisi in the Perugian country, Saint Francis
himself—the nearest approach the Western world ever made
to an Oriental incarnation of the divine essence—loved the
French *romans,,* and typified himself in the "Chanson de
Roland." With Mont-Saint-Michel, the "Chanson de Roland"
is almost one. The "Chanson" is in poetry what the Mount is
in architecture. Without the "Chanson," one cannot
approach the feeling which the eleventh century built into the
Archangel's church. Probably there was never a day,
certainly never a week, during several centuries, when

portions of the "Chanson" were not sung, or recited, at the
Mount, and if there was one room where it was most at
home, this one, supposing it to be the old refectory, claims to
be the place.

Mark Twain:
Versailles and Père la Chaise

Samuel Langhorne Clemens (1835-1910), who wrote under the pseudonym of Mark Twain, reported in 1869 on a trip to Europe and North Africa in The Innocents Abroad. *It was a pleasure trip, a "record of a picnic," later to supply anecdotes for the lectures he was obliged to give to meet his debts. In Europe, as elsewhere, he was a familiar figure in his white suit and straw hat, smoking the inevitable cigar. Since Twain's report, Versailles has been restored and refurbished through the use of Rockefeller funds. The famous cemetery of Père La Chaise in Paris, also described by Twain, now includes the grave of Oscar Wilde and, in the special Jewish quarter, that of the great actress Sarah Bernhardt.*

Versailles! It is wonderfully beautiful! You gaze and stare and try to understand that it is real, that it is on the earth, that it is not the Garden of Eden—but your brain grows giddy, stupefied by the world of beauty around you, and you half believe you are the dupe of an exquisite dream. The scene thrills one like military music! A noble palace, stretching its ornamental front, block upon block away, till it seemed that it would never end; a grand promenade before it, whereon the armies of an empire might parade; all about it rainbows of flowers, and colossal statues that were almost numberless and yet seemed only scattered over the ample space; broad flights of stone steps leading down from the promenade to lower grounds of the park—stairways that whole regiments might stand to arms upon and have room to

spare; vast fountains whose great bronze effigies discharged
rivers of sparkling water into the air and mingled a hundred
curving jets together in forms of matchless beauty; wide
grass-carpeted avenues that branched hither and thither in
every direction and wandered to seemingly interminable
distances, walled all the way on either side with compact
ranks of leafy trees whose branches met above and formed
arches as faultless and as symmetrical as ever were carved in
stone; and here and there were glimpses of sylvan lakes with
miniature ships glassed in their surfaces. And everywhere — on
the palace steps, and the great promenade, around the
fountains, among the trees, and far under the arches of the
endless avenues — hundreds and hundreds of people in gay
costumes walked or run or danced, and gave to the fairy
picture the life and animation which was all of perfection it
could have lacked.

It was worth a pilgrimage to see. Everything is on so
gigantic a scale. Nothing is small — nothing is cheap. The
statues are all large; the palace is grand; the park covers a
fair-sized country; the avenues are interminable. All the
distances and all the dimensions about Versailles are vast. I
used to think the pictures exaggerated these distances and
these dimensions beyond all reason, and that they made
Versailles more beautiful than it was possible for any place in
the world to be. I know now that the pictures never came up
to the subject in any respect, and that no painter could
represent Versailles on canvas as beautiful as it is in reality. I
used to abuse Louis XIV for spending two hundred millions
of dollars in creating this marvelous park when bread was so
scarce with some of his subjects, but I have forgiven him now.
He took a tract of land sixty miles in circumference and set to
work to make this park and build this palace and a road to it
from Paris. He kept 36,000 men employed daily on it, and
the labor was so unhealthy that they used to die and be
hauled off by cartloads every night. The wife of a nobleman of
the time speaks of this as an *"inconvenience,"* but naively
remarks that "it does not seem worthy of attention in the
happy state of tranquillity we now enjoy."

I always thought ill of people at home who trimmed their

shrubbery into pyramids and squares and spires and all manner of unnatural shapes, and when I saw the same thing being practiced in this great park I began to feel dissatisfied. But I soon saw the idea of the thing and the wisdom of it. They seek the *general* effect. We distort a dozen sickly trees into unaccustomed shapes in a little yard no bigger than a dining room, and then surely they look absurd enough. But here they take two hundred thousand tall forest trees and set them in a double row; allow no sign of leaf or branch to grow on the trunk lower down than six feet above the ground; from that point the boughs begin to project, and very gradually they extend outward further and further till they meet overhead, and a faultless tunnel of foliage is formed. The arch is mathematically precise. The effect is then very fine. They make trees take fifty different shapes, and so these quaint effects are infinitely varied and picturesque. The trees in no two avenues are shaped alike, and consequently the eye is not fatigued with anything in the nature of monotonous uniformity. I will drop this subject now, leaving it to others to determine how these people manage to make endless ranks of lofty forest trees grow to just a certain thickness of trunk (say a foot and two-thirds); how they make them spring to precisely the same height for miles; how they make them grow so close together; how they compel one huge limb to spring from the same identical spot on each tree and form the main sweep of the arch; and how all these things are kept exactly in the same condition and in the same exquisite shapeliness and symmetry month after month and year after year — for I have tried to reason out the problem and have failed.

We walked through the great hall of sculpture and the one hundred and fifty galleries of paintings in the palace of Versailles, and felt that to be in such a place was useless unless one had a whole year at his disposal. These pictures are all battle scenes, and only one solitary little canvas among them all treats of anything but great French victories. We wandered, also, through the Grand Trianon and the Petit Trianon, those monuments of royal prodigality, and with histories so mournful — filled, as it is, with souvenirs of

Napoleon the first, and three dead kings and as many
queens. In one sumptuous bed they had all slept in
succession, but no one occupies it now. In a large dining
room stood the table at which Louis XIV and his mistress
Madame Maintenon, and after them Louis XV, and
Pompadour, had sat at their meals naked and unattended —
for the table stood upon a trapdoor, which descended with it
to regions below when it was necessary to replenish its dishes.
In a room of the Petit Trianon stood the furniture, just as
poor Marie Antoinette left it when the mob came and
dragged her and the King to Paris, never to return. Near at
hand, in the stables, were prodigious carriages that showed
no color but gold — carriages used by former kings of France
on state occasions, and never used now save when a kingly
head is to be crowned or an imperial infant christened. And
with them were some curious sleighs, whose bodies were
shaped like lions, swans, tigers, etc. — vehicles that had once
been handsome with pictured designs and fine workmanship,
but were dusty and decaying now. They had their history.
When Louis XIV had finished the Grand Trianon, he told
Maintenon he had created a paradise for her, and asked if
she could think of anything now to wish for. He said he
wished the Trianon to be perfection — nothing less. She said
she could think of but one thing — it was summer, and it was
balmy France — yet she would like well to sleigh ride in the
leafy avenues of Versailles! The next morning found miles
and miles of grassy avenues spread thick with snowy salt and
sugar, and a procession of those quaint sleighs waiting to
receive the chief concubine of the gaiest and most
unprincipled court that France has ever seen!

From sumptuous Versailles, with its palaces, its statues, its
gardens, and its fountains, we journeyed back to Paris and
sought its antipodes — the Faubourg St. Antoine. Little,
narrow streets; dirty children blockading them; greasy,
slovenly women capturing and spanking them; filthy dens on
first floors, with rag stores in them (the heaviest business in
the Faubourg is the chiffonier's); other filthy dens where
whole suits of second- and third-hand clothing are sold at
prices that would ruin any propiertor who did not steal his

VERSAILLES. — Vue générale du Palais. — General View of Palace.

Ile-de-France. — Versailles. The Castle.

stock; still other filthy dens where they sold groceries — sold them by the halfpennyworth — five dollars would buy the man out, goodwill and all. Up these little crooked streets they will murder a man for seven dollars and dump the body in the Seine. And up some other of these streets — most of them, I should say — live *lorettes*.

All through this Faubourg St. Antoine, misery, poverty, vice, and crime go hand in hand, and the evidences of it stare one in the face from every side. Here the people live who begin the revolutions. Whenever there is anything of that kind to be done, they are always ready. They take as much genuine pleasure in building a barricade as they do in cutting a throat or shoving a friend into the Seine. It is these savage-looking ruffians who storm the splendid halls of the Tuileries occasionally, and swarm into Versailles when a king is to be called to account.

But they will build no more barricades; they will break no more soldiers' heads with paving stones. Louis Napoleon has taken care of all that. He is annihilating the crooked streets and building in their stead noble boulevards as straight as an arrow — avenues which a cannon ball could traverse from end to end without meeting an obstruction more irresistible than the flesh and bones of men — boulevards whose stately edifices will never afford refuges and plotting places for starving, discontented revolution breeders. Five of these great thorough-fares radiate from one ample center — a center which is exceedingly well adapted to the accommodation of heavy artillery. The mobs used to riot there, and they must seek another rallying place in future. And this ingenious Napoleon paves the streets of his great cities with a smooth, compact composition of asphaltum and sand. No more barricades of flagstones — no more assaulting his majesty's troops with cobbles. I cannot feel friendly toward my quondam fellow American Napoleon III, especially at this time, when in fancy I see his credulous victim, Maximilian, lying stark and stiff in Mexico, and his maniac widow watching eagerly from her French asylum for the form that will never come — but I do admire his ,nerve, his calm self-reliance, his shrewd good sense.

Père La Chaise

One of our pleasantest visits was to Père la Chaise, the national burying ground of France, the honored resting place of some of her greatest and best children, the last home of scores of illustrious men and women who were born to no titles, but achieved fame by their own energy and their own genius. It is a solemn city of winding streets and of miniature temples and mansions of the dead gleaming white from out a wilderness of foliage and fresh flowers. Not every city is so well peopled as this or has so ample an area within its walls. Few palaces exist in any city that are so exquisite in design, so rich in art, so costly in material, so graceful, so beautiful.

We had stood in the ancient church of St. Denis, where the marble effigies of thirty generations of kings and queens lay stretched at length upon the tombs, and the sensations invoked were startling and novel; the curious armor, the obsolete customes, the placid faces, the hands placed palm to palm in eloquent supplication—it was a vision of gray antiquity. It seemed curious enough to be standing face to face, as it were, with old Dagobert I, and Clovis and Charlemagne, those vague, collosal heroes, those shadows, those myths of a thousand years ago! I touched their dust-covered faces with my finger, but Dagobert was deader than the sixteen centuries that have passed over him, Clovis slept well after his labor for Christ, and old Charlemagne went on dreaming of his paladins, of bloody Roncesvalles, and gave no heed to me.

The great names of Père la Chaise impress one, too, but differently. There the suggestion brought constantly to his mind that this place is sacred to a nobler royalty—the royalty of heart and brain. Every faculty of mind, every noble trait of human nature, every high occupation which men engage in, seems represented by a famous name. The effect is a curious medley. Davoust and Massena, who wrought in many a battle tragedy, are here, and so also is Rachel, of equal renown in mimic tragedy on the stage. The Abbé Sicard sleeps here—the first great teacher of the deaf and dumb—a man whose heart went out to every unfortunate, and whose life was given to kindly offices in their service; and not far off, in repose and peace at last, lies Marshal Ney, whose stormy spirit knew no music like the 'bugle call to arms. The man who originated public gas-lighting, and that other benefactor who introduced the cultivation of the potato and thus blessed millions of his starving countrymen, lie with the Prince of Masserano, and with exiled queens and princes of Further India. Gay-Lussac the chemist, Laplace the astronomer, Larrey the surgeon, DeSeze the advocate, are here, and with them are Talma, Bellini, Rubini; de Balzac, Beaumarchais, Beranger; Molière and La Fontaine, and scores of other men whose names and whose worthy labors are as familiar in the remote byplaces of civilization as are the historic deeds of the kings and princes that sleep in the marble vaults of St. Denis.

But among the thousands and thousands of tombs in Père la Chaise, there is one that no man, no woman, no youth of either sex, ever passes by without stopping to examine. Every visitor has a sort of indistinct idea of the history of its dead and comprehends that homage is due there, but not one in twenty thousand clearly remembers the story of that tomb and its romantic occupants. This is the grave of Abelard and Héloïse — a grave which has been more revered, more widely known, more written and sung about and wept over, for seven hundred years, than any other in Christendom save only that of the Saviour. All visitors linger pensively about it; all young people capture and carry away keepsakes and mementos of it; all Parisian youths and maidens who are disappointed in love come there to bail out when they are full of tears; yea, many sticken lovers make pilgrimages to this shrine from distant provinces to weep and wail and "grit" their teeth over their heavy sorrows, and to purchase the sympathies of the chastened spirits of that tomb with offerings of immortelles and budding flowers.

Go when you will, you find somebody snuffing over that tomb. Go when you will, you find it furnished with those bouquets and immortelles. Go when you will, you find a gravel train from Marseilles arriving to supply the deficiencies caused by memento-cabbaging vandals whose affections have miscarried.

Charles Dickens: Lyons, Avignon and Marseilles

On July 1, 1844, Charles Dickens (1812-1870), his wife Catherine, his sister-in-law Georgina Hogarth, five children, two nurses, and the family dog left London in a large carriage and started over the Dover road. He was following the Grand Tour, earlier traced by Fielding, Smollett, Goldsmith, Hazlitt, and many other English writers. Dickens sent letters to his friend John Forster depicting his experiences and impressions. His genius as a storyteller is reflected in his accounts of his journey.

What a city Lyons is! Talk about people feeling, at certain unlucky times, as if they had tumbled from the clouds! Here is a whole town that has tumbled, anyhow, out of the sky; having been first caught up, like other stones that tumble down from that region, out of fens and barren places, dismal to behold! The two great streets through which the two great rivers dash, and all the little streets whose name is Legion, were scorching, blistering, and sweltering. The houses, high and vast, dirty to excess, rotten as old cheeses, and as thickly peopled. All up the hills that hem the city in, these houses swarm; and the mites inside were lolling out of the windows, and drying their ragged clothes on poles; and crawling in and out at the doors; and coming out to pant and gasp upon the pavement; and creeping in and out among huge piles of fusty, musty, stifling goods; and living, or rather not dying, till their time should come, in an exhausted receiver. Every

manufacturing town, melted into one, would hardly convey
an impression of Lyons as it presented itself to me; for all the
undrained, unscavengered, qualities of a foreign town,
seemed grafted, there, upon the native miseries of a
manufacturing one; and it bears such fruit as I would go
some miles out of my way to avoid encountering again.

In the cool of the evening: or rather in the faded heat of
the day: we went to see the Cathedral; where divers old
women, and a few dogs, were engaged in contemplation.
There was no difference, in point of cleanliness, between its
stone pavement and that of the streets; and there was a wax
saint, in a little box like a berth aboard ship, with a glass
front to it, whom Madame Tussaud would have nothing to
say to, on any terms, and which even Westminster Abbey
might be ashamed of. If you would know all about the
architecture of this church, or any other, its dates,
dimensions, endowments, and history, is it not written in Mr.
Murray's 'Guide-Book', and may you not read it there, with
thanks to him, as I did!

For this reason, I should abstain from mentioning the
curious clock in Lyons Cathedral, if it were not for a small
mistake I made, in connexion with that piece of mechanism.
The keeper of the church was very anxious it should be
shown; partly for the honour of the establishment and the
town; and partly, perhaps, because of his deriving a
percentage from the additional consideration. However that
may be, it was set in motion, and thereupon a host of little
doors flew open, and innumerable little figures staggered out
of them, and jerked themselves back again, with that special
unsteadiness of purpose, and hitching in the gait, which
usually attaches of figures that are moved by clock-work.
Meanwhile, the Sacristan stood explaining these wonders,
and pointing them out, severally, with a wand. There was a
centre puppet of the Virgin Mary; and close to her, a small
pigeon-hole, out of which another and very ill-looking puppet
made one of the most sudden plunges I ever saw
accomplished; instantly flopping back again at sight of her,
and banging his little door violently after him. Taking this to
be emblematic of the victory over Sin and Death: and not at

Charles Dickens

all unwilling to shew that I perfectly understood the subject,
in anticipation of the showman, I rashly said, 'Aha! The Evil
Spirit. To be sure. He is very soon disposed of.' 'Pardon,
Monsieur,' said the Sacristan, with a polite motion of his
hand towards the little door, as if introducing somebody —
'The Angel Gabriel!'

Soon after day-break next morning, we were steaming
down the arrowy Rhone, at the rate of twenty miles an hour,
in a very dirty vessel full of merchandise, and with only three
or four other passengers for our companions: among whom,
the   most   remarkable   was   a   silly,   old,   garlic-
eating, immeasureably-polite Chevalier, with a dirty scrap of
red ribbon hanging at his button-hole, as if he had tied it
there, to remind himself of something: as Tom Noddy in the
farce ties knots in his pocket-handkerchief.

For the last two days, we had seen great sullen hills; the
first indications of the Alps: lowering in the distance. Now,
we were rushing on beside them: sometimes close beside
them: sometimes with an intervening slope, covered with
vineyards. Villages and small towns hanging in mid-air, with
great woods of olives seen through the light open towers of
their churches; and clouds moving slowly on, upon the steep
acclivity behind them; ruined castles perched on every
eminence; and scattered houses in the clefts and gullies of the
hills; made it very beautiful. The great height of these, too,
making the buildings look so tiny, that they had all the
charm of elegant models; their excessive whiteness, as
contrasted with the brown rocks, or the sombre, deep, dull,
heavy green of the olive-tree; and the puny size, and little
slow walk of the Lilliputian men and women on the bank;
made a charming picture. There were ferries out of number
too; bridges; the famous Pont d'Esprit, with I don't know how
many arches; towns were memorable wines are made;
Vallence, where Napoleon studied; and the noble river,
bringing at every winding turn new beauties into view.

There lay before us, that same afternoon, the broken
bridge of Avignon, and all the city baking in the sun; yet with
an under-done-pie-crust, battlemented wall, that never will
be brown, though it bake for centuries.

The grapes were hanging in clusters in the streets, and the brilliant Oleander was in full bloom everywhere. The streets are old and very narrow, but tolerably clean, and shaded by awnings stretched from house to house. Bright stuffs, and handkerchiefs: curiosities, ancient frames of carved wood, old chairs, ghostly tables, saints, virgins, angels, and staring daubs of portraits, being exposed for sale beneath, it was very quaint and lively. All this was much set off, too, by the glimpses one caught, through rusty gates standing ajar, of quiet sleepy courtyards, having stately old houses within, as silent as tombs. It was all very like one of the descriptions in the 'Arabian Nights.' The three one-eyed Calenders might have knocked at any one of the doors till the street rang again, and the porter who persisted in asking questions — the man who had the delicious purchases put into his basket in the morning — might have opened it quite naturally.

After breakfast next morning, we sallied forth to see the lions. Such a delicious breeze was blowing in, from the north, as made the walk delightful: though the pavement-stones, and stones of the walls and houses, were far too hot to have a hand laid on them comfortably.

We went, first of all, up a rockly height, to the cathedral: where Mass was performing to an auditory very like that of Lyons, namely, several old women, a baby, and a very self-possessed dog, who had marked out for himself a little course or platform for exercise: beginning at the altar-rails and ending at the door; up and down which constitutional walk, he trotted, during the service, as methodically and calmly, as any old gentleman out of doors, It is a bare old church, and the paintings in the roof are sadly defaced by time and damp weather; but the sun was shining in, splendidly, through the red curtains of the windows, and glittering on the altar furniture; and it looked as bright and cheerful as need be.

Going apart, in this Church, to see some painting which was being executed in fresco by a French artist and his pupil, I was led to observe more closely than I might otherwise have done, a great number of votive offerings with which the walls of the different chapels were profusely hung. I will not say decorated, for they were very roughly and comically got up; most likely by poor sign-painters, who eke out their living in that way. They were all little pictures: each representing some sickness or calamity from which the person placing it there, had escaped, through the interposition of his or her patron saint, or of the Madonna; and I may refer to them as good specimens of the class generally. They are abundant in Italy.

In a grotesque squareness of outline, and impossibility of perspective, they were not unlike the woodcuts in old books; but they were oil-paintings, and the artist, like the painter of the Primrose family, had not been sparing of his colours. In one, a lady was having a toe amputated — an operation which a saintly personage had sailed into the room, upon a cloud, to superintend. In another, a lady was lying in bed, tucked up very tight and prim, and staring with much composure at a tripod, with a slop-basin on it: the usual form of washing-stand, and the only piece of furniture, besides the bedstead, in her chamber. One would never have supposed her to be labouring under any complaint, beyond the inconvenience of being miraculously wide awake, if the painter had not hit upon the idea of putting all her family on their knees in one corner, with their legs sticking out behind them on the floor, like boot-trees. Above whom, the Virgin, on a kind of blue divan, promised to restore the patient. In another case, a lady was in the very act of being run over, immediately outside the city walls, by a sort of piano-forte van. But the Madonna was there again. Whether the supernatural appearance had startled the horse (a bay griffin), or whether it was invisible to him, I don't know; but he was galloping away, ding-dong, without the smallest reverence or compunction. On every picture 'Ex voto' was painted in yellow capitals in the sky.

Though votive offerings were not unknown in Pagan Temples, and are evidently among the many compromises made between the false religion and the true, when the true was in its infancy, I could wish that all the other compromises were as harmless. Gratitude and Devotion are Christian qualities; and a grateful, humble, Christian spirit may dictate the observance.

Hard by the cathedral, stands the ancient Palace of the Popes, of which one portion is now a common jail, and another a noisy barrack: while gloomy suites of state apartments, shut up and deserted, mock their own old state and glory, like the embalmed bodies of kings. But we neither went there, to see state-rooms, nor soldiers' quarters, nor a common jail, though we dropped some money into a prisoners' box outside, whilst the prisoners, themselves, looked through the iron bars, high up, and watched us eagerly. We went to see the ruins of the dreadful rooms in which the Inquisition used to sit.

A little, old, swarthy woman, with a pair of flashing black eyes, — proof that the world hadn't conjured down the devil within her, though it had been between sixty and seventy years to do it in, — came out of the Barrack Cabaret, of which she was the keeper, with some large keys in her hands, and marshalled us the way that we should go. How she told us, on the way, that she was a Government Officer (*concierge du palais apostolique*), and had been, for I don't know how many years; and how she had shown these dungeons to princes; and how she was the best of dungeon demonstrators; and how she had resided in the palace from an infant, — had been born there, if I recollect right, — I needn't relate. But such a fierce, little, rapid, sparkling, energetic, she-devil I never beheld. She was alight and flaming, all the time. Her action was violent in the extreme. She never spoke, without stopping expressly for the purpose. She stamped her feet, clutched us by the arms, flung herself into attitudes, hammered against walls with her keys, for mere emphasis: now whispered as if the Inquisition were there still: now shrieked as if she were on the rack herself; and had a mysterious, hag-like way with her forefinger, when approaching the remains of some new horror — looking back and walking stealthily and making horrible grimaces — that might alone have qualified her to walk up and down a sick man's counterpane, to the exclusion of all other figures, through a whole fever.

Passing through the court-yard, among groups of idle soldiers, we turned off by a gate, which this She-Goblin unlocked for our admission, and locked again behind us: and entered a narrow court, rendered narrower by fallen stones and heaps of rubbish; part of it choking up the mouth of a ruined subterranean passage, that once communicated (or is said to have done so) with another castle on the opposite bank of the river. Close to this court-yard, is a dungeon — we stood within it, in another minute — in the dismal tower *des oubliettes*, where Rienzi was imprisoned, fastened by an iron chain to the very wall that stands there now, but shut out from the sky which now looks down into it. A few steps brought us to the Cachots, in which the prisoners of the Inquisition were confined for forty-eight hours after their capture, without food or drink, that their constancy might be shaken, even before they were confronted with their gloomy judges. The day has not got in there yet. They are still small cells, shut in by four unyielding, close, hard walls; still profoundly dark; still massively doored and fastened, as of old.

Goblin, looking back as I have described, went softly on, into a vaulted chamber, now used as a store-room: once the Chapel of the Holy Office. The place where the tribunal sat, was plain. The platform might have been removed but yesterday. Conceive the parable of the Good Samaritan having been painted on the wall of one of these Inquisition chambers! But it was, and may be traced there yet.

High up in the jealous wall, are niches where the faltering replies of the accused were heard and noted down. Many of them had been brought out of the very cell we had just looked into, so awfully; along with the same stone passage. We had trodden in their very footsteps.

I am gazing round me, with the horror that the place inspires, when Goblin clutches me by the wrist, and lays, not her skinny finger, but the handle of a key, upon her lip. She invites me, with a jerk, to follow her. I do so. She leads me out into a room adjoining — a rugged room, with a funnel-shaped, contracting roof, open at the top, to the bright day. I ask her what it is. She folds her arms, leers hideously, and stares. I ask again. She glances round, to see that all the little company are there; sits down upon a mound of stones: throws up her arms, and yells out, like a fiend, 'La Salle de la Question!'

The Chamber of Torture! And the roof was made of that shape to stifle the victim's cries! Oh Goblin, Goblin, let us think of this awhile, in silence. Peace, Goblin! Sit with your short arms crossed on your short legs, upon that heap of stones, for only five minutes, and then flame out again.

Minutes! Seconds are not marked upon the Palace clock, when, with her eyes flashing fire, Goblin is up, in the middle of the chamber: describing, with her sun-burnt arms, a wheel of heavy blows. Thus it ran round! cries Goblin. Mash, mash, mash! An endless routine of heavy hammers. Mash, mash, mash! upon the sufferer's limbs. See the stone trough! says Goblin. For the water torture! Gurgle, swill, bloat, burst, for the Redeemer's honour! Suck the bloody rag, deep down into your unbelieving body, Heretic, at every breath you draw! And when the executioner plucks it out, reeking with the smaller mysteries of God's own Image, know us for His chosen servants; true believers in the Sermon on the Mount; elect disciples of Him who never did a miracle but to heal: who never struck a man with palsy, blindness, deafness, dumbness, madness, any one affliction of mankind; and never stretched His blessed hand out, but to give relief and ease!

See! cries Goblin. There the furnace was. There they made the irons red-hot. Those holes supported the sharp stake, on which the tortured persons hung poised: dangling with their whole weight from the roof. 'But;' and Goblin whispers this; 'Monsieur has heard of this tower? Yes? Let Monsieur look down, then!'

A cold air, laden with an earthy smell, falls upon the face of Monsieur; for she has opened, while speaking, a trap-door in the wall. Monsieur looks in. Downward to the bottom, upward to the top, of a steep, dark, lofty tower: very dismal, very dark, very cold. The Executioner of the Inquisition, says Goblin, edging in her head to look down also, flung those who were past all further torturing, down here. 'But look! does Monsieur see the black stains on the wall?' A glance, over his shoulder, at Goblin's keen eye, shows Monsieur — and would without the aid of the directing-key — where they are. 'What are they?' 'Blood!'

In October, 1791, when the Revolution was at its height

here, sixty persons: men and women ('and priests,' says
Goblin, 'priests'): were murdered, and hurled, the dying and
the dead, into this dreadful pit, where a quantity of
quick-lime was tumbled down upon their bodies. Those
ghastly tokens of the massacre were soon no more; but while
one stone of the strong building in which the deed was done,
remains upon another, there they will lie in the memories of
men, as plain to see as the splashing of their blood upon the
wall is now.

Was it a portion of the great scheme of Retribution, that
the cruel deed should be committed in this place? That a part
of the atrocities and monstrous institutions, which had been,
for scores of years, at work to change men's nature, should in
its last service, tempt them with the ready means of gratifying
their furious and beastly rage! Should enable them to show
themselves, in the height of their frenzy, no worse than a
great, solemn, legal establishment, in the height of its power!
No worse! Much better. They used the Tower of the
Forgotten, in the name of Liberty — their liberty; and
earth-born creature, nursed in the black mud of the Bastille
moats and dungeons, and necessarily betraying many
evidences of its unwholesome bringing-up — but the Inquisition used it in the name of Heaven.

Goblin's finger is lifted; and she steals out again, into the
Chapel of the Holy Office. She stops at a certain part of the
flooring. Her great effect is at hand. She waits for the rest.
She darts at the brave Courier, who is explaining something;
hits him a sounding rap on the hat with the largest key; and
bids him be silent. She assembles us all, round a little trap-
door in the floor, as round a grave. 'Voilà!' she darts down at
the ring, and flings the door open with a crash, in her goblin
energy, though it is no light weight. 'Voilà les oubliettes!
Voilà les oubliettes! Subterranean! Frightful! Black! Terrible!
Deadly! Les oubliettes de l'Inquisition!'

My blood ran cold, as I looked from Goblin, down into the
vaults, where these forgotten creatures, with recollections of
the world outside: of wives, friends, children, brothers:
starved to death, and made the stones ring with their
unavailing groans. But, the thrill I felt on seeing the accursed

wall below, decayed and broken through, and the sun shining
in through its gaping wounds, was like a sense of victory and
triumph. I felt exalted with the proud delight of living, in
these degenerate times, to see it. As if I were the hero of some
high achievement! The light in the doleful vaults was typical
of the light that has streamed in, on all persecution in God's
name, but which is not yet at its noon! It cannot look more
lovely to a blind man newly restored to sight, than to a
traveller who sees it, calmly and majestically, treading down
the darkness of that Infernal Well.

Avignon and Marseilles

Goblin, having shown *les oubliettes,* felt that her great
coup was struck. She let the door fall with a crash, and stood
upon it with her arms a-kimbo, sniffing prodigiously.

When we left the place, I accompanied her into her house,
under the outer gateway of the fortress, to buy a little history
of the building. Her cabaret, a dark low room, lighted by
small windows, sunk in the thick wall — in the softened light,
and with its forge-like chimney; its little counter by the door,
with bottles, jars, and glasses on it; its household implements
and scraps of dress against the walls; and a sober-looking
woman (she must have a congenial life of it, with Goblin),
knitting at the door — looked exactly like a picture by Ostade.

I walked round the building on the outside, in a sort of
dream, and yet with the delightful sense of having awakened
from it, of which the light, down in the vaults, had given me
the assurance. The immense thickness and giddy height of
the walls; the enormous strength of the massive towers; the
great extent of the building; its gigantic proportions,
frowning aspect, and barbarous irregularity, awaken awe and
wonder. The recollection of its opposite old uses: an
impregnable fortress, a luxurious palace, a horrible prison, a
place of torture, the court of the Inquisition: at one and the
same time, a house of feasting, fighting, religion, and blood:
gives to every stone in its huge form a fearful interest, and
imparts new meaning to its incongruities. I could think of
little, however, then, or long afterwards, but the sun in the

dungeons. The palace coming down to be the lounging-place of noisy soldiers, and being forced to echo their rough talk and common oaths, and to have their garments fluttering from its dirty windows, was some reduction of its state, and something to rejoice at; but the day in its cells, and the sky for the roof of its chambers of cruelty — that was its desolation and defeat! If I had seen it in a blaze from ditch to rampart, I should have felt that not that light, nor all the light in all the fire that burns, could waste it, like the sunbeams in its secret council-chamber, and its prisons.

Before I quit this Palace of the Popes, let me translate from the little history I mentioned just now, a short anecdote, quite appropriate to itself, connected with its adventures.

'An ancient tradition relates, that in 1441, a nephew of Pierre de Lude, the Pope's legate, seriously insulted some distinguished ladies of Avignon, whose relations, in revenge, seized the young man, and horribly mutilated him. For several years the legate kept *his* revenge within his own breast, but he was not the less resolved upon its gratification at last. He even made, in the fullness of time, advances towards a complete reconciliation; and when their apparent sincerity had prevailed, he invited to a splendid banquet, in this palace, certain families, whole families, whom he sought to exterminate. The utmost gaiety animated the repast; but the measures of the legate were well taken. When the dessert was on the board, a Swiss presented himself, with the announcement that a strange ambassador solicited an extraordinary audience. The legate, excusing himself, for the moment, to his guests, retired, followed by his officers. Within a few moments afterwards, five hundred persons were reduced to ashes: the whole of that wing of the building having been blown into the air with a terrible explosion!'

After seeing the churches (I will not trouble you with churches just now), we left Avignon that afternoon. The heat being very great, the roads outside the walls were strewn with people fast asleep in every little slip of shade, and with lazy groups, half asleep and half awake, who were waiting until the sun should be low enough to admit of their playing bowls among the burnt-up trees, and on the dusty road. The harvest here, was already gathered in, and mules and horses were treading out the corn in the fields. We came, at dusk, upon a wild and hilly country, once famous for brigands: and travelled slowly up a steep ascent. So we went on, until eleven at night, when we halted at the town of Aix (within two stages of Marseilles) to sleep.

The hotel, with all the blinds and shutters closed to keep the light and heat out, was comfortable and airy next morning and the town was very clean; but so hot, and so intensely light, that when I walked out at noon it was like coming suddenly from the darkened room into crisp blue fire. The air was so very clear, that distant hills and rocky points appeared within an hour's walk: while the town immediately at hand — with a kind of blue wind between me and it — seemed to be white hot, and to be throwing off a fiery air from its surface.

We left this town towards evening, and took the road to Marseilles. A dusty road it was; the houses shut up close; and the vines powdered white. At nearly all the cottage doors, women were peeling and slicing onions into earthen bowls for supper. So they had been doing last night all the way from Avignon. We passed one or two shady dark chateaux, surrounded by trees, and embellished with cool basins of water: which were the more refreshing to behold, from the great scarcity of such residences on the road we had travelled. As we approached Marseilles, the road began to be covered with holiday people. Outside the public houses were parties smoking, drinking, playing draughts and cards, and (once) dancing. But dust, dust, dust, everywhere. We went on, through a long, straggling, dirty suburb, thronged with people; having on our left a dreary slope of land, on which the country houses of the Marseilles merchants, always staring white, are jumbled and heaped without the slightest order: backs, fronts, sides, and gables towards all points of the compass; until, at last, we entered the town.

I was there, twice or thrice afterwards, in fair weather and foul; and I am afraid there is no doubt that it is a dirty and disagreeable place. But the prospect, from the fortified heights, of the beautiful Mediterranean, with its lovely rocks and islands, is most delightful. These heights are a desirable retreat, for less pictureque reasons — as an escape from a compound of vile smells perpetually arising from a great harbour full of stagnant water, and befouled by the refuse of innumerable ships with all sorts of cargoes: which, in hot weather, is dreadful in the last degree.

There were foreign sailors, of all nations, in the streets; with red shirts, blue shirts, buff shirts, tawny shirts, and shirts of orange colour; with red caps, blue caps, green caps, great beards, and no beards; in Turkish turbans, glazed English hats, and Neapolitan head-dresses. There were townspeople sitting in clusters on the pavement, or airing themselves on the tops of their houses, or walking up and down the closest and least airy of Boulevards; and there were crowds of fierce-looking people of the lower sort, blocking up the way, constantly. In the very heart of all this stir and uproar, was the common madhouse; a low, contracted, miserable building, looking straight upon the street, without the smallest screen or court-yard; where chattering madmen and mad-women were peeping out, through rusty bars, at the staring faces below, while the sun, darting fiercely aslant into their little cells, seemed to dry up their brains, and worry them, as if they were baited by a pack of dogs.

We were pretty well accommodated at the Hôtel du Paradis, situated in a narrow street of very high houses, with a hairdresser's shop opposite, exhibiting in one of its windows two full-length waxen ladies, twirling round and round: which so enchanted the hairdresser himself, that he and his family sat in arm-chairs, and in cool undresses, on the pavement outside, enjoying the gratification of the passers-by, with lazy dignity. The family had retired to rest when we went to bed, at midnight; but the hairdresser (a corpulent man, in drab slippers) was still sitting there, with his legs stretched out before him; and evidently couldn't bear to have the shutters put up.

Next day we went down to the harbour, where the sailors of all nations were discharging and taking in cargoes of all kinds: fruits, wines, oils, silks, stuffs, velvets, and every manner of merchandise. Taking one of a great number of

lively little boats with gay-striped awnings, we rowed away;
under the sterns of great ships; under tow-ropes and cables;
against and among other boats; and very much too near the
sides of vessels that were faint with oranges, to the *Marie
Antoinette,* a handsome steamer bound for Genoa, lying near
the mouth of the harbour. By-and-by, the carriage, that
unwieldy 'trifle from the Pantechnicon,' on a flat barge,
bumping against everything, and giving occasion for a
prodigious quantity of oaths and grimaces, came stupidly
alongside; and by five o'clock we were steaming out in the
open sea. The vessel was beautifully clean; the meals were
served under an awning on deck; the night was calm and
clear; the quiet beauty of the sea and sky, unspeakable.

Part Three:
Italy

Charles Dickens: Rome

Charles Dickens took a respite from writing magazine serials in London, and settled with his family in Italy for a year. His impressions are recounted in Pictures from Italy, *published in 1846. "This book," said Dickens, "is a series of faint reflections—mere shadows in the water—of places to which the imaginations of most people are attracted in a greater or less degree. If they have ever a fanciful and idle air, perhaps the reader will suppose them written in the shade of a Sunny Day."*

We entered the Eternal City, at about four o'clock in the afternoon, on the thirtieth of January, by the Porta del Popolo, and came immediately—it was a dark muddy day, and there had been heavy rain—on the skirts of the Carnival. We did not, then, know that we were only looking at the fag end of the masks, who were driving slowly round and round the Piazza, until they could find a promising opportunity for falling into the stream of carriages, and getting, in good time, into the thick of the festivity; and coming among them so abruptly, all travel-stained and weary, was not coming very well prepared to enjoy the scene.

We had crossed the Tiber by the Ponte Molle, two or three miles before. It had looked as yellow as it ought to look, and hurrying on between its worn-away and miry banks, had a promising aspect of desolation and ruin. The masquerade dresses on the fringe of the Carnival, did great violence to this promise. There were no great ruins, no solemn tokens of antiquity, to be seen; — they all lie on the other side of the city. There seemed to be long streets of commonplace shops and houses, such as are to be found in any European town; there were busy people, equipages, ordinary walkers to and fro; a multitude of chattering strangers. It was no more *my* Rome: the Rome of anybody's fancy, man or boy; degraded and fallen and lying asleep in the sun among a heap of ruins: than the Place de la Concorde in Paris is. A cloudy sky, a dull cold rain, and muddy streets, I was prepared for, but not for this: and I confess to having gone to bed, that night, in a very indifferent humour, and with a very considerably quenched enthusiasm.

Immediately on going out next day, we hurried off to St. Peter's. It looked so immense in the distance, but distinctly and decidely small, by comparison, on a near approach. The beauty of the Piazza in which it stands, with its clusters of exquisite columns, and its gushing fountains — so fresh, so broad, and free, and beautiful — nothing can exaggerate. The first burst of the interior, in all its expansive majesty and glory: and, most of all, the looking up into the Dome: is a sensation never to be forgotten. But, there were preparations for a Festa; the pillars of stately marble were swathed in some impertinent frippery of red and yellow; the altar, and entrance to the subterranean chapel: which is before it: in the centre of the church: were like a goldsmith's shop, or one of the opening scenes in a very lavish pantomime. And though I had as high a sense of beauty of the building (I hope) as it is possible to entertain, I felt no very strong emotion. I have been infinitely more affected in many English cathedrals when the organ has been playing, and in many English country churches when the congregation have been singing. I had a much greater sense of mystery and wonder, in the Cathedral of San Mark at Venice.

When we came out of the church again (we stood nearly an hour staring up into the dome: and would not have 'gone over' the Cathedral then, for any money), we said to the coachman, 'Go to the Coliseum.' In a quarter of an hour or so, he stopped at the gate, and we went in.

It is no fiction, but plain, sober, honest Truth, to say: so suggestive and distinct is it at this hour: that, for a moment — actually in passing in — they who will, may have the whole great pile before them, as it used to be, with thousands of eager faces staring down into the arena, and such a whirl of strife, and blood, and dust, going on there, as no language can describe. Its solitude, its awful beauty, and its utter desolation, strike upon the stranger, the next moment, like a softened sorrow; and never in his life, perhaps, will he be so moved and overcome by any sight, not immediately connected with his own affections and afflictions.

To see it crumbling there, an inch a year; its walls and arches overgrown with green; its corridors open to the day; the long grass growing in its porches; young trees of yesterday, springing up on its ragged parapets, and bearing fruit; chance produce of the seeds dropped there by the birds who build their nests within its chinks and crannies; to see its Pit of Fight filled up with earth, and the peaceful Cross planted in the centre; to climb into its upper halls, and look down on ruin, ruin, ruin, all about it; the triumphal arches of Constantine, Septimus, Severus, and Titus; the Roman Forum; the Palace of the Cæsars; the temples of the old Rome, wicked wonderful old city; haunting the very ground on which its people trod. It is the most impressive, the most stately, the most solemn, grand, majestic, mournful sight, conceivable. Never, in its bloodiest prime, can the sight of the gigantic Coliseum, full and running over with the lustiest life, have moved one heart, as it must move all who look upon it now, a ruin. God be thanked: a ruin!

As it tops the other ruins: standing there, a mountain among graves: so do its ancient influences outlive all other remnants of the old mythology and old butchery of Rome, in the nature of the fierce and cruel Roman people. The Italian face changes as the visiter approaches the city; its beauty becomes devilish; and there is scarcely one countenance in a hundred, among the common people in the streets, that would not be at home and happy in a renovated Coliseum to-morrow.

Here was Rome indeed at last; and such a Rome as no one can imagine in its full and awful grandeur! We wandered out upon the Appian Way, and then went on, through miles of ruined tombs and broken walls, with here and there a desolate and uninhabited house: past the Circus of Romulus, where the course of the chariots, the stations of the judges, competitors, and spectators, are yet as plainly to be seen as in old time: past the tomb of Cecilia Metella: past all inclosure, hedge, or stake, wall or fence: away upon the open Campagna, where on that side of Rome, nothing is to be beheld but Ruin. Except where the distant Apennines bound the view upon the left, the whole wide prospect is one field of ruin. Broken aqueducts, left in the most picturesque and beautiful clusters of arches; broken temples; broken tombs. A desert of decay, sombre and desolate beyond all expression; and with a history in every stone that strews the ground.

The Corso is a street a mile long; a street of shops, and palaces, and private houses, sometimes opening into a broad piazza. There are virandas and balconies, of all shapes and sizes, to almost every house — not on one story alone, but often to one room or another on every story — put there in general with so little order or regularity, that if, year after year, and season after season, it had rained balconies, hailed balconies, snowed balconies, blown balconies, they could scarcely have come into existence in a more disorderly manner.

This is the great fountain-head and focus of the Carnival. But all the streets in which the Carnival is held, being vigilantly kept by dragoons, it is necessary for carriages, in the first instance, to pass, in line, down another thorough-fare, and so come into the Corso at the end remote from the Piazza del Popolo; which is one of its terminations. Accordingly, we fell into the string of coaches, and, for some time, jogged on quietly enough; now crawling on at a very slow walk; now trotting half a dozen yards; now backing fifty; and now stopping altogether: as the pressure in front obliged us. If any impetuous carriage dashed out of the rank and clattered forward, with the wild idea of getting on faster, it was suddenly met, or overtaken, by a trooper on horseback, who, deaf as his own drawn sword to all remonstrances,

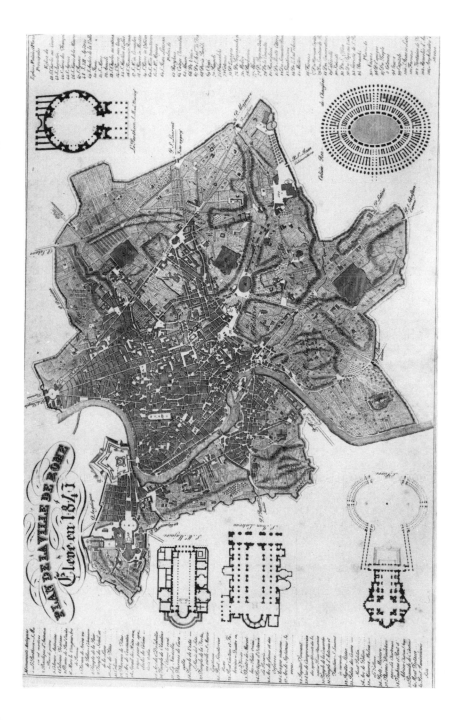

PLAN DE LA VILLE DE ROME
Élevé en 1841.

immediately escorted it back to the very end of the row, and made it a dim speck in the remotest perspective. Occasionally, we interchanged a volley of confetti with the carriage next in front, or the carriage next behind; but, as yet, this capturing of stray and errant coaches by the military, was the chief amusement.

Presently, we came into a narrow street, where, besides one line of carriages going, there was another line of carriages returning. Here the sugar-plums and the nosegays began to fly about, pretty smartly; and I was fortunate enough to observe one gentleman attired as a Greek warrior, catch a light-whiskered brigand on the nose (he was in the very act of tossing up a bouquet to a young lady in a first-floor window) with a precision that was much applauded by the by-standers. As this victorious Greek was exchanging a facetious remark with a stout gentleman in a door-way — one-half black and one-half white, as if he had been peeled up the middle — who had offered him his congratulations on this achievement, he received an orange from a house-top, full on his left ear, and was much surprised, not to say discomfited. Especially, as he was standing up at the time; and in consequence of the carriage moving on suddenly, at the same moment, staggered ignominiously, and buried himself among his flowers.

Some quarter of an hour of this sort of progress, brought us to the Corso; and anything so gay, so bright, and lively as the whole scene there, it would be difficult to imagine. From all the innumerable balconies: from the remotest and highest, no less than from the lowest and nearest: hangings of bright red, bright green, bright blue, white and gold, were fluttering in the brilliant sunlight. From windows, and from parapets, and tops of houses, streamers of the richest colours, and draperies of the gaudiest and most sparkling hues, were floating out upon the street. The buildings seemed to have been literally turned inside out, and to have all their gaiety towards the highway. Shop-fronts were taken down, and the windows filled with company, like boxes at a shining theatre; doors were carried off their hinges, and long tapestried groves, hung with garlands of flowers and evergreens, displayed within; builders' scaffoldings were gorgeous temples, radiant

in silver, gold, and crimson; and in every nook and corner,
from the pavement to the chimney-tops, where women's eyes
could glisten, there they danced, and laughed, and sparkled,
like the light in water. Every sort of bewitching madness of
dress was there. Little preposterous scarlet jackets; quaint old
stomachers, more wicked than the smartest boddices; Polish
pelisses, strained and tight as ripe gooseberries: tiny Greek
caps, all awry, and clinging to the dark hair. Heaven knows
how; every wild, quaint, bold, shy, pettish, madcap fancy
had its illustration in a dress; and every fancy was as dead
forgotten by its owner, in the tumult of merriment, as if the
three old aqueducts that still remain entire, had brought
Lethe into Rome, upon their sturdy arches, that morning.

The carriages were now three abreast; in broader places
four; often stationary for a long time together; always one
close mass of variegated brightness; showing, the whole street-
full, through the storm of flowers, like flowers of a larger
growth themselves. In some, the horses were richly
caparisoned in magnificent trappings; in others they were
decked from head to tail, with flowing ribbons. Some were
driven by coachmen with enormous double faces: one face
leering at the horses: the other cocking its extraordinary eyes
into the carriage: and both rattling again, under the hail of
sugar-plums. Other drivers were attired as women, wearing
long ringlets and no bonnets, and looking more ridiculous in
any real difficulty with the horses (of which, in such a
concourse, there were a great many) than tongue can tell, or
pen describe. Instead of sitting *in* the carriages, upon the
seats, the handsome Roman women, to see and to be seen the
better, sit in the heads of the barouches, at this time of
general license, with their feet upon the cushions — and oh the
flowing skirts and dainty wrists, the blessed shapes and
laughing faces, the free, good-humoured, gallant figures that
they make! There were great vans, too, full of handsome
girls — thirty, or more together, perhaps — and the broadsides
that were poured into, and poured out of, these fairy fire-
ships, splashed the air with flowers and bonbons for ten
minutes at a time. Carriages, delayed long in one place,
would begin a deliberate engagement with other carriages, or

with people at the lower windows; and the spectators at some upper balcony or windows; and the spectators at some upper balcony or window, joining in the fray, and attacking both parties, would empty down great bags of confetti, that descended like a cloud, and in an instant made them white as millers. Still, carriages on carriages, dresses on dresses, colours on colours, crowds upon crowds, without end. Men and boys clinging to the wheels of coaches, and holding on behind, and following in their wake, and diving in among the horses' feet to pick up scattered flowers to sell again; maskers on foot (the drollest, generally) in fantastic exaggerations of court-dresses, surveying the throng through enormous eye-glasses, and always transported with an ecstasy of love, on the discovery of any particularly old lady at a window; long strings of Policinelli, laying about them with blown bladders at the ends of sticks; a waggon-full of madmen, screaming and tearing to the life; a coach-full of grave mamelukes, with their horse-tail standard set up in the midst; a party of gipsy-women engaged in terrific conflict with a shipful of sailors; a man-monkey on a pole, surrounded by strange animals with pigs' faces, and lions' tails, carried under their arms, or worn gracefully over their shoulders; carriages on carriages, dresses on dresses, colours on colours, crowds upon crowds, without end. Not many actual characters sustained, or represented, perhaps, considering the number dressed, but the main pleasure of the scene consisting in its perfect good temper; in its bright, and infinite, and flashing variety; and in its entire abandonment to the mad humour of the time — an abandonment so perfect, so contagious, so irresistible, that the steadiest foreigner fights up to his middle in flowers and sugar-plums, like the wildest Roman of them all, and thinks of nothing else till half-past four o'clock, when he is suddenly reminded (to his great regret) that this is not the whole business of his existence, by hearing the trumpets sound, and seeing the dragoons begin to clear the street.

How it ever *is* cleared for the race that takes place at five, or how the horses ever go through the race, without going over the people, is more than I can say. But the carriages get into the by-streets, or up into the Piazza del Popolo, and

some people sit in temporary galleries in the latter place, and
tens of thousands line the Corso on both sides, when the
horses are brought out into the Piazza — to the foot of that
same column which, for centuries, looked down upon the
games and chariot-races in the Circus Maximus.

At a given signal, they are started off. Down the live lane,
the whole length of the Corso, they fly like the wind:
riderless, as all the world knows: with shining ornaments
upon their backs, and twisted in their plaited manes: and
with heavy little balls stuck full spikes, dangling at their sides,
to goad them on. The jingling of these trappings, and the
rattling of their hoofs upon the hard stones; the dash and
fury of their speed along the echoing street; nay, the very
cannon that are fired — these noises are nothing to the roaring
of the multitude: their shouts: the clapping of their hands.
But it is soon over — almost instantaneously. More cannon
shake the town. The horses have plunged into the carpets put
across the street to stop them; the goal is reached; the prizes
are won (they are given, in part, by the poor Jews, as a
compromise for not running foot-races themselves); and there
is an end to that day's sport.

But if the scene be bright, and gay, and crowded, on the
last day but one, it attains, on the concluding day, to such a
height of glittering colour, swarming life, and frolicsome
uproar, that the bare recollection of it makes me giddy at this
moment. The same diversions, greatly heightened and
intensified in the ardour with which they are pursued, go on
until the same hour. The race is repeated; the cannon are
fired; the shouting and clapping of hands are renewed; the
cannon are fired again; the race is over; and the prizes are
won. But the carriages: ankle-deep in sugar-plums within,
and so beflowered and dusty without, as to be hardly
recognisable for the same vehicles that they were, three hours
ago: instead of scampering off in all directions, throng into
the Corso, where they are soon wedged together in a scarcely
moving mass. For the diversion of the Moccoletti, the last gay
madness of the Carnival, is now at hand; and sellers of little
tapers, like what are called Christmas candles in England, are
shouting lustily on every side, 'Moccoli, Moccoli! Ecco

Moccoli!' — a new item in the tumult; quite abolishing that other item of 'Ecco Fiori! Ecco Fior — r — r!' which has been making itself audible over all the rest, at intervals, the whole day through.

As the bright hangings and dresses are all fading into one dull, heavy, uniform colour in the decline of the day, lights begin flashing, here and there: in the windows, on the house-tops, in the balconies, in the carriages, in the hands of the foot-passengers: little by little: gradually, gradually: more and more: until the whole long street is one great glare and blaze of fire. Then, everybody present has but one engrossing object; that is, to extinguish other people's candles, and to keep his own alight; and everybody: man, woman, or child, gentleman or lady, prince or peasant, native or foreigner: yells and screams, and roars incessantly, as a taunt to the subdued, 'Senza Moccolo, Senza Moccolo!' (Without a light! Without a light!) until nothing is heard but a gigantic chorus of those two words, mingled with peals of laughter.

The spectacle, at this time, is one of the most extraordinary that can be imagined. Carriages coming slowly by, with everybody standing on the seats or on the box, holding up their lights at arms' length, for greater safety; some in paper shades; some with a bunch of undefended little tapers, kindled altogether; some with blazing torches; some with feeble little candles; men on foot, creeping along, among the wheels, watching their opportunity, to make a spring at some particular light, and dash it out; other people climbing up into carriages, to get hold of them by main force; others, chasing some unlucky wanderer, round and round his own coach, to blow out the light he has begged or stolen somewhere, before we can ascend to his own company, and enable them to light their extinguished tapers; others, with their hats off, at a carriage-door, humbly beseeching some kindhearted lady to oblige them with a light for a cigar, and when she is in the fulness of doubt whether to comply or no, blowing out the candle she is guarding so tenderly with her little hand; other people at the windows, fishing for candles with lines and hooks, or letting down long willow-wands with handkerchiefs at the end, and flapping them out,

dexterously, when the bearer is at the height of his triumph;
others, biding their time in corners, with immense extin-
guishers like halbreds, and suddenly coming down upon
glorious torches; others, gathered round one coach, and
sticking to it; others, raining oranges and nosegays at an
obdurate little lantern, or regularly storming a pyramid of
men, holding up one man among them, who carries one
feeble little wick above his head, with which he defies them
all! Senza Moccolo! Senza Moccolo! Beautiful women,
standing up in coaches, pointing in derision at extinguished
lights and clapping their hands, as they pass on, crying,
'Senza Moccoloa! Senza Moccolo!'; low balconies full of lovely
faces and gay dresses, struggling with assailants in the steets;
some repressing them as they climb up, some bending down,
some leaning over, some shrinking back — delicate arms and
bosoms — graceful figures — glowing lights, fluttering dresses,
Senza Moccolo, Senza Moccolo, Senza Moc-co-lo-o-o-o! —
when in the wildest enthusiasm of the cry, and fullest ecstasy
of the sport, the Ave Maria rings from the church steeples,
and the Carnival is over in an instant — put out like a taper,
with a breath!

There was a masquerade at the theatre at night, as dull
and senseless as a London one, and only remarkable for the
summary way in which the house was cleared at eleven
o'clock: which was done by a line of soldiers forming along
the wall, at the back of the stage, and sweeping the whole
company out before them, like a broad broom. The game of
the Moccoletti (the word, in the singular, Moccoletto, is the
diminutive of Moccolo, and means a little lamp or candle-
snuff) is supposed by some to be a ceremony of burlesque
mourning for the death of the Carnival: candles being
indispensable to Catholic grief. But whether it be so, or be a
remnant of the ancient Saturnalia, or an incorporation of
both, or have its origin in anything else, I shall always
remember it, and the frolic, as a brilliant and most
captivating sight: no less remarkable for the unbroken good-
humour of all concerned, down to the very lowest (and
among those who scaled the carriages, were many of the
commonest men and boys) than for its innocent vivacity. For,

odd as it may seem to say so, of a sport so full of thoughtlessness and personal display, it is as free from any taint of immodesty as any general mingling of the two sexes can possibly be; and there seems to prevail, during its progress, a feeling of general, almost childish, simplicity and confidence, which one thinks of with a pang, when the Ave Maria has rung it away, for a whole year.

Availing ourselves of a part of the quiet interval between the termination of the Carnival and the beginning of the Holy Week: when everybody had run away from the one, and few people had yet begun to run back again for the other: we went conscientiously to work, to see Rome. And, by dint of going out early every morning, and coming back late every evening, and labouring hard all day, I believe we made acquaintance with every post and pillar in the city, and the country round; and, in particular, explored so many churches that I abandoned that part of the enterprise at last, before it was half finished, lest I should never, of my own accord, go to church again, as long as I lived. But, I managed, almost every day, at one time or other, to get back to the Coliseum, and out upon the open Campagna, beyond the Tomb of Cecilia Metella.

Among what may be called the Cubs or minor Lions of Rome, there was one that amused me mightily. It is always to be found there; and its den is on the great flight of steps that lead from the Piázza di Spágna, to the church of Trinita del Monte. In plainer words, these steps are the great place of resort for the artists' 'Models,' and there they are constantly waiting to be hired. The first time I went up there, I could not conceive why the faces seemed familiar to me; why they appeared to have beset me, for years, in every possible variety of action and costume; and how it came to pass that they started up before me, in Rome, in the broad day, like so many saddled and bridled nightmares. I soon found that we had made acquaintance, and improved it, for several years, on the walls of various Exhibition Galleries. There is one old gentleman, with long white hair and an immense beard, who, to my knowledge, has gone half through the catalogue of the Royal Academy. This is the venerable, or patriarchal model.

He carries a long staff; and every knot and twist in that staff I
have seen, faithfully delineated, innumerable times. There is
another man in a blue cloak, who always pretends to be
asleep in the sun (when there is any) and who, I need not say,
is always very wide awake, and very attentive to the
disposition of his legs. This is the *dolce far' niente* model.
There is another man in a brown cloak, who leans against a
wall, with his arms folded in his mantle, and looks out of the
corners of his eyes: which are just visible beneath his broad
slouched hat. This is the assassin model. There is another
man, who constantly looks over his own shoulder, and is
always going away, but never goes. This is the haughty or
scornful model. As to Domestic Happiness, and Holy
Families, they should come very cheap, for there are lumps of
them, all up the steps; and the cream of the thing, is, that
they are all the falsest vagabonds in the world, especially
made up for the purpose, and having no counterparts in
Rome or any other part of the habitable globe.

My recent mention of the Carnival, reminds me of its being
said to be a mock mourning (in the ceremony with which it
closes), for the gaieties and merry-makings before Lent; and
this again reminds me of the real funerals and mourning
processions of Rome, which, like those in most other parts of
Italy, are rendered chiefly remarkable to a Foreigner, by the
indifference with which the mere clay is universally regarded,
after life has left it. And this is not from the survivors having
had time to dissociate the memory of the dead from their
well-remembered appearance and form on earth; for the
interment follows too speedily after death, for that: almost
always taking place within four-and-twenty hours, and,
sometimes, within twelve.

At Rome, there is the same arrangement of Pits in a great
bleak, open, dreary space, that I have already described as
existing in Genoa. When I visited it, at noonday, I saw a
solitary coffin of plain deal: uncovered by any shroud or pall,
and so slightly made, that the hoof of any wandering mule
would have crushed it in: carelessly tumbled down, all on one
side, on the door of one of the pits — and there left, by itself,
in the wind and sunshine. 'How does it come to be left here?'

I asked the man who showed me the place. 'It was brought here half an hour ago, Signore,' he said. I remembered to have met the procession, on its return: straggling away at a good round pace. 'When will it be put in the pit?' I asked him. 'When the cart comes, and it is opened to-night,' he said. 'How much does it cost to be brought here in this way, instead of coming in the cart?' I asked him. 'Ten scudi,' he said (about two pounds, two-and-sixpence, English). 'The other bodies, for whom nothing is paid, are taken to the church of the Santa Maria della Consolázione,' he continued, 'and brought here, altogether, in the cart at night.' I stood a moment, looking at the coffin, which had two initial letters scrawled upon the top; and turned away, with an expression in my face, I suppose, of not much liking its exposure in that manner: for he said, shrugging his shoulders with great vivacity, and giving a pleasant smile, 'But he's dead, Signore, he's dead. Why not?'

Among the innumerable churches, there is one I must select for separate mention. It is the church of the Ara Cœli, supposed to be built on the site of the old Temple of Jupiter Feretrius; and approached, on one side, by a long steep flight of steps, which seem incomplete without some group of bearded soothsayers on the top. It is remarkable for the possession of a miraculous Bambíno, or wooden doll, representing the Infant Saviour; and I first saw this miraculous Bambíno, in legal phrase, in manner following, that is to say:

We had strolled into the church one afternoon, and were looking down its long vista of gloomy pillars (for all these ancient churches built upon the ruins of old temples, are dark and sad), when the Brave came running in, with a grin upon his face that stretched it from ear to ear, and implored us to follow him, without a moment's delay, as they were going to show the Bambíno to a select party. He accordingly hurried off to a sort of chapel, or sacristy, hard by the chief altar, but not in the church itself, where the select party: consisting of two or three Catholic gentlemen and ladies (not Italians) were already assembled: and where one hollow-cheeked young monk was lighting up divers candles, while another was putting on some clerical robes over his coarse brown habit. The candles were on a kind of altar, and above it were two delectable figures, such as you would see at any English fair, representing the Holy Virgin, and Saint Joseph, as I suppose, bending in devotion over a wooden box, or coffer; which was shut.

The hollow-cheeked monk, number One, having finished lighting the candles, went down on his knees, in a corner, before this set-piece; and the monk number Two, having put on a pair of highly ornamented and gold-bespattered gloves, lifted down the coffer, with great reverence, and set it on the altar. Then, with many genuflexions, and muttering certain prayers, he opened it, and let down the front, and took off sundry coverings of satin and lace from the inside. The ladies had been on their knees from the commencement; and the gentlemen now dropped down devoutly, as he exposed to view, a little wooden doll, in face very like General Tom Thumb, the American Dwarf: gorgeously dressed in satin and gold lace, and actually blazing with rich jewels. There was scarcely a spot upon its little breast, or neck, or stomach, but was sparkling with the costly offerings of the Faithful. Presently, he lifted it out of the box, and, carrying it round among the kneelers, set its face against the forehead of every one, and tendered its clumsy foot to them to kiss—a ceremony which they all performed, down to a dirty little ragamuffin of a boy who had walked in from the street. When this was done, he laid it in the box again: and the company, rising, drew near, and commended the jewels in whispers. In good time, he replaced the coverings, shut up the box, put it back in its place, locked up the whole concern (Holy Family and all) behind a pair of folding-doors; took off his priestly vestments; and received the customary 'small charge,' while his companion, by means of an extinguisher fastened to the end of a long stick, put out the lights, one after another. The candles being all extinguished, and the money all collected, they retired, and so did the spectators.

I met this same Bambino, in the street, a short time afterwards, going, in great state, to the house of some sick person. It is taken to all parts of Rome for this purpose, constantly; but, I understand that it is not always as successful as could be wished; for, making its appearance at the bedside of weak and nervous people in extremity, accompanied by a numerous escort, it not unfrequently frightens them to death. It is most popular in cases of child-birth, where it has done such wonders, that if a lady be longer than usual in getting through her difficulties, a messenger is despatched, with all speed, to solicit the immediate attendance of the Bambino. It is a very valuable property, and much confided in — especially by the religious body to whom it belongs.

I am happy to know that it is not considered immaculate, by some who are good Catholics, and who are behind the scenes, from what was told me by the near relation of a Priest, himself a Catholic, and a gentleman of learning and intelligence. This Priest made my informant promise that he would, on no account, allow the Bambino to be borne into the bedroom of a sick lady, in whom they were both interested. 'For,' said he, 'if they (the monks) trouble her with it, and intrude themselves into her room, it will certainly kill her.' My informant accordingly looked out of the window when it came; and, with many thanks, declined to open the door. He endeavored, in another case of which he had no other knowledge than such as he gained as a passer-by at the moment, to prevent its being carried into a small unwholesome chamber, where a poor girl was dying. but, he strove against it unsuccessfully, and she expired while the crowd were pressing round her bed.

Among the people who drop into St. Peter's at their leisure, to kneel on the pavement, and say a quiet prayer, there are certain schools and seminaries, priestly and otherwise, that come in, twenty or thirty-strong. These boys, always kneel down in single file, one behind the other, with a tall grim master in a black gown, bringing up the rear: like a pack of cards arranged to be tumbled down at a touch, with a disproportionately large Knave of clubs at the end. When they have had a minute or so at the chief altar, they scramble up, and filing off to the chapel of the Madonna, or the sacrament, flop down again in the same order; so that if anybody *did* stumble against the master, a general and sudden overthrow of the whole line must inevitably ensue.

The scene in all the churches is the strangest possible. The same monotonous, heartless, drowsy chaunting, always going on; the same dark building, darker from the brightness of the street without; the same lamps dimly burning; the self-same people kneeling here and there; turned towards you, from one altar or other, the same priest's back, with the same large cross embroidered on it; however different in size, in shape, in wealth, in architecture, this church is from that, it is the same thing still. There are the same dirty beggars stopping in their muttered prayers to beg; the same miserable cripples exhibiting their deformity at the doors; the same blind men, rattling little pots like kitchen pepper-castors; their depositories for alms; the same preposterous crowns of silver stuck upon the painted heads of single saints and Virgins in crowded pictures, so that a little figure on a mountain has a head-dress bigger than the temple in the foreground, or adjacent miles of landscape; the same favourite shrine or figure, smothered with little silver hearts and crosses, and the like: the staple trade and show of all the jewellers; the same odd mixture of respect and indecorum, faith and phlegm: kneeling on the stones, and spitting on them, loudly; getting up from prayers to beg a little, or to pursue some other worldly matter: and then kneeling down again, to resume the contrite supplication at the point where it was interrupted. In one church, a kneeling lady got up from her prayers, for a moment, to offer us her card, as a teacher of Music; and in another, a sedate gentleman with a very thick walking-staff, arose from his devotions to belabour his dog, who was growling at another dog: and whose yelps and howls resounded through the church, as his master quietly relapsed into his former trains of meditation—keeping his eye upon the dog, at the same time, nevertheless.

Above all, there is always a receptable for the contributions of the Faithful, in some form or other. Sometimes, it is a money-box, set up between worshipper, and the wooden life-size figure of the Redeemer; sometimes, it is a little chest for the maintenance of the Virgin; sometimes a bag at the end of a long stick, thrust among the people here and there, and vigilantly jingled by an active Sacristan; but there it always is, and, very often, in many shapes in the same church, and doing pretty well in all. Nor, is it wanting in the open air — the streets and roads — for, often as you are walking along, thinking about anything rather than a tin canister, that object pounces out upon you from a little house by the wayside; and on its top is painted, 'For the Souls in Purgatory;' an appeal which the bearer repeats a great many times, as he rattles it before you, much as Punch rattles the cracked bell which his sanguine disposition makes an organ of.

And this reminds me that some Roman altars of peculiar sanctity, bear the inscription, 'Every Mass performed at this altar, frees a soul from Purgatory.' I have never been able to find out the charge for one of these services, but they should needs be expensive. There are several Crosses in Rome too, the kissing of which, confers indulgences for varying terms. That in the centre of the Coliseum, is worth a hundred days; and people may be seen kissing it, from morning to night. It is curious that some of these crosses seem to acquire an arbitrary popularity; this very one among them. In another part of the Coliseum there is a cross upon a marble slab, with the inscription, 'Who kisses this cross shall be entitled to Two hundred and forty days' indulgence.' But I saw no one person kiss it, though, day after day, I sat in the arena, and saw scores upon scores of peasants pass it, on their way to kiss the other.

To single out details from the great dream of Roman Churches, would be the wildest occupation in the world. But St. Stefano Rotondo, a damp mildewed vault of an old church in the outskirts of Rome, will always struggle uppermost in my mind, by reason of the hideous paintings with which its walls are covered. These represent the martyrdoms of saints and early Christians; and such a panorama of horror and butchery no man could imagine in his sleep, though he were to eat a whole pig, raw, for supper. Grey-bearded men being boiled, fried, grilled, crimped, singed, eaten by wild beasts, worried by dogs, buried alive, torn asunder by horses, chopped up small with hatchets: women having their breasts torn with iron pincers, their tongues cut out, their ears screwed off, their jaws broken, their bodies stretched upon the rack, or skinned upon the stake, or crackled up and melted in the fire: these are among the mildest subjects. So insisted on, and laboured at, besides, that every sufferer gives you the same occasion for wonder as poor old Duncan awoke, in Lady Macbeth, when she marvelled at his having so much blood in him.

There is an upper chamber in the Mamertine prisons, over what is said to have been—and very possibly may have been—the dungeon of St. Peter. This chamber is now fitted up as an oratory, dedicated to that saint; and it lives, as a distinct and separate place, in my recollection, too. It is very small and low-roofed; and the dread and gloom of the ponderous, obdurate old prison are on it, as if they had come up in a dark mist through the floor. Hanging on the walls, among the clustered votive offerings, are objects, at once strangely in keeping, and strangely at variance, with, the place—rusty daggers, knives, pistols, clubs, divers instruments of violence and murder, brought here, fresh from use, and hung up to propitiate offended Heaven: as if the blood upon them would drain off in consecrated air, and have no voice to cry with. It is all so silent and so close, and tomb-like; and the dungeons below, are so black, and stealthy, and stagnant, and naked; that this little dark spot becomes a dream within a dream: and in the vision of great churches which come rolling past me like a sea, it is a small wave by itself, that melts into no other wave, and does not flow on with the rest.

It is an awful thing to think of the enormous caverns that are entered from some Roman churches, and undermine the city. Many churches have crypts and subterranean chapels of great size, which, in the ancient time, were baths, and secret chambers of temples, and what not; but I do not speak of them. Beneath the church of St. Giovanni and St. Paolo, there are the jaws of a terrific range of caverns, hewn out of the rock, and said to have another outlet underneath the Coliseum—tremendous darknesses of vast extent, half-buried in the earth and unexplorable, where the dull torches, flashed by the attendants, glimmer down long ranges of distant vaults branching to the right and left, like streets in a city of the dead; and show the cold damp stealing down the walls, drip-drop, drip-drop, to join the pools of water that lie here and there, and never saw, and never will see, one ray of the sun. Some accounts make these the prisons of the wild beasts destined for the amphitheatre; some, the prisons of the condemned gladiators; some, both. But the legend most appalling to the fancy is, that is the upper range (for there are two stories of these caves) the Early Christians destined to be eaten at the Coliseum Shows, heard the wild beasts, hungry for them, roaring down below; until, upon the night and solitude of their captivity, there burst the sudden noon and life of the vast theatre crowded to the parapet, and of these, their dreaded neighbours, bounding in!

Below the church of San Sebastiano, two miles beyond the gate of San Sebastiano, on the Appian way, is the entrance to the catacombs of Rome — quarries in the old time, but afterwards the hiding-places of the Christians. These ghastly passages have been explored for twenty miles; and form a chain of labyrinths, sixty miles in circumference.

A gaunt Franciscan friar, with a wild bright eye, was our only guide, down into this profound and dreadful place. The narrow ways and openings hither and thither, coupled with the dead and heavy air, soon blotted out, in all of us, any recollection of the track by which we had come; and I could not help thinking, 'Good Heavens, if, in a sudden fit of madness he should dash the torches out, or if he should be seized with a fit, what would become of us!' On we wandered, among martyrs' graves: passing great subterranean vaulted roads, diverging in all directions, and choked up with heaps of stones, that thieves and murderers may not take refuge there, and form a population under Rome, even worse than that which lives between it and the sun. Graves, graves, graves; graves of men, of women, of their little children, who ran crying to the persecutors, 'We are Christians! We are Christians!' that they might be murdered with their parents; Graves with the palm of martyrdom roughly cut into their

stone boundaries, and little niches, made to hold a vessel of
the martyrs' blood; Graves of some who lived down here, for
years together, ministering to the rest, and preaching truth,
and hope, and comfort, from the rude altars, that bear
witness to their fortitude at this hour; more roomy graves,
but far more terrible, where hundreds, being surprised, were
hemmed in and walled up: buried before Death, and killed
by slow starvation.

'The Triumphs of the Faith are not above ground in our
splendid churches,' said the friar, looking round upon us, as
we stopped to rest in one of the low passages, with bones and
dust surrounding us on every side. 'They are here! Among the
Martyrs' Graves! He was a gentle, earnest man, and said it
from his heart; but when I thought how Christian men have
dealt with one another; how, perverting our most merciful
religion, they have hunted down and tortured, burnt and
beheaded, strangled, slaughtered, and oppressed each other;
I pictured to myself an agony surpassing any that this Dust
had suffered with the breath of life yet lingering in it, and
how these great and constant hearts would have been
shaken—how they would have quailed and drooped—if a
fore-knowledge of the deeds that professing Christians would
commit in the Great Name for which they died, could have
rent them with its own unutterable anguish, on the cruel
wheel, and bitter cross, and in the fearful fire.

Such are the spots and patches in my dream of churches,
that remain apart, and keep their separate identity. I have a
fainter recollection, sometimes, of the relics; of the fragment
of the pillar of the Temple that was rent in twain; of the
portion of the table that was spread for the Last Supper; of
the well at which the woman of Samaria gave water to Our
Saviour; of two columns from the house of Pontius Pilate; of
the stone to which the sacred hands were bound, when the
scourging was performed; of the gridiron of Saint Lawrence,
and the stone below it, marked with the frying of his fat and
blood; these set a shadowy mark on some cathedrals, as an
old story, or a fable might, and stop them for an instant, as
they flit before me. The rest is a vast wilderness of
consecrated buildings of all shapes and fancies, blending one

with another; of battered pillars of old Pagan temples, dug
up from the ground, and forced, like giant captives, to
support the roofs of Christian churches; of pictures, bad, and
wonderful, and impious, and ridiculous; of kneeling people,
curling incense, tinkling bells, and sometimes (but not often)
of a swelling organ; of Madonne, with their breasts stuck full
of swords, arranged in a half-circle like a modern fan; of
actual skeletons of dead saints, hideously attired in gaudy
satins, silks, and velvets trimmed with gold: their withered
crust of skull adorned with precious jewels, or with chaplets
of crushed flowers; sometimes, of people gathered round the
pulpit, and a monk within it stretching out the crucifix, and
preaching fiercely: the sun just streaming down through some
high window on the sail-cloth stretched above him and across
the church, to keep his high-pitched voice from being lost
among the echoes of the roof. Then my tired memory comes
out upon a flight of steps, where knots of people are asleep,
or basking in the light; and strolls away, among the rags, and
smells, and palaces, and hovels, of an old Italian street.

At the head of the collections in the palaces of Rome, the
Vatican, of course, with its treasures of art, its enormous
galleries, and staircases, and suites upon suites of immense
chambers, ranks highest and stands foremost. Many most
noble statues, and wonderful pictures, are there; nor is it
heresy to say that there is a considered amount of rubbish
there, too. When any old piece of sculpture dug out of the
ground, finds a place in a gallery because it *is* old, and
without any reference to its intrinsic merits: and finds
admirers by the hundred, because it is there, and for no other
reason on earth: there will be no lack of objects, very
indifferent in the plain eyesight of any one who employs so
vulgar a property, when he may wear the spectacles of Cant
for less than nothing, and establish himself as a man of taste
for the mere trouble of getting them on.

I unreservedly confess, for myself, that I cannot leave my
natural perception of what is natural and true, at a palace-
door, in Italy or elsewhere, as I should leave my shoes if I
were travelling in the East. I cannot forget that there are
certain expressions of face, natural to certain passions, and as

unchangeable in their nature as the gait of a lion, or the flight of an eagle. I cannot dismiss from my certain knowledge, such common-place facts as the ordinary proportions of men's arms, and legs, and heads; and when I meet with performances that do violence to these experiences and recollections, no matter where they may be, I cannot honestly admire them, and think it best to say so; in spite of high critical advice that we should sometimes feign an admiration, though we have it not.

Therefore, I freely acknowledge that when I see a Jolly young Waterman representing a cherubim, or a Barclay and Perkin's Drayman depicted as an Evangelist, I see nothing to commend or admire in the performance, however great its reputed Painter. Neither am I partial to libellous Angels, who play on fiddles and bassoons, for the edification of sprawling monks apparently in liquor. Nor to those Monsieur Tonsons of galleries, Saint Francis and Saint Sebastian; both of whom I submit should have very uncommon and rare merits, as works of art, to justify their compound multiplication by Italian Painters.

It seems to me, too, that the indiscriminate and determined raptures in which some critics indulge, is incompatible with the true appreciation of the really great and transcendent works. I cannot imagine, for example, how the resolute champion of undeserving pictures can soar to the amazing beauty of Titian's great picture of the Assumption of the Virgin at Venice; or how the man who is truly affected by the sublimity of that exquisite production, or who is truly sensible of the beauty of Tintoretto's great picture of the Assembly of the Blessed in the same place, can discern in Michael Angelo's Last Judgment, in the Sistine chapel, any general idea, or one pervading thought, in harmony with the stupendous subject. He who will contemplate Raphael's masterpiece, the Transfiguration, and will go away into another chamber of that same Vatican, and contemplate another design of Raphael, representing (in incredible caricature) the miraculous stopping of a great fire by Leo the Fourth — and who will say that he admires them both, as works of extraordinary genius — must, as I think, be wanting in his powers of perception in one of the instances, and, probably, in the high and lofty one.

It is easy to suggest a doubt, but I have a great doubt whether, sometimes, the rules of art are not too strictly observed, and whether it is quite well or agreeable that we should know beforehand, where this figure will be turning round, and where that figure will be lying down, and where there will be drapery in folds, and so forth. When I observe heads inferior to the subject, in pictures of merit, in Italian galleries, I do not attach that reproach to the Painter, for I have a suspicion that these great men, who were, of necessity, very much in the hands of monks and priests, and painted monks and priests a great deal too often. I frequently see, in pictures of real power, heads quite below the story and the painter: and I invariably observe that those heads are of the Convent stamp, and have their counterparts among the Convent inmates of this hour; so, I have settled with myself that, in such cases, the lameness was not with the painter, but with the vanity and ignorance of certain of his employers, who would be apostles — on canvass, at all events.

The exquisite grace and beauty of Canova's statues; the wonderful gravity and repose of many of the ancient works in sculpture, both in the Capitol and the Vatican; and the strength and fire of many others; are, in their different ways, beyond all reach of words. They are especially impressive and delightful, after the works of Bernini and his disciples, in which the churches of Rome, from St. Peter's downward, abound; and which are, I verily believe, the most detestable class of productions in the wide world. I would infinitely rather (as mere works of art) look upon the three deities of the Past, the Present, and the Future, in the Chinese Collection, than upon the best of these breezy maniacs; whose every fold of drapery is blown inside-out; whose smallest vein, or artery, is as big as an ordinary forefinger; whose hair is like a nest of lively snakes; and whose attitudes put all other extravagance to shame. Insomuch that I do honestly believe, there can be no place in the world, where such intolerable abortions, begotten of the sculptor's chisel, are to be found in such profusion, as in Rome.

There is a fine collection of Egyptian antiquities, in the Vatican; and the ceilings of the rooms in which they are arranged, are painted to represent a star-light sky in the Desert. It may seem an odd idea, but it is very effective. The grim, half-human monsters from the temples, look more grim and monstrous underneath the deep dark blue; it sheds a strange uncertain gloomy air on everything—a mystery adapted to the objects; and you leave them, as you find them, shrouded in a solemn night.

In the private palaces, pictures are seen to the best advantage. There are seldom so many in one place that the attention need become distracted, or the eye confused. You see them very leisurely; and are rarely interrupted by a crowd of people. There are portraits innumerable, by Titian, and Rembrandt, and Vandyke; heads of Guido, and Domenichino, and Carlo Dolci; various subjects by Correggio, and Murillo, and Rapheal, and Salvator Rosa, and Spagnoletto— many of which it would be difficult, indeed, to praise too highly, or to praise enough; such is their tenderness and grace; their noble elevation, purity, and beauty.

The portrait of Beatrice de Cenci, in the Palazzo Barberini, is a picture almost impossible to be forgotten. Through the transcendent sweetness and beauty of the face, there is a something shining out, that haunts me. I see it now, as I see this paper, or my pen. The head is loosely draped in white; the light hair falling down below the linen folds. She has turned suddenly towards you; and there is an expression in the eyes—although they are very tender and gentle—as if the wildness of a momentary terror, or distraction, had been struggled with and overcome, that instant; and nothing but a celestial hope, and a beautiful sorrow, and a desolate earthly helplessness remained. Some stories say that Guido painted it, the night before her execution; some other stories, that he painted it from memory, after having seen her, on her way to the scaffold. I am willing to believe that, as you see her on his canvass, so she turned towards him, in the crowd, from the first sight of the axe, and stamped upon his mind a look which he has stamped on mine as though I had stood beside him in the concourse. The guilty palace of the Cenci:

blighting a whole quarter of the town, as it stands withering away by grains: had that face, to my fancy, in its dismal porch, and at its black blind windows, and flitting up and down its dreary stairs, and growing out of the darkness of its ghostly galleries. The History is written in the Painting; written, in the dying girl's face, by Nature's own hand. And oh! how in that one touch she puts to flight (instead of making kin) the puny world that claim to be related to her, in right of poor conventional forgeries!

I saw in the Palazzo Spada, the statue of Pompey; the statue at whose base, Cæsar fell. A stern, tremendous figure! I imagined one of greater finish: of the last refinement: full of delicate touches: losing its distinctness, in the giddy eyes of one whose blood was ebbing before it, and settling into some such rigid majesty as this, as Death came creeping over the upturned face.

The excursions in the neighbourhood of Rome are charming, and would be full of interest were it only for the changing views they afford, of the wild Campagna. But, every inch of ground, in every direction, is rich in associations, and in natural beauties. There is Albano, with its lovely lake and wooded shore, and with its wine, that certainly has not improved since the days of Horace, and in these times hardly justifies his panegyric. There is squalid Tivoli, with the river Anio, diverted from its course, and plunging down, headlong, some eighty feet in search of it. With its picturesque Temple of the Sibyl, perched high on a crag; its minor waterfalls glancing and sparkling in the sun; and one good cavern yawning darkly, where the river takes a fearful plunge and shoots on, low down under beetling rocks. There, too, is the Villa d'Este, deserted and decaying among groves of melancholy pine and cypress trees, where it seems to lie in state. Then, there is Frascati, and, on the steep above it, the ruins of Tusculum, where Cicero lived, and wrote, and adorned his favourite house (some fragments of it may yet be seen there), and where Cato was born. We saw its ruined amphitheatre on a grey dull day, when a shrill March wind was blowing, and when the scattered stones of the old city lay strewn about the lonely eminence, as desolate and dead as the ashes of a long extinguished fire.

One day, we walked out, a little party of three, to Albano, fourteen miles distant; possessed by a great desire to go there, by the ancient Appian way, long since ruined and overgrown. We started at half past seven in the morning, and within an hour or so, were out upon the open Campagna. For twelve miles, we went climbing on, over an unbroken succession of mounds, and heaps, and hills, or ruin. Tombs and temples, overthrown and prostrate; small fragments of columns, friezes, pediments; great blocks of granite and marble; mouldering arches, grass-grown and decayed; ruin enough to build a spacious city from; lay strewn about us. Sometimes, loose walls, built up from these fragments by the shepherds, came across our path; sometimes, a ditch between two mounds of broken stones, obstructed our progress; sometimes, the fragments themselves, rolling from beneath our feet, made it a toilsome matter to advance; but it was always ruin. Now, we tracked a piece of the old road, above the ground; now traced it, underneath a grassy covering, as if that were its grave; but all the way was ruin. In the distance, ruined aqueducts went stalking on their giant course along the plain; and every breath of wind that swept towards us, stirred early flowers and grasses, springing up, spontaneously, on miles of ruin. The unseen larks above us, who alone disturbed the awful silence, had their nests in ruin; and the fierce herdsmen, clad in sheepskins, who now and then scowled out upon us from their sleeping nooks, were housed in ruin. The aspect of the desolate Campagna in one direction, where it was most level, reminded me of an American prairie; but what is the solitude of a region where men have never dwelt, to that of a Desert, where a mighty race have left their foot-prints in the earth from which they have vanished; where the resting-places of their Dead, have fallen like their Dead; and the broken hour-glass of Time is but a heap of idle dust! Returning, by the road, at sunset; and looking, from the distance, on the course we had taken in the morning, I almost felt (as I had felt when I first saw it, at that hour) as if the sun would never rise again, but looked its last, that night, upon a ruined world.

To come again on Rome, by moonlight, after such an expedition, is a fitting close to such a day. The narrow streets, devoid of footways, and choked, in every obscure corner, by heaps of dunghill-rubbish, contrast so strongly, in their cramped dimensions, and their filth, and darkness, with the broad square before some haughty church: in the centre of which, a hieroglyphic-covered obelisk, brought from Egypt in the days of the Emperors, looks strangely on the foreign scene about it: or perhaps an ancient pillar, with its honoured statue overthrown, supports a Christian saint: Marcus Aurelius giving place to Paul, and Trajan to St. Peter. Then, there are the ponderous buildings reared from the spoliation of the Coliseum, shutting out the moon, like mountains: while, here and there, are broken arches and rent walls, through which it gushes freely, as the life comes pouring from a wound. The little town of miserable houses, walled, and shut in by barred gates, is the quarter where the Jews are locked up nightly, when the clock strikes eight—a miserable place, densely populated, and reeking with bad odours, but where the people are industrious and money-getting. In the day-time, as you make your way long the narrow streets, you see them all at work: upon the pavement, oftener than in their dark and frouzy shops: furbishing old clothes, and driving bargains.

Crossing from these patches of thick darkness, out into the moon once more, the fountain of Trevi, welling from a hundred jets, and rolling over mimic rocks, is silvery to the eye and ear. In the narrow little throat of street, beyond, a booth, dressed out with flaring lamps, and boughs of trees, attracts a group of sulky Romans round its smoking coppers of hot broth, and cauliflower stew; its trays of fried fish, and its flasks of wine. As you rattle round the sharply-twisting corner, a lumbering sound is heard. The coachman stops abruptly, and uncovers, as a van comes slowly by, preceded by a man who bears a large cross; by a torch-bearer; and a priest: the latter chaunting as he goes. It is the Dead Cart, with the bodies of the poor, on their way to burial in the Sacred Field outside the walls, where they will be thrown into the pit that will be covered with a stone to-night, and sealed up for a year.

But whether, in this ride, you pass by obelisks, or columns:

ancient temples, theatres, houses, porticoes, or forums: it is
strange to see, how every fragment, whenever it is possible,
has been blended into some modern structure, and made to
serve some modern purpose—a wall, a dwelling-place, a
granary, a stable—some use for which it never was designed,
and associated with which it cannot otherwise than lamely
assort. It is stranger still, to see how many ruins of the old
mythology: how many fragments of obsolete legend and
observance: have been incorporated into the worship of
Christian altars here; and how, in numberless respects, the
false faith and the true are fused into a monstrous union.

From one part of the city, looking out beyond the walls, a
squat and stunted pyramid (the burial-place of Caius Cestius)
makes an opaque triangle in the moonlight. But, to an
English traveller, it serves to mark the grave of Shelley too,
whose ashes lie beneath a little garden near it. Nearer still,
almost within its shadow, lie the bones of Keats, 'whose name
is writ in water,' that shines brightly in the landscape of a
calm Italian night.

The Holy Week in Rome is supposed to offer great attrac-
tions to all visitors; but, saving for the sights of Easter Sunday, I would counsel those who go to Rome for its own
interest, to avoid it at that time. The ceremonies, in general,
are of the most tedious and wearisome kind; the heat and
crowd at every one of them, painfully oppressive; the noise,
hubbub, and confusion, quite distracting. We abandoned the
pursuit of these shows, very early in the proceedings, and
betook ourselves to the Ruins again. But, we plunged into the
crowd for a share of the best of the sights; and what we saw, I
will describe to you.

At the Sistine chapel, on the Wednesday, we saw very little,
for by the time we reached it (though we were early) the
besieging crowd had filled it to the door, and overflowed into
the adjoining hall, where they were struggling, and
squeezing, and mutually expostulating, and making great
rushes every time a lady was brought out faint, as if at least
fifty people could be accommodated in her vacant
standing-room. Hanging in the doorway of the chapel, was a

heavy curtain, and this curtain, some twenty people nearest
to it, in their anxiety to hear the chaunting of the Miserere,
were continually plucking at, in opposition to each other,
that it might not fall down and stifle the sound of the voices.
The consquence was, that it occasioned the most extraordinary confusion, and seemed to wind itself about the
unwary, like a Serpent. Now, a lady was wrapped up in it,
and couldn't be unwound. Now, the voice of a stifling
gentleman was heard inside it, beseeching to be let out. Now,
two muffled arms, no man could say of which sex, struggled
in it as in a sack. Now, it was carried by a rush, bodily
overhead into the chapel, like an awning. Now, it came out
the other way, and blinded one of the Pope's Swiss Guard
who had arrived, that moment, to set things to rights.

Being seated at a little distance, among two or three of the
Pope's gentlemen, who were very weary and counting the
minutes — as perhaps His Holiness was too — we had better
opportunities of observing this eccentric entertainment, than
of hearing the Miserere. Sometimes, there was a swell of
mounful voices that sounded very pathetic and sad, and died
away, into a low strain again; but that was all we heard.

At another time, there was the Exhibition of the Relics in
Saint Peter's, which took place at between six and seven
o'clock in the evening, and was striking from the cathedral
being dark and gloomy, and having a great many people in
it. The place into which the relics were brought, one by one,
by a party of three priests, was a high balcony near the chief
altar. This was the only lighted part of the church. There a
are always a hundred and twelve lamps burning near the
altar, and there were two tall tapers, besides, near the black
statue of St. Peter; but these were nothing in such an
immense edifice. The gloom, and the general upturning of
faces to the balcony, and the prostration of true believers on
the pavement, as shining objects, like pictures or looking-
glasses, were brought out and shown, had something effective
in it, despite the very preposterous manner in which they
were held up for the general edification, and the great
elevation at which they were displayed; which one would
think rather calculated to diminish the comfort derivable
from a full conviction of their being genuine.

On the Thursday, we went to see the Pope convey the
Sacrament from the Sistine chapel, to deposit it in the
Capella Paolina, another chapel in the Vatican; — a ceremony
emblematical of the entombment of the Saviour before His
Resurrection. We waited in a great gallery with a great crowd
of people (three-fourths of them English) for an hour or so,
while they were chaunting the Miserere, in the Sistine chapel
again. Both chapels opened out of the gallery; and the
general attention was concentrated on the occasional opening
and shutting of the door of the one for which the Pope was
ultimately bound. None of these openings disclosed anything
more tremendous than a man on a ladder, lighting a great
quantity of candles; but at each and every opening, there was
a terrific rush made at this ladder and this man, something
like (I should think) a charge of the heavy British cavalry at
Waterloo. The man was never brought down, however, nor
the ladder; for it performed the strangest antics in the world
among the crowd — where it was carried by the man, when
the candles were all lighted; and finally it was stuck up
against the gallery wall, in a very disorderly manner, just
before the opening of the other chapel, and the commencement of a new chaunt, announced the approach of His
Holiness. At this crisis, the soldiers of the guard, who had
been poking the crowd into all sorts of shapes, formed down
the gallery: and the procession came up, between the two
lines they made.

There were a few choristers, and then a great many priests,
walking two and two, and carrying — the good-looking priests
at least — their lighted tapers, so as to throw the light with a
good effect upon their faces: for the room was darkened.
Those who were not handsome, or who had not long beards,
carried *their* tapers anyhow, and abandoned themselves to
spiritual contemplation. Meanwhile, the chaunting was very
monotonous and dreary. The procession passed on, slowly,
into the chapel, and the drone of voices went on, and came
on, with it, until the Pope himself appeared, walking under a
white satin canopy, and bearing the covered Sacrament in
both hands; cardinals and canons clustered round him,
making a brilliant show. The soldiers of the guard knelt down
as he passed; all the bystanders bowed; and so he passed on

into the chapel: the white satin canopy being removed from over him at the door, and a white satin parasol hoisted over his poor old head, in place of it. A few more couples brought up the rear, and passed into the chapel also. Then, the chapel door was shut; and it was all over; and everybody hurried off headlong, as for life or death, to see something else, and say it wasn't worth the trouble.

I think the most popular and most crowded sight (excepting those of Easter Sunday and Monday, which are open to all classes of people) was the Pope washing the feet of Thirteen men, representing the twelve apostles, and Judas Iscariot. The place in which this pious office is performed, is one of the chapels of St. Peter's, which is gaily decorated for the occasion; the thirteen sitting 'all of a row,' on a very high bench, and looking particularly uncomfortable, with the eyes of Heaven knows how many English, French, Americans, Swiss, Germans, Russians, Swedes, Norwegians, and other foreigners, nailed to their faces all the time. They are robed in white; and on their heads they wear a stiff white cap, like a large English porter-pot, without a handle. Each carries in his hand, a nosegay, of the size of a fine cauliflower; and two of them, on this occasion, wore spectacles: which, remembering the characters they sustained, I thought a droll appendage to the costume. There was a great eye to character. St. John was represented by a good-looking young man. St. Peter, by a grave-looking old gentleman, with a flowing brown beard; and Judas Iscariot by such an enormous hypocrite (I could not make out, though, whether the expression of his face was real or assumed) that if he had acted the part to the death and had gone away and hanged himself, he would have left nothing to be desired.

As the two large boxes, appropriate to ladies, at this sight, were full to the throat, and getting near was hopeless, we posted off, along with a great crowd, to be in time at the Table, where the Pope, in person, waits on these Thirteen; and after a prodigious struggle at the Vatican staircase, and several personal conflicts with the Swiss guard, the whole crowd swept into the room. It was a long gallery hung with drapery of white and red, with another great box for ladies

ROME. — LA PLACE NAVONE ET L'ÉGLISE SAINTE-AGNÈS, dessin de H. CLERGET, d'après une photographie.

(who are obliged to dress in black at these ceremonies, and to wear black veils), a royal box for the King of Naples, and his party; and the table itself, which, set out like a ball supper, and ornamented with golden figures of the real apostles, was arranged on an elevated platform on one side of the gallery. The counterfeit apostles' knives and forks were laid out on that side of the table which was nearest to the wall, so that they might be stared at again, without let or hindrance.

The body of the room was full of male strangers; the crowd immense; the heat very great; and the pressure sometimes frightful. It was at its height when the stream came pouring in, from the feet-washing; and then there were such shrieks and outcries, that a party of Piedmontese dragoons went to the rescue of the Swiss guard, and helped them to calm the tumult.

The ladies were particularly ferocious, in their struggles for places. One lady of my acquaintance was seized round the waist, in the ladies' box, by a strong matron, and hoisted out of her place; and there was another lady (in the back row in the same box) who improved her position by sticking a large pin into the ladies before her.

The gentlemen about me were remarkably anxious to see what was on the table; and one Englishman seemed to have embarked the whole energy of his nature in the determination to discover whether there was any mustard. 'By Jupiter there's vinegar!' I heard him say to his friend, after he had stood on tiptoe an immense time, and had been crushed and beaten on all sides. 'And there's oil!! I saw them distinctly, in cruets! Can any gentleman, in front· there, see mustard on the table? Sir, will you oblige me! *Do* you see a Mustard-Pot?'

The apostles and Judas appearing on the platform, after much expectation, were marshalled, in line, in front of the table, with Peter at the top; and a good long stare was taken at them by the company, while twelve of them took a long smell at their nosegays, and Judas—moving his lips very obtrusively—engaged in inward prayer. Then, the Pope, clad in a scarlet robe, and wearing on his head a skull-cap of white satin, appeared in the midst of a crowd of Cardinals and other dignitaries, and took in his hand a little golden ewer, from which he poured a little water over one of Peter's hands, while one attendant held a golden basin; a second, a fine cloth; a third, Peter's nosegay, which was taken from him during the operation. This His Holiness performed, with considerable expedition, on every man in the line (Judas, I observed, to be particularly overcome by his condescension); and then the whole Thirteen sat down to dinner. Grace said by the Pope. Peter in the chair.

There was white wine, and red wine; and the dinner looked very good. The courses appeared in portions, one for each apostle; and these being presented to the Pope, by Cardinals upon their knees, were by him handed to the Thirteen. The manner in which Judas grew more white-livered over his victuals, and languished, with his head on one side, as if he had no appetite, defies all description. Peter was a good, sound, old man, and went in, as the saying is, 'to win;' eating everything that was given him (he got the best: being first in the row) and saying nothing to anybody. The dishes appeared to be chiefly composed of fish and vegetables. The Pope helped the Thirteen to wine also; and, during the whole dinner, somebody read something aloud, out of a large book — the Bible, I presume — which nobody could hear, and to which nobody paid the least attention. The Cardinals, and other attendants, smiled to each other from time to time, as if the thing were a great farce; and if they thought so, there is little doubt they were perfectly right. His Holiness did what he had to do, as a sensible man gets through a troublesome ceremony, and seemed very glad when it was all over.

The Pilgrim's Suppers: where lords and ladies waited on the Pilgrims, in token of humility, and dried their feet when they had been well washed by deputy: were very attractive. But, of all the many spectacles of dangerous reliance on outward observances, in themselves mere empty forms, none struck me half so much as the Scala Santa, or Holy Staircase, which I saw several times, but to the greatest advantage, or disadvantage, on Good Friday.

This holy staircase is composed of eight-and-twenty steps, said to have belonged to Pontius Pilate's house, and to be the identical stairs on which Our Saviour trod, in coming down from the judgment-seat. Pilgrims ascend it, only on their knees. It is steep; and, at the summit, is a chapel, reported to be full of relics; into which they peep through some iron bars, and then come down again, by one of the two side staircases, which are not sacred, and may be walked on.

On Good Friday, there were, on a moderate computation, a hundred people, slowly shuffling up these stairs, on their knees, at one time; while others who were going up, or had come down — and a few who had done both, and were going up again for the second time — stood loitering in the porch below, where an old gentleman in a sort of watch-box, rattled a tin cannister, with a slit in the top, incessantly, to remind them that he took the money. The majority were country-people, male and female. There were four or five Jesuit priests, however, and some half-dozen well-dressed women. A whole school of boys, twenty at least, were about half-way up — evidently enjoying it very much. They were all wedged together, pretty closely; but the rest of the company gave the boys as wide a berth as possible, in consequence of their betraying some recklessness in the management of their boots.

I never, in my life, saw anything at once so ridiculous, and so unpleasant, as this sight — ridiculous in the absurd incidents inseparable from it; and unpleasant in its senseless and unmeaning degradation. There are two steps to begin with, and then a rather broad landing. The more rigid climbers went along this landing on their knees, as well as up the stairs; and the figures they cut, in their shuffling progress over the level surface, no description can paint. Then, to see them watch their opportunity from the porch, and cut in where there was a place next the wall! And to see one man with an umbrella (brought on purpose, for it was a fine day) hoisting himself, unlawfully, from stair to stair! And to observe a demure lady of fifty-five or so, looking back, every now and then, to assure herself that her legs were properly disposed!

There were such odd differences in the speed of different people too. Some got on as if they were doing a match against time; others stopped to say a prayer on every step. This man touched every stair with his forehead, and kissed it; that man scratched his head all the way. The boys got on brilliantly, and were up and down again before the old lady had accomplished her half dozen stairs. But most of the Penitents came down, very sprightly and fresh, as having done a real good substantial deed which it would take a good deal of sin to counterbalance; and the old gentleman in the watch-box was down upon them with his cannister while they were in this humour, I promise you.

As if such a progress were not in its nature inevitably droll enough, there lay, on the top of the stairs, a wooden figure on a crucifix, resting on a sort of great iron saucer: so ricketty and unsteady, that whenever an enthusiastic person kissed the figure, with more than usual devotion, or threw a coin into the saucer, with more than common readiness (for it served in this respect as a second or supplementary cannister), it gave a great leap and rattle, and nearly shook the attendant lamp out: horribly frightening the people further down, and throwing the guilty party into unspeakable embarrassment.

On Easter Sunday, as well as on the preceding Thursday, the Pope bestows his benediction on the people, from the balcony in from of St. Peter's. This Easter Sunday was a day so bright and blue: so cloudless, balmy, wonderfully bright: that all the previous bad weather vanished from the recollection in a moment. I had seen the Thursday's Benediction dropping damply on some hundreds of umbrellas, but there was not a sparkle then, in all the hundred fountains of Rome — such fountains as they are! — and on this Sunday morning, they were running diamonds. The miles of miserable streets through which we drove (compelled to a certain course by the Pope's dragoons: the Roman police on such occasions) were so full of colour, that nothing in them was capable of wearing a faded aspect. The common people came out in their gayest dresses; the richer people in their smartest vehicles; Cardinals rattled to the church of the Poor Fishermen in their state carriages; shabby magnificence flaunted its thread-bare liveries and tarnished cocked hats, in the sun; and every coach in Rome was put in requisition for the Great Piazza of St. Peter's.

One hundred and fifty thousand people were there, at

least! Yet there was ample room. How many carriages were there, I don't know; yet there was room for them too, and to spare. The great steps of the church were densely crowded. There were many of the Contadini, from Albano (who delight in red) in that part of the square; and the mingling of bright colours in the crowd, was beautiful. Below the steps, the troops were ranged. In the magnificent proportions of the place, they looked like a bed of flowers. Sulky Romans, lively peasants from the neighbouring country, groups of pilgrims from distant parts of Italy, sight-seeing foreigners of all nations, made a murmur in the clear air, like so many insects; and high above them all, plashing and bubbling, and making rainbow colours in the light, the two delicious fountains welled and tumbled bountifully.

A kind of bright carpet was hung over the front of the balcony; and the sides of the great window were bedecked with crimson drapery. An awning was stretched too, over the top, to screen the old man from the hot rays of the sun. As noon approached, all eyes were turned up to this window. In due time, the chair was seen approaching to the front, with the gigantic fans of peacock's feathers, close behind. The doll within it (for the balcony is very high) then rose up, and stretched out its tiny arms, while all the male spectators in the square uncovered, and some, but not by any means the greater part, kneeled down. The guns upon the ramparts of the Castle of St. Angelo proclaimed, next moment, that the benediction was given; drums beat; trumpets sounded; arms clashed; and the great mass below, suddenly breaking into smaller heaps, and scattering here and there in rills, was stirred like partycoloured sand.

What a bright noon it was, as we rode away! The Tiber was no longer yellow, but blue. There was a blush on the old bridges, that made them fresh and hale again. The Pantheon, with its majestic front, all seamed and furrowed like an old face, had summer light upon its battered walls. Every squalid and desolate Hut in the Eternal City (bear witness every grim old palace, to the filth and misery of the plebeian neighbour that elbows it, as certainly as Time has laid its grip on its Patrician head!) was fresh and new with some ray of the sun.

The very prison in the crowded street, a whirl of carriages and people, had some stray sense of the day, dropping through its chinks and crevices: and dismal prisoners who could not wind their faces round the barricading of the blocked-up windows, stretched out their hands, and clinging to the rusty bars, turned *them* towards the overflowing street: as if it were a cheerful fire, and could be shared in, that way.

But, when the night came on, without a cloud to dim the full moon, what a sight it was to see the Great Square full once more, and the whole church, from the cross to the ground, lighted with innumerable lanterns, tracing out the architecture, and winking and shining all round the colonnade of the piazza! And what a sense of exultation, joy, delight, it was, when the great bell struck half-past seven — on the instant — to behold one bright red mass of fire, soar gallantly from the top of the cupola to the extremest summit of the cross, and the moment it leaped into its place, become the signal of a bursting out of countless lights, as great, and red, and blazing as itself, from every part of the gigantic church; so that every cornice, capital, and smallest ornament of stone, expressed itself in fire: and the black solid ground-work of the enormous dome, seemed to grow transparent as an egg-shell!

A train of gunpowder, an electric chain — nothing could be fired, more suddenly and swiftly, than this second illumination; and when we had got away, and gone upon a distant height, and looked towards it two hours afterwards, there it still stood, shining and glittering in the calm night like a Jewel! Not a line of its proportions wanting; not an angle blunted; not an atom of its radiance lost.

The next night — Easter Monday — there was a great display of fireworks from the Castle of St. Angelo. We hired a room in an opposite house, and made our way to our places, in good time, through a dense mob of people choking up the square in front, and all the avenues leading to it; and so loading the bridge by which the castle is approached, that it seemed ready to sink into the rapid Tiber below. There are statues on this bridge (execrable works) and, among them, great vessels full of burning tow were placed: glaring strangely on the faces of the crowd, and not less strangely on the stone counterfeits above them.

The show began with a tremendous discharge of cannon; and then, for twenty minutes, or half an hour, the whole castle was one incessant sheet of fire, and labyrinth of blazing wheels of every colour, size, and speed: while rockets streamed into the sky, not by ones or twos, or scores, but hundreds at a time. The concluding burst — the Girandola — was like the blowing up into the air, of the whole massive castle, without smoke or dust.

In half an hour afterwards, the immense concourse had dispursed; the moon was looking calmly down upon her wrinkled image in the river; and half a dozen men and boys, with bits of lighted candle in their hands: moving here and there, in search of anything worth having, that might have been dropped in the press: had the whole scene to themselves.

By way of contrast, we rode out into old ruined Rome, after all this firing and booming, to take our leave of the Coliseum. I had seen it by moonlight before (I never could get through a day without going back to it), but its tremendous solitude, that night, is past all telling. The ghostly pillars in the Forum; the triumphal arches of Old Emperors; those enormous masses of ruin which were once their palaces; the grass-grown mounds that mark the graves of ruined temples; the stones of the Via Sacra, smooth with the tread of feet in ancient Rome; even these were dimmed, in their transcendent melancholy, by the dark ghost of its bloody holidays, erect and grim; haunting the old scene; despoiled by pillaging Popes and fighting Princes, but not laid; wringing wild hands of weed, and grass, and bramble; and lamenting to the night in every gap and broken arch — the shadow of its awful self, immovable!

As we lay down on the grass of the Campagna, next day, on our way to Florence, hearing the larks sing, we saw that a little wooden cross had been erected on the spot where the poor Pilgrim Countess was murdered. So, we piled some loose stones about it, as the beginning of a mound to her memory, and wondered if we should ever rest there again, and look back at Rome.

Mark Twain: Venice

Mark Twain wrote in acid. Even the romance of Venice, the dreamy aura of the canals, the gondolas, and the Bridge of Sighs, cannot obscure man's folly. Twain's wit, as always, is companion to a sting. The following account of Venice is taken from The Innocents Abroad. Venice has changed little—save that it has sunk further into the sea. By law, no alterations may be made in the exterior of Venetian houses. In St. Marks, as in Twain's time, children still feed the pigeons, and painters are at work at their easels. Although the shops of Venetian glass and the restaurants are new, one can take a trip in a gondola along the canals and still see Venice in its pristine though somewhat decayed grandeur.

This Venice, which was a haughty, invincible, magnificent republic for nearly fourteen hundred years, whose armies compelled the world's applause whenever and wherever they battled, whose navies well-nigh held dominion of the seas, and whose merchant fleets whitened the remotest oceans with their sails and loaded these piers with the products of every clime, is fallen a prey to poverty, neglect, and melancholy decay. Six hundred years ago Venice was the Autocrat of Commerce; her mart was the great commercial center, the distributing house from whence the enormous trade of the Orient was spread abroad over the Western world. Today her piers are deserted, her warehouses are empty, her merchant fleets are vanished, her armies and her navies are but memories. Her glory is departed, and with her crumbling grandeur of wharves and palaces about her, she sits among her stagnant lagoons, forlorn and beggared, forgotten of the world. She that in her palmy days commanded the commerce of a hemisphere, and made the weal or woe of nations with a beck of her puissant finger, is become the humblest among the peoples of the earth — a peddler of glass beads for women and trifling toys and trinkets for schoolgirls and children.

The venerable Mother of the Republics is scarce a fit subject for flippant speech or the idle gossiping of tourists. It seems a sort of sacrilege to disturb the glamour of old romance that pictures her to us softly from afar off as through a tinted mist, and curtains her ruin and her desolation from our view. One ought, indeed, to turn away from her rags, her poverty, and her humiliation and think of her only as she was when she sunk the fleets of Charlemagne, when she humbled Frederick Barbarossa or waved her victorious banners above the battlements of Constantinople.

We reached Venice at eight in the evening and entered a hearse belonging to the Grand Hôtel d'Europe. At any rate, it was more like a hearse than anything else, though to speak by the card, it was a gondola. And this was the storied gondola of Venice! — the fairy boat in which the princely cavaliers of the olden time were wont to cleave the waters of the moonlit canals and look the eloquence of love into the soft eyes of patrician beauties, while the gay gondolier in silken doublet touched his guitar and sang as only gondoliers can sing! This the famed gondola and this the gorgeous gondolier! — the one an inky, rusty old canoe with a sable hearse body clapped onto the middle of it, and the other a mangy, barefooted guttersnipe with a portion of his raiment on exhibition which should have been sacred from public scrutiny. Presently, as he turned a corner and shot his hearse into a dismal ditch between two long rows of towering, untenanted buildings, the gay gondolier began to sing, true to the traditions of his race. I stood it a little while. Then I said:

"Now, here, Roderigo Gonzales Michelangelo, I'm a pilgrim and I'm a stranger, but I am not going to have my

Mark Twain

feelings lacerated by any such caterwauling as that. If that
goes on, one of us has got to take water. It is enough that my
cherished dreams of Venice have been blighted forever as to
the romantic gondola and the gorgeous gondolier; this system
of destruction shall go no farther; I will accept the hearse
under protest, and you may fly your flag of truce in peace,
but here I register a dark and bloody oath that you shan't
sing. Another yelp, and overboard you go."

I began to feel that the old Venice of song and story had
departed forever. But I was too hasty. In a few minutes we
swept gracefully out into the Grand Canal, and under the
mellow moonlight the Venice of poetry and romance stood
revealed. Right from the water's edge rose long lines of stately
palaces of marble; gondolas were gliding swiftly hither and
thither and disappearing suddenly through unsuspected gates
and alleys; ponderous stone bridges threw their shadows
athwart the glittering waves. There was life and motion
everywhere, and yet everywhere there was a hush, a stealthy
sort of stillness, that was suggestive of secret enterprises of
bravos and of lovers; and clad half in moonbeams and half in
mysterious shadows, the grim old mansions of the republic
seemed to have an expression about them of having an eye
out for just such enterprises as these at that same moment.
Music came floating over the waters — Venice was complete.

It was a beautiful picture — very soft and dreamy and
beautiful. But what was this Venice to compare with the
Venice of midnight? Nothing. There was a fete — a grand fete
in honor of some saint who had been instrumental in
checking the cholera three hundred years ago, and all Venice
was abroad on the water. It was no common affair, for the
Venetians did not know how soon they might need the saint's
services again, now that the cholera was spreading everywhere. So in one vast space — say a third of a mile wide and
two miles long — were collected two thousand gondolas, and
every one of them had from two to ten, twenty, and even
thirty colored lanterns suspended about it, and from four to a
dozen occupants. Just as far as the eye could reach, these
painted lights were massed together — like a vast garden of
many-colored flowers, except that these blossoms were never

still; they were ceaselessly gliding in and out, and mingling together, and seducing you into bewildering attempts to follow their mazy evolutions. Here and there a strong red, green, or blue glare from a rocket that was struggling to get away splendidly illuminated all the boats around it. Every gondola that swam by us, with its crescents and pyramids and circles of colored lamps hung aloft, and lighting up the faces of the young and the sweet-scented and lovely below, was a picture; and the reflections of those lights, so long, so slender, so numberless, so many-colored, and so distorted and wrinkled by the waves, was a picture likewise, and one that was enchantingly beautiful. Many and many a party of young ladies and gentlemen had their state gondolas handsomely decorated, and ate supper on board, bringing their swallow-tailed, white-cravatted varlets to wait upon them and having their tables tricked out as if for a bridal supper. They had brought along the costly globe lamps from their drawing rooms, and the lace and silken curtains from the same places, I suppose. And they had also brought pianos and guitars, and they played and sang operas, while the plebeian paper-lanterned gondolas from the suburbs and the back alleys crowded around to stare and listen.

There was music everywhere—choruses, string bands, brass bands, flutes, everything. I was so surrounded, walled in, with music, mangificence, and loveliness that I became inspired with the spirit of the scene and sang one tune myself. However, when I observed that the other gondolas had sailed away, and my gondolier was preparing to go overboard, I stopped.

The fete was magnificent. They kept it up the whole night long, and I never enjoyed myself better than I did while it lasted.

What a funny old city this Queen of the Adriatic is! Narrow streets, vast, gloomy marble palaces, black with the corroding damps of centuries, and all partly submerged; no dry land visible anywhere, and no sidewalks worth mentioning; if you want to go to church, to the theater, or to the restaurant, you must call a gondola. It must be a paradise for cripples, for verily a man has no use for legs here.

For a day or two the place looked so like an overflowed Arkansas town, because of its currentless waters laving the very doorsteps of all the houses, and the cluster of boats made fast under the windows or skimming in and out of the alleys and byways, that I could not get rid of the impression that there was nothing the matter here but a spring freshet, and that the river would fall in a few weeks and leave a dirty high-water mark on the houses and the street full of mud and rubbish.

In the glare of day there is little poetry about Venice, but under the charitable moon her stained palaces are white again, their battered sculptures are hidden in shadows, and the old city seems crowned once more with the grandeur that was hers five hundred years ago. It is easy then in fancy to people these silent canals with plumed gallants and fair ladies — with Shylocks in gaberdine and sandals, venturing loans upon the rich argosies of Venetian commerce — with Othellos and Desdemonas, with Iagos and Roderigos — with noble fleets and victorious legions returning from the wars. In the treacherous sunlight we see Venice decayed, forlorn, poverty-stricken, and commerceless — forgotten and utterly insignificant. But in the moonlight her fourteen centuries of greatness fling their glories about her, and once more is she the princeliest among the nations of the earth.

> There is a glorious city in the sea;
> The sea is in the broad, the narrow streets,
> Ebbing and flowing; and the salt-sea weed
> Clings to the marble of her palaces.
> No track of men, no footsteps to and fro,
> Lead to her gates! The path lies o'er the sea,
> Invisible: and from the land we went,
> As to a floating city — steering in,
> And gliding up her streets, as in a dream,
> So smoothly, silently — by many a dome,
> Mosque-like, and many a stately portico,
> The statues ranged along an azure sky;
> By many a pile, in more than Eastern pride,
> Of old the residence of merchant kings;
> The fronts of some, tho' time had shatter'd them,

>Still glowing with the richest hues of art,
>As tho' the wealth within them had run o'er.

What would one naturally wish to see first in Venice? The Bridge of Sighs, of course — and next the Church and the Great Square of St. Mark, the Bronze Horses, and the famous Lion of St. Mark.

We intended to go to the Bridge of Sighs, but happened into the Ducal Palace first — a building which necessarily figures largely in Venetian poetry and tradition. In the Senate Chamber of the ancient republic we wearied our eyes with staring at acres of historical paintings by Tintoretto and Paul Veronese, but nothing struck us forcibly except the one thing that strikes *all* strangers forcibly — a black square in the midst of a gallery of portraits. In one long row, around the great hall, were painted the portraits of the doges of Venice (venerable fellows, with flowing white beards, for of the three hundred Senators eligible to the office, the oldest was usually chosen Doge), and each had its complimentary inscription attached — till you came to the place that should have had Marino Faliero's picture in it, and that was blank and black — blank except that it bore a terse inscription saying that the conspirator had died for his crime. It seemed cruel to keep that pitiless inscription still staring from the walls after the unhappy wretch had been in his grave five hundred years.

At the head of the Giant's Staircase, where Marino Faliero was beheaded, and where the doges were crowned in ancient times, two small slits in the stone wall were pointed out, two harmless, insignificant orifices that would never attract a stranger's attention — yet these were the terrible Lions' Mouths! The heads were gone (knocked off by the French during their occupation of Venice), but these were the throats down which went the anonymous accusation, thrust in secretly at dead of night by an enemy, that doomed many an innocent man to walk the Bridge of Sighs and descend into the dungeon which none entered and hoped to see the sun again. This was in the old days when the patricians alone governed Venice — the common herd had no vote and no voice. There were one thousand five hundred patricians;

from these, three hundred Senators were chosen; from the
Senators a Doge and a Council of Ten were selected, and by
secret ballot the Ten chose from their own number a Council
of Three. All these were government spies then, and every spy
was under surveillance himself — men spoke in whispers in
Venice, and no man trusted his neighbor; not always his own
brother. No man knew who the Council of Three were — not
even the Senate, not even the Doge; the members of that
dread tribunal met at night in a chamber to themselves,
masked, and robed from head to foot in scarlet cloaks, and
did not even know each other unless by voice. It was their
duty to judge heinous political crimes, and from their
sentence there was no appeal. A nod to the executioner was
sufficient. The doomed man was marched down a hall and
out a doorway into the covered Bridge of Sighs, through it
and into the dungeon and unto his death. At no time in his
transit was he visible to any save his conductor. If a man had
an enemy in those old days, the cleverest thing he could do
was to slip a note for the Council of Three into the Lion's
mouth, saying, "This man is plotting against the government." If the awful Three found no proof, ten to one they
would drown him anyhow, because he was a deep rascal,
since his plots were unsolvable. Masked judges and masked
executioners, with unlimited power and no appeal from their
judgments, in that hard, cruel age, were not likely to be
lenient with men they suspected yet could not convict.

We walked through the hall of the Council of Ten and
presently entered the infernal den of the Council of Three.

The table around which they had sat was there still, and
likewise the stations where the masked inquisitors and
executioners formerly stood, frozen, upright, and silent, till
they received a bloody order, and then, without a word,
moved off, like the inexorable machines they were, to carry it
out. The frescoes on the walls were startlingly suited to the
place. In all the other saloons, the halls, the great state
chambers of the palace, the walls and ceilings were bright
with gilding, rich with elaborate carving, and resplendent
with gallant pictures of Venetian victories in war and
Venetain display in foreign courts, and hallowed with

portraits of the Virgin, the Saviour of men, and the holy saints that preached the gospel of peace upon earth, but here, in dismal contrast, were none but pictures of death and dreadful suffering!—not a living figure but was writhing in torture, not a dead one but was smeared with blood, gashed with wounds, and distorted with the agonies that had taken away its life!

From the palace to the gloomy prison is but a step—one might almost jump across the narrow canal that intervenes. The ponderous stone Bridge of Sighs crosses it at the second story—a bridge that is a covered tunnel—you cannot be seen when you walk in it. It is partitioned lengthwise, and through one compartment walked such as bore light sentences in ancient times, and through the other marched sadly the wretches whom the Three had doomed to lingering misery and utter oblivion in the dungeons or to sudden and mysterious death. Down below the level of the water, by the light of smoking torches, we were shown the damp, thick-walled cells where many a proud patrician's life was eaten away by the long-drawn miseries of solitary imprisonment—without light, air, books: naked, unshaven, uncombed, covered with vermin; his useless tongue forgetting its office, with none to speak to; the days and nights of his life no longer marked, but merged into one eternal eventless night; far away from all cheerful sounds, buried in the silence of a tomb; forgotten by his helpless friends, and his fate a dark mystery to them forever; losing his own memory at last, and knowing no more who he was or how he came there; devouring the loaf of bread and drinking the water that were thrust into the cell by unseen hands, and troubling his worn spirit no more with hopes and fears and doubts and longings to be free; ceasing to scratch vain prayers and complainings on walls where none, not even himself could see them, and resigning himself to hopeless apathy, driveling childishness, lunacy! Many and many a sorrowful story like this these stony walls could tell if they could but speak.

In a little narrow corridor nearby they showed us where many a prisoner, after lying in the dungeons until he was forgotten by all save his persecutors, was brought by masked

executioners and garroted or sewed up in a sack, passed
through a little window to a boat, at dead of night, and taken
to some remote spot and drowned.

They used to show to visitors the implements of torture
wherewith the Three were wont to worm secrets out of the
accused — villainous machines for crushing thumbs; the stocks
where a prisoner sat immovable while water fell drop by drop
upon his head till the torture was more than humanity could
bear; and a devilish contrivance of steel, which enclosed a prisoner's head like a shell and crushed it slowly by means of a
screw. It bore the stains of blood that had trickled through its
joints long ago, and on one side it had a projection whereon
the torturer rested his elbow confortably and bent down his ear
to catch the moanings of the sufferer perishing within.

Of course we went to see the venerable relic of the ancient
glory of Venice, with its pavements worn and broken by the
passing feet of a thousand years of plebeians and
patricians — the Cathedral of St. Mark. It is built entirely of
precious marbles brought from the Orient — nothing in its
composition is domestic. Its hoary traditions make it an
object of absorbing interest to even the most careless stranger,
and thus far it had interest for me; but no further. I could not
go into ecstasies over its coarse mosaics, its unlovely Byzantine
architecture, or its five hundred curious interior columns
from as many distant quarries. Everything was worn
out — every block of stone was smooth and almost shapeless
with the polishing hands and shoulders of loungers who
devoutly idled here in bygone centuries and have died and
gone to the dev — no, simply died, I mean.

Under the altar repose the ashes of St. Mark — and
Matthew, Luke, and John, too, for all I know. Venice
reveres those relics above all things earthly. For fourteen
hundred years St. Mark has been her patron saint. Everything
about the city seems to be named after him or so named as to
refer to him in some way — so named or some purchase rigged
in some way to scrape a sort of hurrahing acquaintance with
him. That seems to be the idea. To be on good terms with St.
Mark seems to be the summit of Venetian ambition. They say
St. Mark had a tame lion and used to travel with him — and

everywhere that St. Mark went, the lion was sure to go. It was his protector, his friend, his librarian. And so the Winged Lion of St. Mark, with the open Bible under his paw, is a favorite emblem in the grand old city. It casts its shadow from the most ancient pillar in Venice, in the Grand Square of St. Mark, upon the throngs of free citizens below, and has so done for many a long century. The winged lion is found everywhere — and doubtless here, where the winged lion is, no harm can come.

St. Mark died at Alexandria, in Egypt. He was martyred, I think. However, that has nothing to do with my legend. After the founding of the city of Venice — say four hundred and fifty years after Christ (for Venice is much younger than any other Italian city) — a priest dreamed that an angel told him that until the remains of St. Mark were brought to Venice, the city could never rise to high distinction among the nations; that the body must be captured, brought to the city, and a magnificent church build over it; and that if ever the Venetians allowed the saint to be removed from his new resting place, in that day Venice would perish from off the face of the earth. The priest proclaimed his dream, and forthwith Venice set about procuring the corpse of St. Mark. One expedition after another tried and failed, but the project was never abandoned during four hundred years. At last it was secured by stratagem, in the year eight hundred and something. The commander of a Venetian expedition disguised himself, stole the bones, separated them, and packed them in vessels filled with lard. The religion of Muhammad causes its devotees to abhor anything that is in the nature of pork, and so when the Christian was stopped by the officers at the gates of the city, they only glanced once into his precious baskets, then turned up their noses at the unholy lard, and let him go. The bones were buried in the vaults of the grand chthedral, which had been waiting long years to receive them, and thus the safety and the greatness of Venice was secured. And to this day there be those in Venice who believe that if those holy ashes were stolen away, the ancient city would vanish like a dream and its foundations be buried forever in the unremembering sea.

The Venetian gondola is as free and graceful in its gliding movement as a serpent. It is twenty or thirty feet long, and is narrow and deep like a canoe; its sharp bow and stern sweep upward from the water like the horns of a crescent with the abruptness of the curve slightly modified.

The bow is ornamented with a steel comb with a battle-ax attachment which threatens to cut passing boats in two occasionally, but never does. The gondola is painted black because in the zenith of Venetian magnificence the gondolas became too gorgeous altogether, and the Senate decreed that all such display must cease, and a solemn, unembellished black be substituted. If the truth were known, it would doubtless appear that rich plebeians grew too prominent in their affection of patrician show on the Grand Canal, and required a wholesome snubbing. Reverence for the hallowed Past and its traditions keeps the dismal fashion in force now that the compulsion exists no longer. So let it remain, it is the color of mourning. Venice mourns. The stern of the boat is decked over and the gondolier stands there. He uses a single oar — a long blade, of course, for he stands nearly erect. A wooden peg, a foot and a half high, with two slight crooks or curves in one side of it and one in the other, projects above the starboard gunwale. Against that peg the gondolier takes a purchase with his oar, changing it at intervals to the other side of the peg or dropping in into another of the crooks, as the steering of the craft may demand — and how in the world he can back and fill, shoot straight ahead, or flirt suddenly around a corner, and make the oar stay in those insignificant notches is a problem to me and a never-diminishing matter or interest. I am afraid I study the gondolier's marvelous skill more than I do the sculptured palaces we glide among. He cuts a corner so closely, now and then, or misses another gondola by such an imperceptible hairbreadth that I feel myself "scrooching," as the children say, just as one does when a buggy wheel grazes his elbow. But he makes all his calculations with the nicest precision, and goes darting in and out among a Broadway confusion of busy craft with the easy confidence of the educated hackman. He never makes a mistake.

Sometimes we go flying down the great canals at such a gait that we can get only the merest glimpses into front doors, and again, in obscure alleys in the suburbs, we put on a solemnity suited to the silence, the mildew, the stagnant waters, the clinging weeds, the deserted houses, and the general lifelessness of the place, and move to the spirit of grave meditation.

The gondolier *is* a picturesque rascal for all he wears no satin harness, no plumed bonnet, no silken tights. His attitude is stately; he is lithe and supple; all his movements are full of grace. When his long canoe and his fine figure, towering from its high perch on the stern, are cut against the evening sky, they make a picture that is very novel and striking to a foreign eye.

We sit in the cushioned carriage body of a cabin, with the curtains drawn and smoke or read or look out upon the passing boats, the houses, the bridges, the people, and enjoy ourselves much more than we could in a buggy jolting over our cobblestone pavements at home. This is the gentlest, pleasantest locomotion we have ever known.

But it seems queer — ever so queer — to see a boat doing duty as a private carriage. We see businessmen come to the front door, step into a gondola instead of a streetcar, and go off downtown to the counting room.

We see visiting young ladies stand on the stoop, and laugh, and kiss good-bye, and flirt their fans, and say, "Come soon — now *do* — you've been just as mean as ever you can be — Mother's dying to see you — and we've moved into the new house, oh such a love of a place! — so convenient to the post office and the church, and the Young Men's Christian Association; and we do have such fishing, and such carrying on, and *such* swimming matches in the backyard — oh, you *must* come — no distance at all, and if you go down through by St. Mark's and the Bridge of Sighs, and cut through the alley and come up by the Church of Santa Maria dei Frari and into the Grand Canal, there isn't a *bit* of current — now *do* come, Sally Maria — bye-bye!" And then the little humbug trips down the steps, jumps into the gondola, says under her breath, "Disagreeable old thing, I hope she *won't!*" goes skimming away, round the corner; and the other girl slams the street door and says, "Well, *that* infliction's over, anyway — but I suppose I've got to go and see her — tiresome, stuck-up thing!" Human nature appears to be just the same all over the world. We see the diffident young man, mild of moustache, affluent of hair, indigent of brain, elegant of costume, drive up to *her* father's mansion, tell his hackman to bail out and wait, start fearfully up the steps and meet "the old gentleman" right on the threshold! — hear him ask what street the new British bank is in — as if *that* were what he came for — and then bounce into his boat and skurry away with his coward heart in his boots! — see him come sneaking around the corner again directly, with a crack of the curtain open toward the old gentleman's disappearing gondola, and out scampers his Susan with a flock of little Italian endearments fluttering from her lips, and goes to drive with him in the watery avenues down toward the Rialto.

We see the ladies go out shopping in the most natural way, and flit from street to street and from store to store, just in the good old fashion, except that they leave the gondola, instead of a private carriage, waiting at the curbstone a couple of hours for them — waiting while they make the nice young clerks pull down tons and tons of silks and velvets and musty antiques and those things; and then they buy a paper of pins and go paddling away to confer the rest of their disastrous patronage on some other firm. And they always have their purchases sent home just in the good old way. Human nature is *very* much the same all over the world; and it is *so* like my dear native home to see a Venetian lady go into a store and buy ten cents' worth of blue ribbon and have it sent home in a scow. Ah, it is these little touches of nature that move one to tears in these far-off foreign lands.

We see little girls and boys go out in gondolas with their nurses for an airing. We see staid families, with prayer book and beads, enter the gondola dressed in their Sunday best and float away to church. And at midnight we see the theater break up and discharge its swarm of hilarious youth and beauty; we hear the cries of the hackman-gondoliers and behold the struggling crowd jump aboard, and the black multitude of boats go skimming down the moonlit avenues; we see them separate here and there and disappear up divergent streets; we hear the faint sounds of laughter and of shouted farewells floating up out of the distance; and then, the strange pageant being gone, we have lonely stretches of glitterying water — of stately buildings — of blotting shadows — of wierd stone faces creeping into the moonlight — of deserted bridges — of motionless boats at anchor. And over all broods that mysterious stillness, that stealthy quiet, that befits so well this old dreaming Venice.

We have been pretty much everywhere in our gondola. We have bought beads and photographs in the stores and wax matches in the Great Square of St. Mark. The last remark suggests a digression. Everybody goes to this vast square in the evening. The military bands play in the center of it and countless couples of ladies and gentlemen promenade up and down on either side, and platoons of them are constantly drifting away toward the old cathedral, and by the venerable column with the Winged Lion of St. Mark on its top, and out to where the boats lie moored: and other platoons are as constantly arriving from the gondolas and joining the great throng. Between the promenaders and the sidewalks are seated hundreds and hundreds of people at small tables, smoking and taking *granita* (a first cousin to ice cream); on the sidewalks are more employing themselves in the same way. The shops in the first floor of the tall rows of buildings that wall in three sides of the square are brilliantly lighted, the air is filled with music and merry voices, and altogether the scene is as bright and spirited and full of cheerfulness as any man could desire. We enjoy it thoroughly. Very many of the young women are exceedingly pretty and dress with rare good taste. We are gradually and laboriously learning the ill manners of staring them unflinchingly in the face — not because such conduct is agreeable to us, but because it is the custom of the country and they say the girls like it. We wish to learn all the curious, outlandish ways of all the different countries, so that we can "show off" and astonish people when we get home. We wish to excite the envy of our untraveled friends with our strange

foreign fashions which we can't shake off. All our passengers
are paying strict attention to this thing, with the end in view
which I have mentioned. The gentle reader will never, never
know what a consummate ass he can become until he goes
abroad. I speak now, of course, in the supposition that the
gentle reader has not been abroad, and therefore is not
already a consummate ass. If the case be otherwise, I beg his
pardon and extend to him the cordial hand of fellowship and
call him brother. I shall alwasy delight to meet an ass after
my own heart when I have finished my travels.

On this subject let me remark that there are Americans
abroad in Italy who have actually forgotten their mother
tongue in three months — forgot it in France. They cannot
even write their address in English in a hotel register. I
append these evidences, which I copied verbatim from the
register of a hotel in a certain Italian city:

> John P. Whitcomb, *Etats Unis.*
> Wm. L. Ainsworth, *travailleur* (he meant traveler, I
> suppose) *Etats Unis.*
> George P. Morton, *et fils, d'Amerique.*
> Lloyd B. Williams, *et trois amis, ville de* Boston,
> *Amerique.*
> J. Ellsworth Baker, *tout de suite de France, place de
> naissance Amerique, destination la Grand Bretagne.*

I love this sort of people. A lady passenger of ours tells of a
fellow citizen of hers who spent eight weeks in Paris and then
returned home and addressed his dearest old bosom friend
Herbert as Mr. "Er-bare!". He apologized, though, and said,
"Pon my soul, it is aggravating, but I cahn't help it — I have got
so used to speaking nothing but French, my dear Erbare —
damme, there it goes again! — got so used to French
pronunciation that I cahn't get rid of it — it is positively
annoying, I assure you." This entertaining idiot, whose name
was Gordon, allowed himself to be hailed three times in the
street before he paid any attention and then begged a
thousand pardons and said he had grown so accustomed to
hearing himself addressed as 'M'sieu Gor-r-*dong*," with a roll
to the r, that he had forgotten the legitimate sound of his

name! He wore a rose in his buttonhole; he gave the French salutation — two flips of the hand in front of the face; he called Paris *Pairree* in ordinary English conversation; he carried envelopes bearing foreign postmarks protruding from his breast pocket; he cultivated a moustache and imperial, and did what else he could to suggest to the beholder his pet fancy that he resembled Louis Napoleon — and in a spirit of thankfulness which is entirely unaccountable, considering the slim foundation there was for it, he praised his Maker that he was *as* he was, and went on enjoying his little life just the same as if he really *had* been deliberately designed and erected by the great Architect of the Universe.

Think of our Whitcombs and our Ainsworths and our Williamses writing themselves down in dilapidated French in foreign hotel registers! We laugh at Englishmen, when we are at home, for sticking so sturdily to their national ways and customs, but we look back upon it from abroad very forgivingly. It is not pleasant to see an American thrusting his nationality forward *obtrusively* in a foreign land, but oh, it is pitiable to see him making of himself a thing that is neither male nor female, neither fish, flesh, nor fowl — a poor, miserable, hermaphrodite Frenchman!

Among a long list of churches, art galleries, and such things visited by us in Venice, I shall mention only one — the Church of Santa Maria dei Frari. It is about five hundred years old, I believe, and stands on twelve hundred thousand piles. In it lie the body of Canova and the heart of Titian, under magnificent monuments. Titian died at the age of almost one hundred years. A plague which swept away fifty thousand lives was raging at the time, and there is notable evidence of the reverence in which the great painter was held, in the fact that to him alone the state permitted a public funeral in all that season of terror and death.

In this church, also, is a monument to the doge Foscari, whose name a once resident of Venice, Lord Byron, has made permanently famous.

The monument to the doge Giovanni Pesaro, in this church, is a curiosity in the way of mortuary adornment. It is eighty feet high and is fronted like some fantastic pagan

temple. Against it stand four colossal Nubians, as black as
night, dressed in white marble garments. The black legs are
bare, and through rents in sleeves and breeches, the skin, of
shiny black marble, shows. The artist was as ingenious as his
funeral designs were absurd. There are two bronze skeletons
bearing scrolls, and two great dragons uphold the sarcophagus. On high, amid all this grotesqueness, sits the departed
doge.

In the conventional buildings attached to this church are
the state archives of Venice. We did not see them, but they
are said to number millions of documents. "They are the
records of centuries of the most watchful, observant, and
suspicious government that ever existed—in which everything
was written down and nothing spoken out." They fill nearly
three hundred rooms. Among them are manuscripts from the
archives of nearly two thousand families, monasteries and
convents. The secret history of Venice for a thousand years is
here—its plots, its hidden trials, its assassinations, its
commissions of hireling spies and masked bravos—food,
ready to hand, for a world of dark and mysterious romances.

Yes, I think we have seen all of Venice. We have seen, in
these old churches, a profusion of costly and elaborate
sepulcher ornamentation such as we never dreamt of before.
We have stood in the dim religious light of these hoary
sanctuaries, in the midst of long ranks of dusty monuments
and effigies of the great dead of Venice, until we seemed
drifting back, back, back, into the solemn past, and looking
upon the scenes and mingling with the peoples of a remote
antiquity. We have been in a half-waking sort of dream all
the time. I do not know how else to describe the feeling. A
part of our being has remained still in the nineteenth century,
while another part of it has seemed in some unaccountable
way walking among the phantoms of the tenth.

We have seen famous pictures until our eyes are weary with
looking at them and refuse to find interest in them any
longer. And what wonder, when there are twelve hundred
pictures by Palma the Younger in Venice and fifteen hundred
by Tintoretto? And behold there are Titians and the works of
other artists in proportion. We have seen Titian's celebrated

"Cain and Able," his "David and Goliath," his "Abraham's Sacrifice." We have seen Tintoretto's monster picture, which is seventy-four feet long and I do not know how many feet high, and thought it a very commodious picture. We have seen pictures of martyrs enough and saints enough to regenerate the world. I ought not to confess it, but still, since one has no opportunity in America to acquire a critical judgment in art, and since I could not hope to become educated in it in Europe in a few short weeks, I may therefore as well acknowledge, with such apologies as may be due, that to me it seemed that when I had seen one of these martyrs I had seen them all. They all have a marked family resemblance to each other, they dress alike, in coarse monkish robes and sandals, they are all bald-headed, they all stand in about the same atitude, and without exception they are gazing heavenward with countenances which the Ainsworths, the Mortons, and the Willaimses *et fils* inform me are full of "expression." To me there is nothing tangible about these imaginary portraits, nothing that I can grasp and take a living interest in. If great Titian had only been gifted with prophecy, and had skipped a martyr, and gone over to England and painted a portrait of Shakespeare, even as a youth, which we could all have confidence in now, the world down to the latest generations would have forgiven him the lost martyr in the rescued seer. I think posterity could have spared one more martyr for the sake of a great historical picture of Titian's time and painted by his brush—such as Columbus returning in chains from the discovery of a world, for instance. The old masters did paint some Venetian historical pictures, and these we did not tire of looking at, notwithstanding representations of the formal introduction of defunct doges to the Virgin Mary in regions beyond the clouds clashed rather harshly with the proprieties, it seemed to us.

But humble as we are, and unpretending, in the matter of art, our researches among the painted monks and martyrs have not been wholly in vain. We have striven hard to learn. We have had some success. We have mastered some things, possibly of trifling import in the eyes of the learned, but to us they give pleasure, and we take as much pride in our little acquirements as do others who have learned far more, and love to display them full as well. When we see a monk going about with a lion and looking tranquilly up to heaven, we know that that is St. Mark. When we see a monk with a book and a pen, looking tranquilly up to heaven, trying to think of a word, we know that that is St. Matthew. When we see a monk sitting on a rock, looking tranquilly up to heaven, with a human skull beside him, and without other baggage, we know that that is St. Jerome. Because we know that he always went flying light in the matter of baggage. When we see a party looking tranquilly up to heaven, unconscious that his body is shot through and through with arrows, we know that that is St. Sebastian. When we see other monks looking tranquilly up to heaven, but having no trademark, we always ask who those parties are. We do this because we humbly wish to learn. We have seen thirteen thousand St. Jeromes, and twenty-two thousand St. Marks, and sixteen thousand St. Matthews, and sixty thousand St. Sebastians, and four millions of assorted monks, undesignated, and we feel encouraged to believe that when we have seen some more of these various pictures and had a larger experience, we shall begin to take an absorbing interest in them like our cultivated countrymen from *Amerique*.

Now it does give me real pain to speak in this almost unappreciative way of the old masters and their martyrs, because good friends of mine in the ship — friends who do thoroughly and conscientiously appreciate them and are in every way competent to discriminate between good pictures and inferior ones — have urged me for my own sake not to make public the fact that I lack this appreciation and this critical discrimination myself. I believe that what I have written and may still write about pictures will give them pain, and I am honestly sorry for it. I even promised that I would hide my uncouth sentiments in my own breast. But alas! I never could keep a promise. I do not blame myself for this weakness, because the fault must lie in my physical organization. It is likely that such a very liberal amount of space was given to the organ which enables me to *make*

promises that the organ which should enable me to keep
them was crowded out. But I grieve not. I like no halfway
things. I had rather have one faculty nobly developed than
two faculties of mere ordinary capacity. I certainly meant to
keep that promise, but I find I cannot do it. It is impossible
to travel through Italy without speaking of pictures, and can
I see them through others' eyes?

If I did not so delight in the grand pictures that are
spread before me every day of my life by that monarch of all
the old masters, Nature, I should come to believe sometimes
that I had in me no appreciation of the beautiful whatsoever.

It seems to me that whenever I glory to think that for once
I have discovered an ancient painting that is beautiful and
worthy of all praise, the pleasure it gives me is an infallible
proof that it is *not* a beautiful picture and not in any wise
worthy of commendation. This very thing has occurred more
times than I can mention in Venice. In every single instance
the guide has crushed out my swelling enthusiasm with the
remark:

"It is nothing—it is of the *Renaissance.*"

I did not know what in the mischief the Renaissance was,
and so always I had to simply say:

"Ah! So it is—I had not observed it before."

I could not bear to be ignorant before a cultivated Negro,
the offspring of a South Carolina slave. But it occurred too
often for even my self-complacency, did that exasperating "It
is nothing—it is of the *Renaissance.*" I said at last: "*Who* is
this Renaissance? Where did he come from? Who gave him
permission to cram the republic with his exerable daubs?"

We learned then that Renaissance was not a man; that
renaissance was a term used to signify what was at best but an
imperfect rejuvenation of art. The guide said that after
Titian's time and the time of the other great names we had
grown so familiar with, high art declined; then it partially
rose again—an inferior sort of painters sprang up, and these
shabby pictures were the work of their hands. Then I said, in
my heat, that I "wished to goodness high art had declined

five hundred years sooner." The Renaissance pictures suit me
very well, though sooth to say its school were too much given
to painting real men and did not indulge enough in martyrs.

The guide I have spoken of is the only one we have had yet
who knew anything. He was born in South Carolina, of slave
parents. They came to Venice while he was an infant. He has
grown up here. He is well educated. He reads, writes, and
speaks English, Italian, Spanish, and French with perfect
facility; is a worshiper of art and thoroughly conversant with
it; knows the history of Venice by heart and never tires of
talking of her illustrious career. He dresses better than any of
us, I think, and is daintily polite. Negroes are deemed as good
as white people in Venice, and so this man feels no desire to
go back to his native land. His judgment is correct.

I have had another shave. I was writing in our front room
this afternoon and trying hard to keep my attention on my
work and refrain from looking out upon the canal. I was
resisting the soft influences of the climate as well as I could,
and endeavoring to overcome the desire to be indolent and
happy. The boys sent for a barber. They asked me if I would
be shaved. I reminded them of my tortures in Genoa, Milan,
Como; of my declaration that I would suffer no more on
Italian soil. I said, "Not any for me, if you please."

I wrote on. The barber began on the doctor. I heard him
say:

"Dan, this is the easiest shave I have had since we left the
ship."

He said again, presently:

"Why, Dan, a man could go to sleep with this man shaving
him."

Dan took the chair. Then he said:

"Why, this is Titian. This is one of the old masters."

I wrote on. Directly Dan said:

"Doctor, it is perfect luxury. The ship's barber isn't
anything to him."

My rough beard was distressing me beyond measure. The
barber was rolling up his apparatus. The temptation was too
strong. I said:

"Hold on, please. Shave me also."

I sat down in the chair and closed my eyes. The barber soaped my face and then took his razor and gave me a rake that well-nigh threw me into convulsions. I jumped out of the chair: Dan and the doctor were both wiping blood off their faces and laughing.

I said it was a mean, disgraceful fraud.

They said that the misery of this shave had gone so far beyond anything they had ever experienced before that they could not bear the idea of losing such a chance of hearing a cordial opinion from me on the subject.

It was shameful. But there was no help for it. The skinning was begun and had to be finished. The tears flowed with every rake, and so did the fervent execrations. The barber grew confused, and brought blood every time. I think the boys enjoyed it better than anything they have seen or heard since they left home.

We have seen the Campanile and Byron's house and Balbi's the geographer, and the palaces of all the ancient dukes and doges of Venice, and we have seen their effeminate descendants airing their nobility in fashionable French attire in the Grand Square of St. Mark, and eating ices and drinking cheap wines, instead of wearing gallant coats of mail and destroying fleets and armies as their great ancestors did in the days of Venetian glory. We have seen no bravos with poisoned stilettos, no masks, no wild carnival; but we have seen the ancient pride of Venice, the grim bronze horses that figure in a thousand legends. Venice may well cherish them, for they are the only horses she ever had. It is said there are hundreds of people in this curious city who never have seen a living horse in their lives. It is entirely true, no doubt.

And so, having satisfied ourselves, we depart tomorrow and leave the venerable Queen of the Republics to summon her vanished ships, and marshal her shadowy armies, and know again in dreams the pride of her old renown.

Mary McCarthy: Florence

Mary McCarthy whose caustic wit has been at the service of theater reviewing (in Partisan Review*), teaching (at Bard and Sara Lawrence colleges), and writing as a novelist and essayist. She is the author of several distinguished novels, and is well known as a keen and knowledgeable critic. Her powers of observation and penetrating commentary are evident in her works on Italy; which are more than travel books and include* Venice Observed, *and* The Stones of Florence, *from which the following chapter is taken.*

"How can you stand it?" This is the first thing the transient visitor to Florence, in summer, wants to know, and the last thing too—the eschatological question he leaves echoing in the air as he speeds on to Venice. He means the noise, the traffic, and the heat, and something else besides, something he hesitates to mention, in view of former raptures: the fact that Florence seems to him dull, drab, provincial. Those who know Florence a little often compare it to Boston. It is full of banks, loan agencies, and insurance companies, of shops selling place mats and doilies and tooled-leather desk sets. The Raphaels and Botticellis in the museums have been copied a thousand times; the architecture and sculpture are associated with the schoolroom. For the contemporary taste, there is too much Renaissance in Florence: too much "David" (copies of Michelangelo's gigantic white nude stand on the

Piazza della Signoria and the Piazzale Michelangelo; the original is in the Academy), too much rusticated stone, too much glazed terracotta, too many Madonnas with Bambinos. In the lackluster cafes of the dreary main piazza (which has a parking lot in the middle), stout women in sensible clothing sit drinking tea, and old gentlemen with canes are reading newspapers. Sensible, stout, countrified flowers like zinnias and dahlias are being sold in the Mercato Nuovo, along with straw carryalls, pocketbooks, and marketing baskets. Along the Arno, near Ponte Vecchio, ugly new buildings fill the cavities where the German mines exploded.

Naples is a taste the contemporary traveler can understand, even if he does not share it. Venice he can understand...Rome...Siena. But Florence? "Nobody comes here any more," says the old Berenson, wryly, in his villa at Settignano, and the echoing sculpture gallery of the Bargello bears him out; almost nobody comes here. The big vaulted main hall seems full of marble wraiths: San Giorgio, San Giovanni, San Giovannino, the dead gods and guardians of the city. The uniformed modern guards standing sentinel over the creations of Donatello, Desiderio, Michelozzo, Luca della Robbia, Agostino di Duccio have grown garrulous from solitude, like people confined in prison: they fall on the rare visitor (usually an art historian) and will scarcely let him go. The Uffizi, on the contrary, is invaded by barbarian hordes from the North, squadrons of tourists in shorts, wearing sandals or hiking shoes, carrying metal canteens and cameras, smelling of sweat and sun-tan oil, who have been hustled in here by their guides to contemplate "Venus on the Half-Shell."

"*Il Diluvio Universale,*" observes a Florentine, sadly, punning on the title of Paolo Uccello's fresco (now in the Belvedere). There is no contradiction. "Nobody comes here any more" is simply the other side, the corollary, of the phenomenon of mass tourism—the universal deluge. The masses rush in where the selective tourist has fled. Almost nobody comes to see Donatello's "David" in the Bargello, the first nude statue of the Renaissance, or San Giorgio or San Giovannino, Donatello's also, or the *cantorias* of dancing

children in the Museum of the Works of the Duomo, but
Michelangelo and Cellini, partly, no doubt, because of
vaguely sensed "off-color" associations, draw crowds of
curiosity-seekers. Florence is scraping the bottom of the
tourist barrel. And the stolid presence of these masses with
their polyglot guides in the Uffizi, in the Pitti, around the
Baptistery doors and the Medici Tombs, in the cell of
Savonarola and the courtyard of Palazzo Vecchio is another
of the "disagreeables," as the Victorians used to call them,
that have made Florence intolerable and, more than that,
inexplicable to the kind of person for whom it was formerly a
passion. "How can you stand it?"

Florence is a manly town, and the cities of art that appeal
to the current sensibility are feminine, like Venice and Siena.
What irritates the modern tourist about Florence is that it
makes no concession to the pleasure principle. It stands four-
square and direct, with no air of mystery, no blandishments,
no furbelows — no Gothic lace or baroque swirls. Against the
green Arno, the ocher-and-dun file of hotels and palazzi has
the spruce, spare look of a regiment drawn up in drill order.
The deep shades of melon and of tangerine that you see in
Rome, the pinks of Venice, the rose of Siena, the red of
Bologna have been ruled out of Florence as if by municipal
decree. The eye turns from mustard, buff, écru, pale yellow,
cream to the severe black-and-white marbles of the Baptistery
and of Santa Maria Novella's facade or the dark-green and
white and flashing gold of San Miniato. On the Duomo and
Giotto's bell tower and the Victorian facade of Santa Croce,
there are touches of pink, which give these buildings a
curious festive air, as though they alone were dressed up for a
party. The general severity is even echoed by the Florentine
bird, which is black and white — the swallow, a bachelor, as
the Florentines say, wearing a tail coat.

The great sculptors and architects who stamped the
outward city with its permanent image or style — Brunelleschi,
Donatello, Michelangelo — were all bachelors. Monks, soldier-
saints, prophets, hermits were the city's heroes. Saint John the
Baptist, in his shaggy skins, feeding on locusts and honey, is
the patron, and, except for the Madonna with her boy-baby,

women saints count for little in the Florentine iconography. Santa Reparata, a little Syrian saint, who once was patron of the Cathedral, was replaced by the Madonna (Santa Maria del Fiore) early in the fifteenth century. The Magdalen as a penitent and desert-wanderer was one of the few female images, outside of the Madonna, to strike the Florentine imagination; Donatello's gaunt sculpture of her stands in the Baptistery: a fearsome brown figure, in wood, clad in a shirt of flowing hair that surrounds her like a beard, so that at first glance she appears to be a man and at second glance almost a beast. Another of these hairy wooden Magdalens, by Desiderio, is in the church of Santa Trinita. Like these wild creatures of the desert, many of the Florentine artists were known for their strange ascetic habits: Paolo Uccello, Donatello, Piero di Cosimo, Michelangelo, Pontormo. When he was doing a statue of Pope Julius II in Bologna, Michelangelo, though an unsociable person, slept four to a bed with his workmen, and in Rome, so he wrote his relations, his quarters were too squalid to receive company.

Many Florentine palaces today are quite comfortable inside and possess pleasant gardens, but outside they bristle like fortresses or dungeons, and, to the passing tourist, their thick walls and bossy surfaces seem to repel the very notion of hospitality. From the Grand Canal, the Venetian palaces, with their windows open to the sun, offer glimpses of sparkling chandeliers and painted ceilings, and it is not hard for the most insensitive tourist to summon up visions of great balls, gaming, love-making in those brilliant rooms. The Florentine palaces, on the contrary, hide their private life like misers, which in fact the Florentines are reputed to be. Consumption is not conspicious here; an unwritten sumptuary law seems to govern outward display. The famous Florentine elegance, which attracts tourists to the shops on Via Tornabuoni and Via della Vigna Nuova, is characterized by austerity of line, simplicity, economy of effect. In this spare city, the rule of *nihil nimis* prevails. A beggar woman who stands soliciting in front of Palazzo Strozzi, when offered alms a second time in the same day, absently, by another Florentine, refuses: "No. You gave me before." Poverty has its own decorum; waste is frowned on. This is a city of endurance, a city of stone. A thing often noticed, with surprise, by foreigners is that the Florentines love their poor, for the poor are the quintessence of Florence—dry in speech, frugal, pessimistic, "queer," disabused. *"Pazienza!"* is their perpetual, shrugging counsel, and if you ask them how they are, the answer is *"Non c'è male."* "Not so bad." The answer to a favorable piece of tidings is *"Meno male,"* literally, "less bad." These people are used to hardship, which begins with a severe climate and overcrowding.

The summers are the worst. The valley of the Arno is a natural oven, in which the city bakes, almost without relief, throughout July and August. Venice has the sea; Rome has a breeze and fountains; Bologna has arcades; Siena is high. But the stony heat of Florence has no extenuation. Some people pretend that it is cooler in Fiesole or near the Boboli Garden, but this is not true, or at least not true enough. For the populace and the tourists, the churches are the only refuge, except for UPIM, the local five-and-ten (a Milanese firm), which is air-cooled, and for an icy swimming pool, surrounded by a flower garden, in the Tennis Club of the Cascine that few tourists hear about and that the native population, on the whole, cannot afford. The Boboli Garden is too hot to walk in until sunset, which is the time it closes. In some Italian cities, the art galleries are cool, but the Uffizi, with its small rooms and long glassed-in corridors, is stifling, and the Pitti stands with wings extended in a glaring gravel courtyard, like a great brown flying lizard, basking in the terrible sun. Closed off, behind blinds and shutters, the city's inhabitants live a nocturnal life by day, like bats, in darkened rooms, wanly lit for the noon meal by electricity. At seven o'clock in the evening, throughout the city, there is a prolonged rumble that sounds as if it were thunder; the blinds are being rolled up to let in the exhausted day. Then the mosquitoes come.

For the tourist, it is too hot, after ten o'clock in the morning, to sight-see, too close, with the windows shut, to sleep after lunch, too dark to read, for electricity is expensive, and the single bulb provided for reading in most Florentine hotels and households is no brighter than a votive candle.

Those who try to sight-see discover the traffic hazard. The sidewalks are mere tilted rims on the edge of the building fronts; if you meet another person coming toward you, you must swerve into the street; if you step backward onto the pavement to look up at a palace, you will probably be run over. "Rambles" through Florence, such as the old guidebooks talk of, are a funny idea under present conditions. Many of the famous monuments have become, quite literally, invisible, for lack of a spot from which they can be viewed with safety. Standing (or trying to stand) opposite Palazzo Rucellai, for example, or Orsanmichele, you constitue a traffic obstruction, to be bumped by pedestrians, honked at by cars, rammed by baby carriages and delivery carts. Driving a car, you are in danger of killing; walking or standing, of being killed. If you walk, you curse the automobiles and motorscooters; if you drive, you curse the pedestrians — above all, old women, children, and tourists with their noses in maps or guidebooks.

A "characteristic" Florentine street — that is, a street which contains points of touristic interest (old palaces, a Michelozzo portal, the room where Dostoievski finished *The Idiot*, et cetera) is not only extremely narrow, poor, and heavily populated, lined with florists and greengrocers who display their wares on the strip of sidewalk, but it is also likely to be one of the principal traffic arteries. The main route today from Siena and Rome, for example, is still the old Roman "way," the Via Romana, which starts at the old arched gate, the Porta Romana (1326; Franciabigio fresco in the archway), bends northeast, passing the gardens of the Annalena (suppressed convent) on the left and the second gate of the Boboli on the right, the church of San Felice (Michelozzo facade) on the left again, to the Pitti Palace, after which it changes it name to Via Guicciardini, passes Palazzo Guicciardini (birthplace of the historian), the ancient church of Santa Felicita ("Deposition" by Pontormo inside, in a Brunelleschi chapel), and continues to Ponte Vecchio, which it crosses, changing its name again to Por Santa Maria and again to Calimala before reaching the city centre. The traffic on Via Romana is highly "characteristic." Along the narrow sidewalk, single file, walks a party of Swiss and German tourists, barelegged, with cameras and other equipment hanging bandoleer-style from various leather straps on their persons; clinging to the buildings, in their cleated shoes, they give the effect of a scaling party in the Alps. They are the only walkers, however, who are not in danger of death. Past them, in both directions (Via Romana is a two-way street), flows a confused stream of human beings and vehicles: baby carriages wheeling in and out of the Boboli Garden, old women hobbling in and out of church, grocery carts, bicycles, Vespas, Lambrettas, motorcycles, *topolinos,* Fiat *seicentos,* a trailer, a donkey cart from the country delivering sacks of laundry that has been washed with ashes, in the old-fashioned way, Cadillacs, Alfa-Romeos, *millecentos,* Chevrolets, a Jaguar, a Rolls-Royce with a chauffeur and a Florence license plate, bands of brawny workmen carrying bureaus, mirrors, and credenzas (for this is the neighborhood of the artisans), plumbers tearing up the sidewalk, pairs of American tourists with guidebooks and maps, children, artists from the Pensione Annalena, clerks, priests, housemaids with shopping baskets stopping to finger the furred rabbits hanging upside down outside the poultry shops, the sanitation brigade (a line of blue-uniformed men riding bicycles that propel wheeled platforms holding two or three garbage cans and a broom made of twigs each), a pair of boys transporting a funeral wreath in the shape of a giant horseshoe, big tourist buses from abroad with guides talking into microphones, trucks full of wine flasks from the Chianti, trucks of crated lettuces, trucks of live chickens, trucks of olive oil, the mail truck, the telegraph boy on a bicycle, which he parks in the street, a tripe-vendor, with a glassed in cart full of smoking-hot entrails, outsize Volkswagen station wagons marked "U.S. Forces in Germany," a man on a motorcycle with an overstuffed armchair strapped to the front of it, an organ-grinder, horse-drawn fiacres from the Pitti Palace. It is as though the whole history of Western locomotion were being recapitulated on a single street; and airplane hums above; missing only is the Roman litter.

But it is a pageant no one can stop to watch, except the

gatekeeper at the Boboli, who sits calmly in his chair at the portal, passing the time of day. In his safe harbor, he appears indifferent to the din, which is truly infernal, demonic. Horns howl, blare, shriek; gears rasp; brakes squeal; Vespas sputter and fart; tires sing. No human voice, not even the voice of a radio, can be distinguished in this mechanical babel, which is magnified as it rings against the rough stone of the palaces. If the Arno valley is a natural oven, the palaces are natural amplifiers. The noise is ubiquitous and goes on all day and night. Far out, in the suburbs, the explosive chatter of a Vespa mingles with the cock's crow at four in the morning; in the city an early worker, warming up his scooter, awakens a whole street.

Everyone complains of the noise; with the windows open, no one can sleep. The morning paper reports the protests of hotel-owners, who say that their rooms are empty; foreigners are leaving the city; something must be done; a law must be passed. And within the hotels, there is a continual shuffling of rooms. Number 13 moves to 22, and 22 moves to 33, and 33 moves to 13 or to Fiesole. In fact, all the rooms are noisy and all are hot, even if an electric fan is provided. The hotel-managers know this, but what can they do? To satisfy the client, they co-operate with polite alacrity in the make-believe of room-shuffling. If the client imagines that he will be cooler or quieter in another part of the hotel, why destroy his illusions? In truth, short of leaving Florence, there is nothing to be done until fall comes and the windows can be shut again. A law already exists forbidding the honking of horns within city limits, but it is impossible to drive in a city like Florence without using your horn to scatter the foot traffic.

As for the Vespas and the Lambrettas, which are the plague of the early hours of the morning, how can a law be framed that will keep their motors quiet? Readers of the morning newspaper write in with suggestions; a meeting is held in Palazzo Vecchio, where more suggestions are aired: merit badges to be distributed to noiseless drivers; state action against the manufacturers; a special police night squad, equipped with radios, empowered to arrest noisemakers of every description; an ordinance that would make a certain type of muffler mandatory, that would make it illegal to race a motor "excessively," that would prohibit motor-scooters from entering the city center. This last suggestion meets with immense approval; it is the only one Draconian enough to offer hope. But the motor-scooterists' organization at once enters a strong protest ("undemocratic," "discriminatory," it calls the proposal), and the newspaper, which has been leading the anti-noise movement, hurriedly backs water, since Florence is a democratic society, and the scooterists are the *popolo minuto* — small clerks and artisans and factory workers. It would be wrong, the paper concedes, to penalize the many well-behaved scooterists for the sins of a few "savages," and unfair, too, to consider only the city center and the tourist trade; residents on the periphery should have the right to sleep also. The idea of the police squad with summary powers and wide discretion is once again brought forward, though the city's finances will hardly afford it. Meanwhile, the newpaper sees no recourse but to appeal to the *gentilezza* of the driving public.

This, however, is utopian: Italians are not civic-minded. "What if *you* were waked up at four in the morning?" — this plea, so typically Anglo-Saxon, for the other fellow as an imagined self, elicits from an Italian the realistic answer: "But I *am* up." A young Italian, out early on a Vespa, does not project himself into the person of a young Italian office worker in bed, trying to sleep, still less into the person of a foreign tourist or a hotel-owner. As well ask the wasp, after which the Vespa is named, to think of itself as the creature it is about to sting. The *popolo minuto,* moreover, *likes* noise, as everyone knows. *"Non fa rumore,"* objected a young Florentine workman, on being shown an English scooter. "It doesn't make any noise."

All ideas advanced to deal with the Florentine noise problem, the Florentine traffic problem, are utopian, and nobody believes in them, just as nobody believed in Machiavelli's Prince, a utopian image of the ideally self-interested despot. They are dreams, to toy with: the dream of prohibiting *all* motor traffic in the city center (on the pattern of Venice) and going back to the horse and the donkey; the

dream that someone (perhaps the Rockefellers?) would like to
build a subway system for the city....Professor La Pira,
Florence's Christian Democratic mayor, had a dream of
solving the housing problem, another of the city's difficulties:
he invited the homeless poor to move into the empty palaces
and villas of the rich. This Christian fantasy collided with the
laws of poverty, and the poor were turned out of the palaces.
Another dream succeeded it, a dream in the modern idiom of
a "satellite" city that would arise southeast of Florence, in a
forest of parasol pines, to house the city's workers, who would
be conveyed back and forth to their jobs by special buses that
would pick them up in the morning, bring them home for
lunch, then back to work, and so on. This plan, which had
something of science fiction about it, was blocked also;
another set of dreamers — professors, architects, and art
historians — rose in protest against the defacement of the
Tuscan countryside, pointing to the impracticalities of the
scheme, the burdening of the already overtaxed roads and
bridges. A meeting was held, attended by other professors
and city-planners from Rome and Venice; fiery speeches were
made; pamphlets distributed; the preservers won. La Pira,
under various pressures (he had also had a dream of
eliminating stray cats from the city), had resigned as mayor
meanwhile.

But the defeat of Sorgane, as the satellite city was to be
called, is only an episode in the factional war being fought
in the city, street by street, building by building, bridge by
bridge, like the old wars of the Blacks and Whites, Guelphs
and Ghibellines, Cerchi and Donati. It is an uncertain,
fluctuating war, with idealists on both sides, which began in
the nineteenth century, when a façade in the then-current
taste was put on the Duomo, the center of the city was
modernized, and the old walls along the Arno were torn down.
This first victory, of the forces of progress over old Florence, is
commemorated by a triumphal arch in the present Piazza
della Repubblica with an inscription to the effect that new
order and beauty have been brought out of ancient squalor.
The inscription today makes Florentines smile, bitterly, for it is
an example of unconscious irony: The present Piazza, with its

neon signs advertising a specific against uric acid, is, as everyone agrees, the ugliest in Italy—a folly of nationalist grandeur committed at a time when Florence was, briefly, the
capital of the new Italy. Those who oppose change have only to
point to it, as an argument for thier side, and because of it the
preservers have won several victories. Nevertheless, the parasol
pines on the hill of Sorgane may yet fall, like the trees in the
last act of *The Cherry Orchard,* unless some other solution is
found for the housing problem, for Florence is a modern,
expanding city—that is partly why the selective tourist dislikes
it.

A false idea of Florence grew up in the nineteenth century,
thanks in great part to the Brownings and their readers—a
tooled-leather idea of Florence as a dear bit of the old world.
Old maids of both sexes, retired librarians, governesses, ladies
with reduced incomes, gentlemen painters, gentlemen
sculptors, gentlemen poets, anemic amateurs and dabblers of
every kind "fell in love" with Florence and settled down to
make it home. Queen Victoria did water colors in the hills at
Vincigliata; Florence Nightingale's parents named her after
the city, where she was born in 1820—a sugary statue of her
stands holding a lamp in the first cloister of Santa Croce.
Early in the present century, a retired colonel, G.H. Young,
formerly in the Indian service, who, it is said, was unable to
read Italian, appointed himself defender of the Medicis and
turned out a spluttering "classic" that went through many
editions, arguing that the Medicis had been misrepresented
by democratic historians. (There is a story in Turgenev of a
retired major who used to practice doctoring on the peasants.
"Has he studied medicine?" someone asks. "No, he hasn't
studied" is the answer. "He does it more from philanthropy."
This was evidently the case with Colonel Young.) Colonel
Young was typical of the Anglo-American visitors who, as it
were, expropriated Florence, occupying villas in Fiesole or
Bellosguardo, studying Tuscan wild flowers, collecting ghost
stories, collecting tiptychs and diptychs, burying their dogs in
the churchyard of the Protestant Epsicopal church, knowing
(for the most part) no Florentines but their servants. The
Brownings, in Casa Guidi, opposite the Pitti Palace, reveled

in Florentine history and hated the Austrian usurper, who
lived across the street, but they did not mingle socially with
the natives; they kept themselves to themselves. George Eliot
spent fifteen days in a Swiss *pensione* on Via Tornabuoni,
conscientiously working up the background for *Romola,* a
sentimental pastiche of Florentine history that was a great
success in its period and is the least read of her novels today.
It smelled of libraries, Henry James complained, and the
foreign colony's notion of Florence, like *Romola,* was
bookish, synthetic, gushing, insular, genteel, and, above all,
proprietary. This sickly love ("our Florence," "my Florence")
on the part of the foreign residents implied, like all such
loves, a tyrannous resistance to change. The rest of the world
might alter, but, in the jealous eyes of its foreign owners,
Florence was supposed to stay exactly as it was when they
found it — a dear bit of the old world.

Florence can never have been that, at any time in its
existence. It is not a shrine of the past, and it rebuffs all
attempts to make it into one, just as it rebuffs tourists.
Tourism, in a certain sense, is an accidental by-product of the
city — at once profitable and a nuisance, adding to the noise
and congestion, raising prices for the population. Florence is
a working city, a market center, a railway junction; it
manufactures furniture (including antiques), shoes, gloves,
handbags, textiles, fine underwear, nightgowns, and table
linens, picture frames, luggage, chemicals, optical equipment, machinery, wrought iron, various novelties in straw.
Much of this work is done in small shops on the Oltrarno, the
Florentine Left Bank, or on the farms of the *contado;* there is
not much big industry but a multitude of small crafts and
trades. Every Friday is market day on the Piazza della
Signoria, and the peasants come with pockets full of samples
from the farms in the Valdarno and the Chianti: grain, oil,
wine, seeds. The small hotels and cheap restaurants are full
of commercial travelers, wine salesmen from Certaldo or
Siena, textile representatives from Prato, dealers in marble
from the Carrara mountains, where Michelangelo quarried.
Everyone is on the move, buying, selling, delivering, and
tourists get in the way of this diversified commerce. The

Florentines, on the whole, would be happy to be rid of them. The shopkeepers on the Lungarno and Ponte Vecchio, the owners of hotels and restaurants, the thieves, and the widows who run *pensiones* might regret their departure, but the tourist is seldom led to suspect this. There is no city in Italy that treats its tourists so summarily, that caters so little to their comfort.

There are no gay bars or smart outdoor cafes, very little night life, very little vice. The food in the restaurants is bad, for the most part, monotonous, and rather expensive. Many of the Florentine specialties — tripe, paunch, rabbit, and a mixture of cockscombs, livers, hearts, and testicles of roosters — do not appeal to the foreign palate. The wine can be good but is not so necessarily. The waiters are slapdash and hurried; like many Florentines, they give the impression of being preoccupied with something else, something more important — a knotty thought, a problem. At one of the "typical" restaurants, recommended by the big hotels, the waiters, who are a family, treat the clients like interlopers, feigning not to notice their presence, bawling orders sarcastically to the kitchen, banging down the dishes, spitting on the floor. "Take it or leave it" is the attitude of the *pensione*-keeper of the better sort when showing a room; the inferior *pensiones* have a practice of shanghaiing tourists. Runners from these establishments lie in wait on the road, just outside the city limits, for cars with foreign license plates; they halt them, leap aboard, and order the driver to proceed to a certain address. Strangely enough, the tourists often comply, and report to the police only later, when they have been cheated in the *pensiones*. These shades of Dante's highwaymen are not the only ones who lie in wait for travelers. One of the best Florentine restaurants was closed by the police, not long ago, for cheating a tourist. Complaints of foreign tourists pour every day into the *questura* and are recorded in the morning newspaper; they have been robbed and victimized everywhere; their cars, parked on the Piazza della Signoria or along the Arno, have been rifled in broad daylight or spirited away. The northern races — Germans and Swedes — appear to the chief prey, and the commonest complaint is the theft of a camera. Other foreigners are the victims of accidents; one old American lady, the mother-in-law of an author, walking on Via Guicciardini, had the distinction of being hit by two bicycles, from the front and rear simultaneously (she was thrown high into the air and suffered a broken arm); some British tourists were injured a few years ago by a piece falling off Palazzo Bartolini Salimbeni (1517-20) in Piazza Santa Trinita. Now the sidewalk in front of that crumbling palace has finally been closed off and a red lantern posted: beware of falling masonry. Recently, during the summer, a piece weighing 132 pounds fell off the cornice of the National Library; a bus-conductor though, rather than a tourist or foreign student, just missed getting killed and, instead, had his picture in the paper.

All summer long, or as long as the tourist season lasts, the *"Cronaca di Firenze"* or city news of the *Nazione,* that excellent morning newspaper, is a daily chronicle of disaster to foreigners, mixed in with a few purely local thefts, frauds, automobile accidents, marital quarrels, and appeals for the preservation of monuments. The newspaper deplores the Florentine thieves, who are giving the city a bad name, like the noisemakers (*selvaggi*). It seeks to promote in its readers a greater understanding of the foreigner, a greater sympathy with his eating habits, his manner of dress, and so on. Yet an undertone of irony, typically Florentine, accompanies this official effort; it is the foreigners with their cameras and wads of currency who appear to be the "savages," and the thieves who are behaving naturally. A series of "sympathetic" articles on tourism was illustrated with decidedly unsympathetic photographs, showing touristic groups masticating spaghetti, tourists entering the Uffizi naked to the waist.

On the street, the Florentines do not like to give directions; if you are lost, you had better ask a policeman. Unlike the Venetians, the Florentines will never volunteer to show a sight to a passing stranger. They do not care to exhibit their city; the monuments are there—let the foreigners find them. Nor is this a sign of indifference, but of a peculiar pride and dignity. Florentine sacristans can never be found to turn on

the lights to illuminate a fresco or an altar painting; they do
not seem to take an interest in the tip. Around the Masolino-
Masaccio-Filippino Lippi frescoes in the Brancacci Chapel of
the Carmine, small groups of tourists wait, uneasily
whispering; they try to find the lights for themselves; they try
looking for someone in the sacristy. Finally a passing priest
flicks on the electricity and hurries off, his robes flying. The
same thing happens with the Ghirlandaio frescoes in Santa
Trinita. Far from hovering, as the normal sacristan does, in
ambush, waiting to expound the paintings, the Florentine
sacristan does not make himself manifest until just before
closing time, at midday, when he becomes very active,
shooing people out of the church with shrill whistles and
threatening gestures of his broom. If there are postcards for
sale in a church, there is usually nobody to sell them.

This lack of co-operative spirit, this absence, this
preoccupation, comes, after a time, and if you are not in a
hurry, to seem one of the blessings of Florence, to make it,
even, a hallowed place. This is one of the few cities where it is
possible to loiter, undisturbed, in the churches, looking at the
works of art. After the din outside, the churches are
extraordinarily peaceful, so that you walk about on tiptoe,
fearful of breaking the silence, of distracting the few old
women, dimly seen, from their prayers. You can pass an
hour, two hours, in the great churches of Brunelleschi —
Santo Spirito and San Lorenzo — and no one will speak to you
or pay you any heed. Touristic parties with guides do not
penetrate here; they go instead to the Medici Chapels, to see
the Michelangelos. The smaller churches — Santa Trinita,
Santa Felicita, Ognissanti, Santissima Annunziata, Santa
Maria Maddalena dei Pazzi, San Giovannino dei Cavalieri —
are rarely visited; neither is the Pazzi Chapel outside Santa
Croce, and the wonderful Giottos, freshly restored, in the
Bardi Chapel of Santa Croce, still surrounded by a shaky
scaffold, are seen only by art critics, their families and
friends. San Miniato, on its hill, is too far away for most
tourists; it is the church that, as they say, they missed. And
the big churches of the preaching orders, Santa Maria
Novella and Santa Croce, and the still bigger Duomo, where

Savonarola delivered sermons to audiences of ten thousand, swallow up touristic parties, leaving hardly a trace. The tourists then complain of feeling "dwarfed" by their architecture. They find it "cold," unwelcoming.

As for the museums, they are the worst-organized, the worst-hung in Italy—a scandal, as the Florentines say themselves, with a certain civic pride. The exception, the new museum that has been opened in the old Fort of the Belvedere, with pale walls, wide views, cool rooms, sparsely hung, immediately became a subject of controversy, as did the new rooms of the Uffizi, which were held to be too white and uncluttered.

In the streets, the famous parti-colored monuments in geometric designs—the Baptistery, Giotto's bell tower, the Duomo, the facade of Santa Maria Novella—are covered with grime and weather stains. The Duomo and the Bell Tower are finally getting a bath, but this is a tedious process that has been going on for years; by the time the Duomo's front is washed, the back will be dirty again. Meanwhile, the green, white, and pink marbles stand in scaffolding, while the traffic whizzes around them. The Badia, the old Benedictine abbey, where the Good Margrave, Ugo of Tuscany (Dante's *"gran barone"*), lies buried and which has now been partly incorporated into the police station, is leaking so badly that on a rainy Sunday parishioners of the Badia church have had to hear mass with their umbrellas up; it was here that Dante is believed to have seen Beatrice. Among the historic places that remain in private hands, many, like Palazzo Bartolini Salimbeni, are literally falling to pieces. The city has no money to undertake repairs; the Soprintendenza delle Belle Arti has no money; private owners say they have no money.

Historic Florence is an incubus on its present population. It is like a vast piece of family property whose upkeep is too much for the heirs, who nevertheless find themselves criticized by strangers for letting the old place go to rack and ruin. History, in Venice, has been transmuted into legend; in Rome, the Eternal City, history is an everlasting present, an orderly perspective of arches whose keystone is the papacy, guaranteeing permanence, decay being but an aspect of grandeur. If St. Peter's were permitted to fall to pieces, it would still inspire awe, as the Forum does, while the dilapidation of Venetian palaces, reflected in lapping waters, is part of the Venetian myth, celebrated already by Guardi and Bellotto in the eighteenth century. Rome had Piranesi; Naples had Salvatore Rosa; but Florentine decay, in the Mercato Vecchio and the crooked byways of the Ghetto (now all destroyed and replaced by the Piazza della Repubblica), inspired only bad nineteenth-century water-colorists, whose work is preserved, not in art galleries, but in the topographical museum under the title of *"Firenze Come Era"* ("Florence as It Was"). History, for Florence, is neither a legend nor eternity, but a massive weight of rough building stone demanding continual repairs, pressing on the modern city like a debt, blocking progress.

This was a city of progress. Nothing could be more un-Florentine, indeed more anti-Florentine, than the protective custody exercised by its foreign residents, most of whom have abandoned the city today, offended by the Vespas, the automobile horns, the Communists, and the rise in the cost of living. Milanese businessmen are moving into their villas and installing new tiled bathrooms with colored bathtubs and toilet seats, linoleum and plastics in the kitchen, television sets and bars. These Milanesi are not popular; they too are *"selvaggi,"* like their Lombard predecessors who descended on Tuscany in the sixth century to brutalize and despoil it. Yet these periodic invasions belong to Florentine life, which is penetrated by the new and transforms it into something newer. Florence has always been a city of extremes, hot in the summer, cold in the winter, traditionally committed to advance, to modernism, yet containing backward elements narrow as its streets, cramped, stony, recalcitrant. It was the only Italian city where, during the last war, the Fascists still held out after the city was taken by the Allies, and kept shooting from the roof tops and loggias at citizens in the streets below. Throughout the Mussolini period, the Fascists in Florence had been the most violent and dangerous in Italy; at the same time, Florence had been the intellectual center of anti-Fascism, and during the Resistance, the city as a whole "redeemed itself" by a series of heroic exploits. The peasants of the *contado* showed a fantastic bravery in hiding enemies of the regime, and in the city many intellectuals and a few aristocrats risked their lives with great hardihood for the Resistance network. Florence, in short, was split, as it had always been, between the best and the worst. Even the Germans here were divided into two kinds. While the S.S. was torturing victims in a house on Via Bolognese (a nineteenth-century upper-middle-class "residential" district), across the city, on the old Piazza Santo Spirito, near Brunelleschi's church, the German Institute was hiding anti-Nazis in its library of reference works on Florentine art and culture. The chief arm of the S.S. was a Florentine devil strangely named "Carità," who acted both as informer and torturer; against the S.S., the chief defense was the German consul, who used his official position to save people who had been denounced. After the Liberation, the consul was given the freedom of the city, in recognition of the risky work he had done. Such divisions, such extremism, such contrasts are *Firenze Come Era*—a terrible city, in many ways, uncomfortable and dangerous to live in, a city of drama, argument, and struggle.

Percy Bysshe Shelley: Rome and Naples

While still married to Harriet Westbrook, Shelley (1792-1822) went to the continent in 1814 with Mary Wollstonecraft Godwin, her half-sister Claire, and the poet Byron. It was then that Mary wrote the novel Frankenstein. *In 1818, Shelley and Mary left England forever. Five years later Shelley was drowned when his boat, christened the* Don Juan *after Byron's poem, overturned in a storm off the Tuscan coast. Meanwhile, he had written many letters, including the one reproduced here, to his close friend, the satirical and romantic novelist Thomas Love Peacock. The letters are rich with his impressions of Italy.*

Naples, 22 December, 1818.

My Dear Peacock,

I have received a letter from you here, dated November 1st; you see the reciprocation of letters from the term of our travels is more slow. I entirely agree with what you say about "Childe Harold." The spirit in which it is written is, if insane, the most wicked and mischievous insanity that ever was given forth. It is a kind of obstinate and self-willed folly in which he hardens himself. I remonstrated with him in vain on the tone of mind from which such a view of things alone arises. For its real root is very different from its apparent one. Nothing can be less sublime than the true source of these expressions of contempt and desperation. The fact is that first, the Italian women with whom he associates are perhaps the most contemptible of all who exist under the moon, the most ignorant, the most disgusting, the most bigoted; countesses smell so strongly of garlic, that an ordinary Englishman cannot approach them. Well. L.B. is familiar with the lowest sort of these women, the people his gondolieri pick up in the streets. He associates with wretches who seem almost to have lost the gait and physiognomy of man, and who do not scruple to avow practices, which are not only not named, but I believe seldom even conceived in England. He says he disapproves, but he endures. He is heartily and deeply discontented with himself; and contemplating in the distorted mirror of his own thoughts the nature and the destiny of man, what can he behold but objects of contempt and despair? But that he is a great poet, I think the Address to Ocean proves. And he has a certain degree of candour while you talk to him, but unfortunately it does not outlast your departure. No, I do not doubt, and for his sake, I ought to hope, that his present career must end soon in some violent circumstance.

Since I last wrote to you, I have seen the ruins of Rome, the Vatican, St. Peter's, and all the miracles of ancient and modern art contained that majestic city. The impression of it exceeds anything I have experienced in my travels. We stayed there only a week, intending to return at the end of February, and devote two or three months to its mines of inexhaustible contemplation, to which period I refer you for a minute account of it. We visited the Forum and the ruins of the Coliseum every day. The Coliseum is unlike any work of human hands I ever saw before. It is of enormous height and circuit, and arches built of many stones are piled on one another, and jut into the blue air shattered into the forms of overhanging rocks. It has been changed by time into the image of an amphitheatre of rocky hills overgrown by the wild olive, the myrtle, and the fig-tree, and threaded by little paths which wind among its ruined stairs and immeasurable galleries: the copse-wood overshadows you as you wander through its labyrinths, and the wild weeds of this climate of flowers bloom under your feet. The arena is covered with grass, and pierces, like the skirts of a natural plan, the chasms of the broken arches, around. But a small part of the exterior circumference remains; it is exquisitely light and beautiful, and the effect of the perfection of its architecture, adorned with ranges of Corinthian pilasters, supporting a bold cornice, is such as to diminish the effect of its greatness. The interior is all ruin. I can scarcely believe that when encrusted with Dorian marble and ornamented by columns of Egyptian granite, its effect could have been so sublime and so impressive as in its present state. It is open to the sky, and it was the clear and sunny weather of the end of November in this climate when we visited it, day after day.

Near it is the Arch of Constantine, or rather the Arch of Trajan; for the servile and avaricious senate of degraded Rome ordered that the monument of his predecessor should be demolished in order to dedicate one to the Christian reptile, who had crept among the blood of his murdered family to the supreme power. It is exquisitely beautiful and perfect. The Forum is a plain in the midst of Rome, a kind of desert full of heaps of stones and pits, and though so near the habitations of men, is the most desolate place you can conceive. The ruins of temples stand in and around it, shattered columns and ranges of others complete, supporting cornices of exquisite workmanship, and vast vaults of shattered domes distinct with regular compartments, once filled with sculptures of ivory or brass. The temples of Jupiter, and Concord, and Peace, and the Sun, and the Moon, and Vesta, are all within a short distance of this spot. Behold the wrecks of what a great nation once dedicated to the abstractions of the mind! Rome is a city, as it were, of the dead, or rather of those who cannot die, and who survive the puny generations which inhabit and pass over the spot which they have made sacred to eternity. In Rome, at least in the first enthusiasm of your recognition of ancient time, you see nothing of the Italians. The nature of the city assists the delusion, for its vast and antique walls describe a circumference of sixteen miles, and thus the population is thinly scattered over this space, nearly as great as London. Wide wild fields are enclosed within it, and there are lanes and copses winding among the ruins, and a great green hill,

lonely and bare, which overhangs the Tiber. The gardens of
the modern palaces are like wild woods of cedar and cypress
and pine, and the neglected walks are overgrown with weeds.
The English burying place is a green slope near the walls,
under the pyramidal tomb of Cestius, and is, I think, the
most beautiful and solemn cemetery I ever beheld. To see the
sun shining on its bright grass, fresh when we first visited it,
with the autumnal dews, and hear the whispering of the wind
among the leaves of the trees which have overgrown the tomb
of Cestius, and the soil which is stirring in the sun-warm
earth, and to mark the tombs, mostly of women and young
people who were buried there, one might, if one were to die,
desire the sleep they seem to sleep. Such is the human mind,
and so it peoples with its wishes vacancy and oblivion.

I have told you little about Rome; but I reserve the
Pantheon, and St. Peter's and the Vatican, and Raphael, for
my return. About a fortnight ago I left Rome, and Mary and
Claire followed in three days, for it was necessary to procure
lodgings here without alighting at an inn. From my peculiar
mode of travelling I saw little of the country, but could just
observe that the wild beauty of the scenery and the barbarous
ferocity of the inhabitants progressively increased. On
entering Naples, the first circumstance that engaged my
attention was an assassination. A youth ran out of a shop,
pursued by a woman with a bludgeon, and a man armed with
a knife. The man overtook him, and with one blow in the
neck laid him dead in the road. On my expressing the
emotions of horror and indignation which I felt, a Calabrian
priest, who travelled with me, laughed heartily, and
attempted to quiz me, as what the English call a *flat*. I never
felt such an inclination to beat any one. Heaven knows I have
little power. But he saw that I looked extremely displeased
and was silent. This same man, a fellow of gigantic strength
and stature, had expressed the most frantic terror of robbers
on the road: he cried at the sight of my pistol, and it had
been with great difficulty that the joint exertions of myself
and the vetturino had quieted his hysterics.

But external nature in these delightful regions contrasts
with and compensates for the deformity and degradation of

humanity. We have a lodging divided from the sea by the Royal Gardens, and from our windows we see perpetually the blue waters of the bay, for ever changing, for ever the same, and encompassed by the mountainous island of Capreae, the lofty peaks which overhang Salerno, and the woody hill of Posilipo, whose promonotories hide from us Misenum and the lofty isle Inarime, which, with its divided summit, forms the opposite horn of the bay. From the pleasant walks of the garden we see Vesuvius; a smoke by day and a fire by night is seen upon its summit, and the glassy sea often reflects its light or shadow. The climate is delicious. We sit without a fire, with the windows open, and have almost all the productions of an English summer. The weather is usually like what Wordsworth calls "the first fine day of March;" sometimes very much warmer, though perhaps it wants that "each minute sweeter than before," which gives an intoxicating sweetness to the awakening of the earth from its winter's sleep in England. We have made two excursions, one to Baiae, and one to Vesuvius, and we propose to visit, successively, the islands, Paestum, Pompeii, and Beneventum.

We set off an hour after sunrise one radiant morning in a little boat; there was not a cloud in the sky, nor a wave upon the sea, which was so translucent that you could see the hollow caverns clothed with the glaucous sea-moss, and the leaves and branches of those delicate weeds that pave the unequal bottom of the water. As noon approached, the heat, and especially the light, became intense. We passed Posilipo, and came first to the eastern point of the Bay of Puzzoli, which is within the great Bay of Naples, and which is within that of Baiae. Here are lofty rocks and craggy islets, with arches and portals of precipice standing in the sea, and enormous caverns, which echoed faintly with the murmur of the languid tide. This is called La Scuola di Virgilio. We then went directly across to the promontory of Misenum, leaving the precipitous island of Nisida on the right. Here we were conducted to see the Mare Morto, and the Elysian Fields; the spot on which Virgil places the scenery of the sixth Aeneid. Though extremely beautiful, as a lake, and woody hills, and this divine sky must make it, I confess my

Percy B. Shelley.

disappointment. The guide showed us an antique cemetery, where the niches used for placing the cinerary urns of the dead yet remain. We then coasted the Bay of Baiae to the left, in which we saw many picturesque and interesting ruins; but I have to remark that we never disembarked but we were disappointed, while from the boat the effect of the scenery was inexpressibly delightful. The colours of the water and the air breathe over all things here in the radiance of their own beauty. After passing the Bay of Baiae, and observing the ruins of its antique grandeur standing like rocks in the transparent sea under boat, we landed to visit Lake Avernus. We passed through the cavern of the sibyl, not Virgil's sibyl, which pierces one of the hills which circumscribe the lake, and came to a calm and lovely basin of water surrounded by dark woody hills and profoundly solitary. Some vast ruins of the temple of Pluto stand on a lawny hill on one side of it, and are reflected in its windless mirror. It is far more beautiful than the Elysian Fields, but there are all the materials for beauty in the latter, and the Avernus was once a chasm of deadly and pestilential vapours. About half a mile from Avernus, a high hill called Monte Novo was thrown up by volcanic fire.

Passing onward we came to Pozzoli, the ancient Dicaearchea, where there are the columns remaining of a temple to Serapis, and the wreck of an enormous amphitheatre, changed, like the Coliseum, into a natural hill of the overteeming vegetation. Here also is the Solfatara, of which there is a poetical description in the "Civil War" of Petronius, beginning "Est locus," and in which the verses of the poet are infinitely finer than what he describes, for it is not a very curious place. After seeing these things we returned by moonlight to Naples in our boat. What colours there were in the sky, what radiance in the evening star, and how the moon was encompassed by a light unknown to our regions!

Our next excursion was to Vesuvius. We went to Resina in a carriage, where Mary and I mounted mules, and Claire was carried in a chair on the shoulders of four men, much like a member of Parliament after he has gained his election, and looking, with less reason, quite as frightened. So we arrived at the hermitage of San Salvador, where an old hermit, belted with rope, set forth the plates for our refreshment.

Vesuvious is, after the glaciers, the most impressive exhibition of the energies of nature I ever saw. It has not the immeasurable greatness, the overpowering magnificence, nor, above all, the radiant beauty of the glaciers; but it has all their character of tremendous and irrestible strength. From Resina to the hermitage you wind up the mountain, and cross a vast stream of hardened lava, which is an actual image of the waves of the sea, changed into hard block by enchantment. The lines of the boiling flood seem to hang in the air, and it is difficult to believe that the billows which seem hurrying down upon you are not actually in motion. This plain was once a sea of liquid fire. From the hermitage we crossed another vast stream of lava, and then went on foot up the cone. This is the only part of the ascent in which there is any difficulty, and that difficulty has been much exaggerated. It is composed of rocks of lava and declivities of ashes; by ascending the former, and descending the latter, there is very little fatigue. On the summit is a kind of irregular plain, the most horrible chaos that can be imagined; riven into ghastly chasms, and heaped up with tumuli of great stones and cinders, and enormous rocks blackened and calcined, which had been thrown from the volcano upon one another in terrible confusion. In the midst stands the conical hill, from which volumes of smoke and fountains of liquid fire, are rolled forth for ever. The mountain is at present in a slight state of eruption; and a thick heavy white smoke is perpetually rolled out, interrupted by enormous columns of an impenetrable black bituminous vapour, which is hurled up, fold after fold, into the sky with a deep hollow sound, and fiery stones are rained down from its darkness, and a black shower of ashes fell even where we sat. The lava, like the glacier, creeps on perpetually, with a crackling sound as of suppressed fire. There are several springs of lava; and in one place it gushes precipitously over a high crag, rolling down the half-molten rocks, and its own overhanging waves: a cataract of quivering fire. We approached the extremity of one of the rivers of lava; it is about twenty feet in breadth and ten in height; and as the inclined plane was not rapid, its motion was very slow. We saw the masses of its dark exterior surface detach themselves as it moved, and betray the depth of the liquid flame. In the day the fire is but slightly seen; you only observe a tremulous motion in the air, and streams and fountains of white sulphurous smoke.

At length we saw the sun sink between Capreae and Inarime, and, as the darkness increased, the effect of the fire became more beautiful. We were, as it were, surrounded by streams, and cataracts of the red and radiant fire; and in the midst, from the column of bituminous smoke shot up into the air, fell the vast masses of rock, white with the light of their intense heat, leaving behind them through the dark vapour trains of splendour. We descended by torch-light, and I should have enjoyed the scenery on my return, but they conducted me, I know not how, to the hermitage in a state of intense bodily suffering, the worst effect of which was spoiling the leisure of Mary and Claire. Our guides on the occasion were complete savages. You have no idea of the horrible cries which they suddenly utter, no one knows why, the clamour, the vociferation, the tumult. Claire in her palanquin suffered most from it; and when I had gone on before they threatened to leave her in the middle of the road, which they would have done had not my Italian servant promised them a beating, after which they became quiet. Nothing, however, can be more picturesque than the gestures and the physiognomies of these savage people. And when, in the darkness of night, they unexpectedly begin to sing in chorus some fragments of their wild but sweet national music, the effect is exceedingly fine.

Since I wrote this I have seen the Museum of this city. Such statues! There is a Venus; an ideal shape of the most winning loveliness. A Bacchus, more sublime than any living being. A Satyr making love to a youth, in which the expressed life of the sculpture, and the inconceivable beauty of the form of the youth, overcome one's repugnance to the subject. There are multitudes of wonderfully fine statues found in Herculaneum and Pompeii. We are going to see Pompeii the first day that the sea is waveless. Herculaneum is almost filled up; no more excavations are made; the King bought the ground and built a palace upon it.

You don't see much of Hunt. I wish you could contrive to see him when you to to town, and ask him what he means to answer to Lord Byron's invitation. He has now an opportunity, if he likes, of seeing Italy. What do you think of joining his party, and paying us a visit next year; I mean as soon as the reign of winter is dissolved? Write to me your thoughts upon this. I cannot express to you the pleasure it would give me to welcome such a party.

I have depression enough of spirits and not good health, though I believe the warm air of Naples does me good. We see absolutely no one here.

Adieu, my dear Peacock,
Affectionately your friend,
P. B. S.

Part Four:
Spain

Washington Irving: The Alhambra

The grounds had grown thick with weeds and the palace of the Alhambra had been neglected until Washington Irving, through his writings, awakened the Spanish government to its neglected treasure. Squatter gypsies, who had chopped up the palace doors for firewood, were evicted, and the grounds were declared open to the public. At once, a grandee claimed the estate as his private property, producing a deed to the Alhambra in his family's name, signed by Ferdinand and Isabella. The court sustained his rights. His honor vindicated and his prestige enhanced, he bestowed the estate upon the country. With its tiered gardens and fountains fed by a mountain stream, the Alhambra is among the most beautiful parks in the world.

The Alhambra has been so often and so minutely described by travelers that a mere sketch will probably be sufficient for the reader to refresh his recollection; I will give, therefore, a brief account of our visit to it the morning after our arrival in Granada.

Leaving our posada of La Espada, we traversed the renowned square of the Vivarrambla, once the scene of Moorish jousts and tournaments, now a crowded market place. From thence we proceeded along the Zacatin, the main street of what was the great Bazaar, in the time of the Moors, where the small shops and narrow alleys still retain their Oriental character. Crossing an open place in front of the palace of the captain-general, we ascended a confined and winding street, the name of which reminded us of the chivalric days of Granada. It is called the *Calle,* or street of the Gomeres: from a Moorish family, famous in chronicle and song. This street led up to a mansion gateway of Grecian architecture, built by Charles V., forming the entrance to the domains of Alhambra.

At the gate were two or three ragged and superannuated soldiers, dozing on a stone bench, the successors of the Zegris and the Abencerrages; while a tall, meager varlet, whose rusty brown cloak was evidently intended to conceal the ragged state of his nether garments, was lounging in the sunshine and gossiping with an ancient sentinel, on duty. He joined us as we entered the gate, and offered his services to show us the fortress.

I have a traveler's dislike to officious ciceroni, and did not altogether like the barb of the applicant:

"You are well acquainted with the place, I presume?"

"Niñguno mas — pues, señor, soy hijo de la Alhambra."

(Nobody better — in fact, sir, I am a son of the Alhambra.)

The common Spaniards have certainly a most poetical way of expressing themselves — "A son of the Alhambra:" the appellation caught me at once; the very tattered garb of my new acquaintance assumed a dignity in my eyes. It was emblematic of the features of the place, and became the progeny of a ruin.

I put some further questions to him, and found his title was legitimate. His family had lived in the fortress from generation to generation ever since the time of the conquest. His name was Mateo Ximenes. "Then, perhaps," said I, "you may be a descendant from the great Cardinal Ximenes."

"Dios sabe! God knows, señor. It may be so. We are the oldest family in the Alhambra. *Viejos Cristianos,* old Christians, without any taint of Moor or Jew. I know we belong to some great family or other, but I forget who. My father knows all about it. He has the coat of arms hanging up in his cottage, up in the fortress." There is never a Spaniard, however poor, but has some claim to high pedigree. The first

title of this ragged worthy, however, had completely capti-
vated me, so I gladly accepted the services of the "son of the
Alhambra."

We now found ourselves in a deep, narrow ravine, filled
with beautiful groves, with a steep avenue and various
footpaths winding through it, bordered with stone seats and
ornamented with fountains. To our left, we beheld the towers
of the Alhambra beetling above us; to our right, on the
opposite side of the ravine, we were equally dominated by rival
towers on a rocky eminence. These we were told, were the
Torres Vermejos, or Vermillion towers, so called from their
ruddy hue. No one knows their origin. They are of a date
much anterior to the Alhambra. Some suppose them to
have been built by the Romans; others, by some wandering
colony of Phoenicians. Ascending the steep and shady
avenue, we arrived at the foot of a huge square Moorish
tower, forming a kind of barbican, through which passed the
main entrance to the fortress. Within the barbican was
another group of veteran invalids, one mounting guard at the
portal, while the rest, wrapped in their tattered cloaks, slept
on the stone benches. This portal is called the Gate of Justice,
from the tribunal held within its porch during the Moslem
domination, for the immediate trial of petty causes; a custom
common to the Oriental nations, and occasionally alluded to
in the sacred Scriptures.

The great vestibule, or porch of the gate, is formed by an
immense Arabian arch of the horseshoe form, which springs
to half the height of the tower. On the keystone of this arch is
engraven a gigantic hand. Within the vestibule, on the
keystone of the portal, is engraven, in like manner, a
gigantic key. Those who pretend to some knowledge of
Mohammedan symbols affirm that the hand is the emblem of
doctrine, and the key of faith; the latter, they add, was
emblazoned on the standard of the Moslems when they
subdued Andalusia, in opposition to the Christian emblem of
the cross. A different explanation, however, was given by the
legitimate "son of the Alhambra," and one more in unison
with the notions of the common people, who attach
something of mystery and magic to everything Moorish, and

have all kinds of superstitions connected with this old Moslem fortress.

According to Mateo, it was a tradition handed down from the oldest inhabitants, and which he had from his father and grandfather, that the hand and key were magical devices on which the fate of the Alhambra depended. The Moorish king who built it was a great magician, and, as some believed, had sold himself to the devil, and had laid the whole fortress under a magic spell. By this means it had remained standing for several hundred years, in defiance of storms and earthquakes, while almost all the other buildings of the Moors had fallen to ruin and disappeared. The spell, the tradition went on to say, would last until the hand on the outer arch should reach down and grasp the key, when the whole pile would tumble to pieces, and all the treasures buried beneath it by the Moors would be revealed.

Notwithstanding this ominous prediction, we ventured to pass through the spellbound gateway, feeling some little assurance against magic art in the protection of the Virgin, a statue of whom we observed above the portal.

After passing through the barbican we ascended a narrow land, winding between walls, and came on an open esplanade within the fortress, called the Plaza de los Algibes, or Place of the Cisterns, from great reservoirs which undermine it, cut in the living rock by the Moors, for the supply of the fortress. Here, also, is a well of immense depth, furnishing the purest and coldest of water, another monument of the delicate taste of the Moors, who were indefatigable in their exertions to obtain that element in its crystal purity.

In front of this esplanade is the splendid pile commenced by Charles V., intended, it is said, to eclipse the residence of the Moslem kings. With all its grandeur and architectural merit, it appeared to us like an arrogant intrusion, and passing by it we entered a simple unostentatious portal, opening into the interior of the Moorish palace.

The transition was almost magical; it seemed as if we were at once transported into other times and another realm, and were treading the scenes of Arabian story. We found ourselves in a great court paved with white marble and decorated at each end with light Moorish peristyles. It is called the court of the Alberca. In the center was an immense basin, or fish-pool, a hundred and thirty feet in length by thirty in breadth, stocked with gold-fish, and bordered by hedges of roses. At the upper end of this court rose the great tower of Comares.

From the lower end, we passed through a Moorish archway into the renowned Court of Lions. There is no part of the edifice that gives us a more complete idea of its original beauty and magnificence than this; for none has suffered so little from the ravages of time. In the center stands the fountain famous in song and story. The alabaster basins still shed their diamond drops, and the twelve lions which support them cast forth their crystal streams as in the days of Boabdil. The court is laid out in flower-beds, and surrounded by light Arabian arcades of open filigree work, supported by slender pillars of white marble. The architecture, like that of all the other parts of the palace, is characterized by elegance rather than grandeur, bespeaking a delicate and graceful taste, and a disposition to indolent enjoyment. When we look upon the fairy tracery of the peristyles and the apparently fragile fretwork of the walls, it is difficult to believe that so much has survived the wear and tear of centuries, the shocks of earthquakes, the violence of war, and the quiet, though no less baneful, pilferings of the tasteful traveler. It is almost sufficient to excuse the popular tradition that the whole is protected by a magic charm.

On one side of the court a portal richly adorned opens into a lofty hall paved with white marble, and called the Hall of the Two Sisters. A cupola or lantern admits a tempered light from above, and a free circulation of air. The lower part of the walls is incrusted with beautiful Moorish tiles, on some of which are emblazoned the escutcheons of the Moorish monarchs: the upper part is faced with the fine stucco work invented at Damascus, consisting of large plates cast in molds and artfully joined, so as to have the appearance of having been laboriously sculptured by the hand into light relievos and fanciful arabesques, intermingled with texts of the Koran, and poetical inscriptions in Arabian and Celtic characters. These decorations of the walls and cupolas are richly gilded, and the interstices paneled with lapis lazuli and other brilliant and enduring colors. On each side of the wall are recesses for ottomans and arches. Above an inner porch is a balcony which communicated with the women's apartment. The latticed balconies still remain, from whence the dark-eyed beauties of the harem might gaze unseen upon the entertainments of the hall below.

It is impossible to contemplate this once favorite abode of Oriental manners without feeling the early associations of Arabian romance, and almost expecting to see the white arm of some mysterious princess beckoning from the balcony, or some dark eye sparkling through the lattice. The abode of beauty is here, as if it had been inhabited but yesterday — but where are the Zoraydas and Linderaxas!

On the opposite side of the Court of Lions is the hall of the Abencerrages, so called from the gallant cavaliers of that illustrious line, who were here perfidiously massacred. There are some who doubt the whole truth of this story, but our humble attendant, Mateo, pointed out the very wicket of the portal through which they are said to have been introduced, one by one, and the white marble fountain in the center of the hall, where they were beheaded. He showed us also certain broad, ruddy stains in the pavement, traces of their blood, which, according to popular belief, can never be effaced. Finding we listened to him with easy faith, he added that there was often heard at night, in the Court of Lions, a low, confused sound, resembling the murmurings of a multitude; with now and then a faint tinkling, like the distant clank of chains. These noises are probably produced by the bubbling currents and tinkling falls of water, conducted under the pavement through the pipes and channels to supply the fountains; but according to the legend of the son of the Alhambra, they are made by the spirits of the murdered Abencerrages, who nightly haunt the scene of their suffering, and invoke the vengeance of Heaven on their destroyer.

From the Court of Lions we retraced our steps through the court of the Alberca, or great fish-pool, crossing which, we proceeded to the tower of Comares, so called from the

name of the Arabian architect. It is of massive strength and
lofty height, domineering over the rest of the edifice and
overhanging the steep hillside, which descends abruptly to the
banks of the Darro. A Moorish archway admitted us into a
vast and lofty hall, which occupies the interior of the tower
and was the grand audience chamber of the Moslem
monarchs, thence called the hall of Ambassadors. It still
bears the traces of past magnificence. The walls are richly
stuccoed and decorated with arabesques, the vaulted ceilings
of cedar wood, almost lost in obscurity from its height, still
gleam with rich gilding and the brilliant tints of the Arabian
pencil. On three sides of the saloon are deep windows, cut
through the immense thickness of the walls, the balconies of
which look down upon the verdant valley of the Darro, the
streets and convents of the Albaycin, and command a
prospect of the distant Vega. I might go on to describe the
other delightful apartments of this side of the palace; the
Tocador or toilet of the Queen, an open belvedere on the
summit of the tower, where the Moorish sultanas enjoyed the
pure breezes from the mountain and the prospect of the
surrounding paradise. The secluded little patio or garden
Lindaraxa, with its alabaster fountain, its thickets of roses
and myrtles, of citrons and oranges. The cool halls and
grottoes of the baths, where the glare and heat of day are
tempered into a self-mysterious light and a pervading
freshness. But I appear to dwell minutely on these scenes. My
object is merely to give the reader a general introduction in
an abode, where, if disposed, he may linger and loiter
with me through the remainder of this work, gradually
becoming familiar with all its beauties.

An abundant supply of water, brought from the mountains
by old Moorish aqueducts, circulates throughout the palace,
supplying its baths and fish-pools, sparkling in jets within its
halls, or murmuring in channels along the marble
pavements.When it has paid its tribute to the royal pile, and
visited its gardens and pastures, it flows down the long avenue
leading to the city, tinkling in rills, gushing in fountains, and
maintaining a perpetual verdure in those groves that
embower and beautify the whole hill of the Alhambra.

Those, only, who have sojourned in the ardent climates of the South can appreciate the delights of an abode combining the breezy coolness of the mountain with the freshness and verdure of the valley.

While the city below pants with the noon-tide heat, and the parched Vega trembles to the eye, the delicate airs from the Sierra Nevada play through the lofty halls, bringing with them the sweetness of the surrounding gardens. Everything invites to that indolent repose, the bliss of Southern climes; and while the half-shut eye looks out from shaded balconies upon the glittering landscape, the ear is lulled by the rustling of groves and the murmer of running streams.

to be entered in many parts; and the rumor of a stranger quartered alone in one of the ruined apartments, out of the hearing of the rest of the inhabitants, might tempt unwelcome visitors in the night, especially as foreigners are always supposed to be well stocked with money. Dolores represented the frightful loneliness of the place; nothing but bats and owls flitting about; then there were a fox and wild cat that kept about the vaults and roamed about at night.

I was not to be diverted from my humor, so calling in the assistance of a carpenter and the ever-officious Mateo Ximenes, the doors and windows were soon placed in a state of tolerable security.

With all these precautions, I must confess the first night I passed in these quarters was inexpressibly dreary. I was escorted by the whole family to my chamber, and their taking leave of me, and retiring along the waste antechamber and echoing galleries reminded me of those hobgoblin stories, where the hero is left to accomplish the adventure of a haunted house.

Soon the thoughts of the fair Elizabetta and the beauties of her court, who had once graced these chambers, now by a perversion of fancy added to the gloom. Here was the scene of their transient gayety and loveliness; here were the very traces of their elegance and enjoyment; but what and where were they?—Dust and ashes! tenants of the tomb! phantoms of the memory!

A vague and indescribable awe was creeping over me. I would fain have ascribed it to the thoughts of robbers, awakened by the evening's conversation, but I felt that it was something more unusual and absurd. In a word, the long-buried impressions of the nursery were reviving and asserting their power over my imagination. Everything began to be affected by the workings of my mind. The whispering of the wind among the citron-trees beneath my window had something sinister. I cast my eyes into the garden of Lindaraxa; the groves presented a gulf of shadows; the thickets had indistinct and ghastly shapes. I was glad to close the window; but my chamber itself became infected. A bat had found its way in, and flitted about my head and athwart my solitary lamp; the

Somerset Maugham: Seville and Granada

Somerset Maugham (1874-1965), the great English writer, who studied medicine and never practiced as a physician, abandoned medicine in 1897 for writing and became a successful novelist, short story writer and playwright. During World War I, he served in England's secret service. The following chapters are taken from his book, The Land of the Blessed Virgin. While he lived on Cape Ferrat, in southern France, he was able to travel widely in Spain—just a stone's skip away. A novelist to the core, Maugham unfolds a dramatic, panoramic account of the country.

On taking up my abode in the Alhambra, one end of a suite of empty chambers of modern architecture, intended for the residence of the governor, was fitted up for my reception. It was in front of the palace, looking forth upon the esplanade. The further end communicated with a cluster of little chambers, partly Moorish, partly modern, inhabited by Tia Antonia and her family. These terminated in a large room which serves the good old dame for parlor, kitchen, and hall of audience. It had boasted of some splendor in the time of the Moors, but a fireplace had been built in one corner, the smoke from which had discolored the walls, nearly obliterated the ornaments, and spread a somber tint over the whole. From these gloomy apartments a narrow blind corridor and a dark winding staircase led down an angle of the tower of Comares; groping down which, and opening a small door at the bottom, you are suddenly dazzled by emerging into the brilliant antechamber of the hall of Ambassadors, with the fountain of the court of the Alberca sparkling before you.

I was dissatisfied with being lodged in a modern and frontier apartment of the palace, and longed to ensconce myself in the very heart of the building.

As I was rambling one day about the Moorish halls I found, in a remote gallery, a door which I had not before noticed, communicating apparently with an extensive apartment, locked up from the public. Here then was a mystery. Here was the haunted wing of the castle. I procured the key, however, without difficulty. The door opened to a range of vacant chambers of European architecture; though built over a Moorish arcade, along with the little garden of Lindaraxa. There were two lofty rooms, the ceilings of which were of deep panel-work of cedar, richly and skillfully carved with fruits and flowers, intermingled with grotesque masks or faces, but broken in many places. The walls had evidently in ancient times, been hung with damask, but were now naked, and scrawled over with the insignificant names of aspiring travelers; the windows, which were dismantled and open to wind and weather, looked into the garden of Lindaraxa, and the orange and citron trees flung their branches into the chambers. Beyond these rooms were two saloons, less lofty, looking also into the garden. In the compartments of the paneled ceiling were baskets of fruit and garlands of flowers, painted by no mean hand, and in tolerable preservation. The walls had also been painted in fresco in the Italian style, but the paintings were nearly obliterated. The windows were in the same shattered state as in the other chambers.

This fanciful suit of rooms terminated in an open gallery with balustrades, which ran at right angles along another side of the garden. The whole apartment had a delicacy and elegance in its decorations, and there was something so choice and sequestered in its situation, along this retired little garden, that awakened an interest in its history. I found on inquiry that it was an apartment fitted up by Italian artists in the early part of the last century, at the time when Philip V.

and the beautiful Elizabetta of Parma were expected at the Alhambra; and was destined for the queen and the ladies of her train. One of the loftiest chambers had been her sleeping-room, and a narrow staircase leading from it, though now walled up, opened to the delightful belvedere, originally a mirador of the Moorish sultanas, but fitted up as a boudoir for the fair Elizabetta, and which still retains the name of the Tocador, or toilette of the queen. The sleeping-room I have mentioned commanded from one window a prospect of the Generaliffe and its embowered terraces; under another window played the alabaster fountain of the garden of Lindaraxa. That garden carried my thoughts still further back, to the period of another reign of beauty—to the days of the Moorish sultanas. "How beauteous is this garden!" says an Arabic inscription, "where the flowers of the earth vie with the stars of heaven! what can compare with the vase of yon alabaster fountain filled with crystal water? Nothing but the moon in her fullness, shining in the midst of an unclouded sky!"

Centuries had elasped, yet how much of this scene of apparently fragile beauty remained! The garden of Lindaraxa was still adorned with flowers; the fountain still presented its crystal mirror; it is true, the alabaster had lost its whiteness, and the basin beneath, overrun with weeds, had become the nestling place of the lizard; but there wa something in the very decay that enhanced the interest of th scene, speaking, as it did, of that mutability which is t irrevocable lot of man and all his works. The desolation, t of these chambers, once the abode of the proud and eleg Elizabetta, had a more touching charm for me than if I beheld them in their pristine splendor, glittering with pageantry of a court—I determined at once to take u quarters in this apartment.

My determination excited great surprise in the famil could not imagine any rational inducement for the cl so solitary, remote and forlorn an apartment. The g Antonia considered it highly dangerous. The neigh she said, was infested by vagrants; the caverns of the hills swarmed with gypsies; the palace was ruinou

grotesque faces carved in the cedar ceiling seemed to mope and mow at me.

Rousing myself and half-smiling at this temporary weakness, I resolved to brave it, and, taking lamp in hand, sallied forth to make a tour of the ancient palace. Notwithstanding every mental exertion, the task was a severe one. The rays of my lamp extended to but a limited distance around me; I walked as it were in a mere halo of light, and all beyond was thick darkness. The vaulted corridors were as caverns; the vaults of the halls were lost in gloom; what unseen foe might not be lurking before or behind me; my own shadow playing about the walls and the echoes of my own footsteps disturbed me.

In this excited state, as I was traversing the great hall of Ambassadors, there were added real sounds to these conjectural fancies. Low moans and indistinct ejaculations seemed to rise as it were from beneath my feet; I paused and listened. They then appeared to resound from without the tower. Sometimes they resembled the howlings of an animal, at others they were stifled shrieks, mingled with articulate ravings. The thrilling effect of these sounds in that still hour and singular place destroyed all inclination to continue my lonely perambulation. I returned to my chamber with more alacrity than I had sallied forth, and drew my breath more freely when once more within its walls and the door bolted behind me.

When I woke in the morning, with the sun shining in at my window and lighting up every part of the building with its cheerful and truth-telling beams, I could scarcely recall the shadows and fancies conjured up by the gloom of the preceding night, or believe that the scenes around me, so naked and apparent, could have been clothed with such imaginary horrors.

Still the dismal howlings and ejaculations I had heard were not ideal; but they were soon accounted for by my handmaid Dolores; being the ravings of a poor maniac, a brother of her aunt, who was subject to violent paroxysms, during which he was confined in a vaulted room beneath the hall of Ambassadors.

Seville

The impression left by strange towns and cities is often a matter of circumstance, depending upon events in the immediate past; or on the chance which, during his earliest visit, there befell the traveller. After a stormy passage across the Channel, Newhaven, from the mere fact of its situation on solid earth, may gain a fascination which closer acquaintance can never entirely destroy; and even Birmingham, first seen by a lurid sunset, may so affect the imagination as to appear for ever like some infernal, splendid city, restless with the hurried toil of gnomes and goblins. So to myself Seville means ten times more than it can mean to others. I came to it after weary years in London, heartsick with much hoping, my mind dull with drudgery; and it seemed a land of freedom. There I became at last conscious of my youth, and it seemed a *belvedere* upon a new life. How can I forget the delight of wandering in the Sierpes, released at length from all imprisoning ties, watching the various movement as though it were a stage-play, yet half afraid that the falling curtain would bring back reality! The songs, the dances, the happy idleness of orange-gardens, the gay turbulence of Seville by night; ah! there at least I seized life eagerly, with both hands, forgetting everything but that time was short and existence full of joy. I sat in the warm sunshine, inhaling the pleasant odours, reminding myself that I had no duty to do them, or the morrow, or the day after. I lay a-bed thinking how happy, effortless and free would be my day. Mounting my horse, I clattered through the narrow streets, over the cobbles, till I came to the country; the air was fresh and sweet, and Aguador loved the spring mornings. When he put his feet to the springy turf he gave a little shake of pleasure, and without a sign from me broke into a gallop. To the amazement of shepherds guarding their wild flocks, to the confusion of herds of brown pigs, scampering hastily as we approached, he and I excited by the wind singing in our ears, we pelted madly through the country. And the whole land laughed with the joy of living.

But I love also the recollection of Seville in the grey days of December, when the falling rain offered a grateful contrast to the unvarying sunshine. Then new sights delighted the eye, new perfumes the nostril. In the decay of that long southern autumn a more sombre opulence was added to the gay colours; a different spirit filled the air, so that I realised suddenly that old romantic Spain of Ferdinand and Isabella. It lay a-dying still, gorgeous in corruption, sober yet flamboyant, rich and poverty-stricken, squalid, magnificent. The white streets, the dripping trees, the clouds gravid with rain, gave to all things an adorable melancholy, a sad, poetic charm. Looking back, I cannot dismiss the suspicion that my passionate emotions were somewhat ridiculous, but at twenty-three one can afford to lack a sense of humour.

But Seville at first is full of disillusion. It has offered abundant material to the idealist who, as might be expected, has drawn of it a picture which is at once common and pretentious. Your idealist can see no beauty in sober fact, but must array it in all the theatrical properties of a vulgar imagination; he must give to things more imposing proportions, he colours gaudily; Nature for him is ever posturing in the full glare of footlights. Really he stands on no higher level than the housemaid who sees in every woman a duchess in black velvet, an Aubrey Plantagenet in plain John Smith. So I, in common with many another traveller, expected to find in the Guadalquivir a river of transparent green, with orange-groves along its banks, were wandered ox-eyed youths and maidens beautiful. Palm-trees, I thought, rose towards heaven, like passionate souls longing for release from earthly bondage; Spanish women, full-breasted and sinuous, danced *boleros, fandangos,* while the air rang with the joyous sound of castanets, and toreadors in picturesque habiliments twanged the light guitar.

Alas! the Guadalquivir is like yellow mud, and moored to the busy quays lie cargo-boats lading fruit or grain or mineral; there no perfume scents the heavy air. The nights, indeed, are calm and clear, and the stars shine brightly; but the river banks see no amours more romantic than those of stokers from Liverpool or Glasgow, and their lady-loves have neither youth nor beauty.

Yet Seville has many a real charm to counter-balance these lost illusions. He that really knows it, like an ardent lover with his mistress' imperfections, would have no difference; even the Guadalquivir, so matter-of-fact, really so prosaic, has an unimagined attractiveness; the crowded shipping, the hurrying porters, add to that sensation of vivacity which is of Seville the most fascinating characteristic. And Seville is an epitome of Andalusia, with its life and death, with its colour and vivid contrasts, with its boyish gaiety.

It is a city of delightful ease, of freedom and sunshine, or torrid heat. There it does not matter what you do, nor when, nor how you do it. There is none to hinder you, none to watch. Each takes his ease, and is content that his neighbour should do the like. Doubtless people are lazy in Seville, but good heavens! why should one be so terribly strenuous? Go into the Plaza Nueva, and you will see it filled with men of all ages, of all classes, 'taking the sun'; they promenade slowly, untroubled by any mental activity, or sit on benches between the palm-trees, smoking cigarettes; perhaps the more energetic read the bull-fighting news in the paper. They are not ambitious, and they do not greatly care to make their fortunes; so long as they have enough to eat and drink — food is very cheap — and cigarettes to smoke, they are quite happy. The Corporation provides seats, and the sun shines down for nothing — so let them sit in it and warm themselves. I daresay it is as good a way of getting through life as most others.

A southern city never reveals its true charm till the summer, and few English know what Seville is under the burning sun of July. It was built for the great heat, and it is only then that the refreshing coolness of the *patio* can be appreciated. In the streets the white glare is mitigated by awnings that stretch from house to house, and the half light in the Sierpes, the High Street, has a curious effect; the people in their summer garb walk noiselessly, as though the warmth made sound impossible. Towards evening the sail-cloths are withdrawn, and a breath of cold air sinks down; the population bestirs itself, and along the Sierpes the *cafes* become suddenly crowded and noisy.

Then, for it was too hot to ride earlier, I would mount my

horse and cross the river. The Guadalquivir had lost its winter russet, and the under the blue sky gained varied tints of liquid gold, of emerald and of sapphire. I lingered in Triana, the gipsy-quarter, watching the people. Beautiful girls stood at the windows, so that the whole way was lined with them, and their lips were not unwilling to break into charming smiles. One especially I remember who was used to sit on a balcony at a street-corner; her hair was irreproachable in its elaborate arrangement, and the red carnation in it gleamed like fire against the night. Her face was long, fairer-complexioned than is common, with regular and delicate features. She sat at her balcony, with a huge book upon her knee, which she read with studied disregard of the passersby; but when I looked back sometimes I saw that she had lifted her eyes, lustrous and dark, and they met mine gravely.

And in the country I passed through long fields of golden corn, which reached as far as I could see; I remembered the spring, when it had all been new, soft, fresh, green. And presently I turned round to look at Seville in the distance, bathed in brilliant light, glowing as though its walls were built of yellow flame. The Giralda arose in its wonderful grace like an arrow; so slim, so comely, it reminded one of an Arab youth, with long, thin limbs. With the setting sun, gradually the city turned rosy-red and seemed to lose all substantiality, till it became a many-shaped mist that was dissolved in the tenderness of the sky.

Late in the night I stood at my window looking at the cloudless heaven. From the earth ascended, like incense, the mellow odours of summertime; the belfry of the neighbouring church stood boldly outlined against the darkness, and the storks that had built their nest upon it were motionless, not stirring even as the bells rang out the hours. The city slept, and it seemed that I alone watched in the silence; the sky still was blue, and the stars shone in their countless millions. I thought of the city that never rested, of London with its unceasing roar, the endless streets, the greyness. And all around me was a quiet serenity, a tranquillity such as the Christian may hope shall reward him in Paradise for the

troublous pilgrimage of life. But that is long ago and passed
for ever.

Arriving at Seville the recollection of Cordova took me
quickly to the Alcazar; but I was a little disappointed. It has
been ill and tawdrily restored, with crude pigments, with gold
that is too bright and too clean; but even before that, Charles
V. and his successors had made additions out of harmony
with Moorish feeling. Of the palace where lived the
Mussulman Kings nothing, indeed, remains; but Pedro the
Cruel, with whom the edifice now standing is more especially
connected, was no less oriental than his predecessors, and he
employed Morisco architects to rebuild it. Parts are said to be
exact reproductions of the older structure, while many of the
beautiful tiles were taken from Moorish houses.

The atmosphere, then, is but half Arabic; the rest belongs
to that flaunting, multi-colored barbarism which is characteristic of Northern Spain before the union of Arragon and
Castile. Wandering in the deserted courts, looking through
horseshoe windows of exquisite design at the wild garden,
Pedro the Cruel and Maria de Padilla are the figures that
occupy the mind.

Seville teems with the anecdotes of the monarch who,
according to the point of view, has been called the Cruel and
the Just. He was an amorist for whom platonic dalliance had
no charm, and there are gruesome tales of ladies buried alive
because they would not quench the flame of his desires, of
others, fiercely virtuous, who poured boiling oil on face and
bosom to make themselves unattractive in his sight. But the
head that wears a crown apparently has fascinations which
few women can resist, and legend tells more frequently of
Pedro's conquests than of his rebuffs. He was an ardent lover
to whom marriage vows were of no importance; that he
committed bigamy is certain — and pardonable, but some
historians are inclined to think that he had at one and the
same time no less than three wives. He was oriental in his
tastes.

In imitation of the Paynim sovereigns Pedro loved to
wander in the streets of Seville at night, alone and disguised,
to seek adventure or to see for himself the humour of his

subjects; and like them also it pleased him to administer justice seated in the porch of his palace. If he was often hard and proud towards the nobles, with the people he was always very gracious; to them he was the redressor of wrongs and a protector of the oppressed; his justice was that of the Mussulman rules, rapid, terrible and passionate, often quaint. For instance; a rich priest had done some injury to a cobbler, who brought him before the ecclesiastical tribunals, where he was for a year suspended from his clerical functions. The tradesman thought the punishment inadequate, and taking the law into his own hands gave the priest a drubbing. He was promptly seized, tried, condemned to death. But he appealed to the king who, with a witty parody of the rival Court, changed the punishment to suspension from his trade, and ordered the cobbler for twelve months to make no boots.

On the other hand, the Alcazar itself has been the scene of Pedro's vilest crimes, in the whole list of which is none more insolent, none more treacherous, than that whereby he secured the priceless ruby which graces still the royal crown of England. There is a school of historians which insists on finding a Baptist Minister in every hero--think what a poor-blooded creature they wish to make of the glorious Nelson — but no casuistry avails to cleanse the memory of Pedro of Castille: even for his own ruthless age he was a monster of cruelty and lust. Indeed the indignation with which his biographers have felt bound to charge their pens has somewhat obscured their judgment; they have so eagerly insisted on the censure with which themselves regard their hero's villainies, that they have found little opportunity to explain a complex character. Yet the story of his early life affords a simple key to his maturity. Till the age of fifteen he lived in prisons, suffering with his mother every insult and humiliation, while his father's mistress kept queenly state, and her children received the honours of royal princes. When he came to the throne he found himself a catspaw between his natural brothers and ambitious nobles. His nearest relatives were even his bitterest enemies, and he was continually betrayed by those he trusted; even his mother delivered to the rebellious peers the strongholds and the treasures he had left in her charge and caused him to be taken prisoner. As a boy he had been violent and impetuous, yet always loyal: but before he was twenty he became suspicious and mistrustful; in his weakness he made craft and perfidy his weapons, practising to compose his face, to feign forgetfulness of injury till the moment of vengeance; he learned to dissemble so that none could tell his mind, and treated no courtiers with greater favour than those upon whose death he had already determined.

Intermingled with this career of vice and perfidy and bloodshed is the love of Maria de Padilla, whom the king met when he was eighteen, and till her death loved passionately — with brief inconstancies, for fidelity has never been a royal virtue; and she figures with gentle pathos in that grim history like wild perfumed flowers on a storm-beaten coast. After the assassination of the unfortunate Blanche, the French Queen whom he loathed with an extraordinary physical repulsion, Pedro acknowledged a secret marriage with Maria de Padilla, which legitimised her children; but for ten years before she had been treated with royal rights. The historian says that she was very beautiful, but her especial charm seems to have been that voluptuous grace which is characteristic of Andalusian women. She was simple and pious, with a nature of great sweetness, and she never abused her power; her influence, as runs the hackneyed phrase, was always for good, and untiringly she did her utmost to incline her despot lover to mercy. She alone sheds a ray of light on Pedro's memory, only her love can save him from the execration of posterity. When she died rich and poor alike mourned her, and the king was inconsolable. He honoured her with pompous obsequies, and throughout the kingdom ordered masses to be sung for the rest of her soul.

The guardians of the Alcazar show you the chambers in which dwelt this gracious lady, and the garden-fountain wherein she bathed in summer. Moralists, anxious to prove that the way of righteousness is hard, say that beauty dies, but they err, for beauty is immortal. The habitations of a lovely women never lose the enchantment she has cast over them, her comeliness lingers in their empty chambers like a subtle odour; and centuries after her very bones have crumbled to dust it is her presence alone that is felt, her footfall that is heard on the marble floors.

Garish colours, alas! have driven the tender spirit of Maria de Padilla from the royal palace, but it has betaken itself to the old garden, and there wanders sadly. It is a charming place of rare plants and exotic odours; cypress and tall palm trees rise towards the blue sky with their irresistible melancholy, their far-away suggestion of burning deserts; and at their feet the ground is carpeted with violets. Yet to me the wild roses brought strangely recollections of England, of long summer days when the air was sweet and balmy; the birds sang heavenly songs, the same songs as they sing in June in the fat Kentish fields. The gorgeous palace had only suggested the long past days of history, and Seville the joy of life and the love of sunshine; but the old quiet garden took me far away from Spain, so that I longed to be again in England. In thought I wandered through a garden that I knew in years gone by, filled also with flowers, but with hollyhocks and jasmine; the breeze carried the sweet scent of the honeysuckle to my nostrils, and I looked at the green lawns, with the broad, straight lines of the grass-mower. The low of cattle reached my ears, and wandering to the fence I looked into the fields beyond; yellow cows grazed idly or lay still chewing the cud; they stared at me with listless, sleepy eyes.

But I glanced up and saw a flock of wild geese flying northwards in long lines that met, making two sides of a huge triangle; they flew quickly in the cloudless sky, far above me, and presently were lost to view. About me was the tall box-wood of the southern garden, and tropical plants with rich flowers of yellow and red and purple. A dark fir-tree stood out, ragged and uneven, like a spirit of the North, erect as a life without reproach; but the foliage of the palms hung down with a sad, adorable grace.

In Seville the Andalusian character thrives in its finest flower; and nowhere can it be more conveniently studied than in the narrow, sinuous, crowded thoroughfare which is the oddest street in Europe. The Calle de las Sierpes is merely a pavement, hardly broader than that of Piccadilly, without a carriage-way. The houses on either side are very irregular; some are tall, four-storeyed, others quite tiny; some are well kept and freshly painted, others dilapidated. It is one of the curiosities of Seville that there is no particularly fashionable quarter; and, as though some moralising ruler had wished to place before his people a continual reminder of the uncertainty of human greatness, by the side of a magnificent palace you will find a hovel.

At no hour of the day does the Calle de las Sierpes lack animation, but to see it at its best you must go towards evening, at seven o'clock, for then there is scarcely room to move. Fine gentlemen stand at the club doors or sit within, looking out of the huge windows; the merchants and the students, smoking cigarettes, saunter, wrapped magnificently in their *capas*. Cigarette-girls pass with roving eyes; they suffer no false modesty and smile with pleasure when a compliment reaches their ears. Admirers do not speak in too low a tone and the fair Sevillan is never hard of hearing.

Newspaper boys with shrill cries announce evening editions: *'Porvenir! Noticiero!'* Vendors of lottery-tickets wander up and down, audaciously offering the first prize: *'Quien quiere el premio gordo?'* Beggars follow you with piteous tales of fasts improbably extended. But most striking is the *gente flamenca,* the bull-fighter, with his numerous hangers-on. The *toreros* — toreador is an unknown word; good for comic opera and persons who write novels of Spanish life and cannot be bothered to go to Spain — *toreros* sit in their especial cafe, the *Cerveceria Nacional,* or stand in little groups talking to one another. They are distinguishable by the *coleta,* which is a little plait of hair used to attach the chignon of full-dress: it is the dearest ambition of the aspirant to the bull-ring to posses this ornament; he grows it as soon as he is full-fledged, and it is solemnly cut off when the weight of years and the responsibility of landed estates induce him to retire from the profession. The bull-fighter dresses peculiarly and the *gente flamenca* imitates him so far as its means allow. A famous *matador* is as well paid as in England a Cabinet Minister or a music-hall artiste. This is his costume:

a broad-brimmed hat with a low crown, which is something like a topper absurdly flattened down, with brims preposterously broadened out. The front of his shirt is befrilled and embroidered, and his studs are the largest diamonds; not even financiers in England wear such important stones. He wears a low collar without a necktie, but ties a silk handkerchief round his neck like an English navvy; an Eton jacket, fitting very tightly, brown, black, or grey, with elaborate frogs and much braiding; the trousers, skin-tight above, loosen below, and show off the lower extremities when, like the heroes of feminine romance, the wearer has a fine leg. Indeed, it is a mode of dress which exhibits the figure to great advantage, and many of these young men have admirable forms.

In their strong, picturesque way they are often very handsome. They have a careless grace of gesture, a manner of actors perfectly at ease in an effective part, a brutal healthiness; there is a flamboyance in their bearing, a melodramatic swagger, which is most diverting. And their faces, so contrasted are the colours, so strongly marked the features, are full of interest. Clean shaven, the beard shows violet through the olive skin; they have high cheek bones and thin, almost hollow cheeks, with eyes set far back in the sockets, dark and lustrous under heavy brows. The black hair, admirably attached to the head, is cut short; shaved on the temples and over the ears, brushed forward as in other countries is fashionable with gentlemen of the box: it fits the skull like a second, tighter skin. The lips are red and sensual, the teeth white, regular and well shaped. The bull-fighter is remarkable also for the diamond rings which decorate his fingers and the massive gold, the ponderous seals, of his watch-chain.

Who can wonder then that maidens fair, their hearts turning to thoughts of love, should cast favourable glances upon this hero of a hundred fights? The conquests of tenors and grand-dukes and fiddlers are insignificant beside those of a bull-fighter; and the certainty of feminine smiles is another inducement for youth to exchange the drudgery of menial occupations for the varied excitement of the ring.

At night the Sierpes is different again. Little by little the
people scatter to their various homes, the shops are closed,
the clubs put out their lights, and by one of the loiterers are
few. The contrast is vivid between the noisy throng of day-
time and this sudden stillness; the emptiness of the winding
street seems almost unnatural. The houses, losing all variety,
are intensely black; and above, the sinuous line of sky is
brilliant with clustering stars. A drunken roysterer reels from
a tavern-door, his footfall echoing noisily along the
pavement, but quickly he sways round a corner; and the
silence, more impressive for the interruption, returns. The
night-watchman, huddled in a cloak of many folds, is
sleeping in a doorway, dimly outlined by the yellow gleam of
his lantern.

Then I, a lover of late hours, returning, seek the *guardia*.
Sevillian houses are locked at midnight by this individual,
who keeps the latch-keys of a whole street, and is supposed to
be on the look-out for tardy comers. I clap my hands, such
being the Spanish way to attract attention, and shout; but he
does not appear. He is a good-natured, round man, bibulous,
with grey hair and a benevolent manner. I know his habits
and resign myself to inquiring for him in the neighbouring
dram-shops. I find him at last and assail him with all the
abuse at my command; he is too tipsy to answer or to care,
and follows me, jangling his keys. He fumbles with them at
the door, blaspheming because they are so much alike, and
finally lets me in.

'Buena noche. Descanse v bien.'

Granada

To go from Seville to Granada is like coming out of the
sunshine into deep shadow. I arrived, my mind full of
Moorish pictures, expecting to find a vivid, tumultuous life;
and I was ready with a prodigal hand to dash on the colours
of my admiration. But Granada is a sad town, grey and
empty; its people meander, melancholy, through the streets,
unoccupied. It is a tradeless place living on the monuments
which attract strangers, and like many a city famous for

stirring history, seems utterly exhausted. Granada gave me an impression that it wished merely to be left alone to drag out its remaining days in peace, away from the advance of civilisation and the fervid hurrying of progress: it seemed like a great adventuress retired from the world after a life of vicissitude, anxious only to be forgotten, and after so much storm and stress to be nothing more than pious. There must be many descendants of the Moors, but the present population is wan and lifeless. They are taciturn, sombre folk, with nothing in them of the chattering and vivacious creatures of Arab history. Indeed, as I wandered through the streets, it was not the Moors that engaged my mind, but rather Ferdinand of Arragon and Isabella of Castille. Their grim strength overpowered the more fraceful shadows of Moordom; and it was only by an effort that I recalled Gazul and Musa, most gallant and amorous of Paynim knights, tilting in the square, displaying incredible valour in the slaughter of savage bulls. I thought of the Catholic Kings, in full armour, riding with clank of steel through the captured streets. And the snowy summits of the Sierra Nevada, dazzling sometimes under the sun and the blue sky, but more often veiled with mist and capped by heavy clouds, grim and terrifying, lent a sort of tragic interest to the scene; so that I felt those grey masses, with their cloak of white, (they seemed near enough to overwhelm one,) made it impossible for the town built at their very feet, to give itself over altogether to flippance.

And for a while I found little of interest in Granada but the Alhambra. The gipsy quarter, with neither beauty, colour, nor even a touch of barbarism, is a squalid, brutal place, consisting of little dens built in the rock of the mountain which stands opposite the Alhambra. Worse than hovels, they are the lairs of wild beasts, fœtid and oppressive, inhabited by debased creatures, with the low forehead, the copper skin, and the shifty cruel look of the Spanish gipsy. They surround the visitor in their rags and tatters, clamouring for alms, and for exorbitant sums proposing to dance. Even in the slums of great cities I have not seen a life more bestial. I tried to imagine what sort of existence these people led. In the old days the rock-dwellings among the cactus served the gipsies for winter quarters only, and when the spring came they set off, scouring the country for something to earn or steal; but that is long ago. For two generations they have remained in these hovels — year in, year out — employed in shoeing horses, shearing, and the like menial occupations which the Spaniard thinks beneath his dignity. The women tell fortunes, or dance for the foreigner, or worse. It is a mere struggle for daily bread. I wondered whether in the spring-time the young men loved the maidens, or if they only coupled like the beasts. I saw one pair who seemed quite newly wed; for their scanty furniture was new and they were young. The man, short and squat, sat scowling, cross-legged on a chair, a cigarette between his lips. The woman was taller and not ill-made, a slattern; her hair fell dishevelled on her back and over her forehead; her dress was open, displaying the bosom; her apron was filthy. But when she smiled, asking for money, her teeth were white and regular, and her eyes flashed darkly. She was attractive in a heavy sensual fashion, attractive and at the same time horribly repellant: she was the sort of woman who might fetter a man to herself by some degrading, insuperable passion, the true Carmen of the famous story whom a man might at once love and hate; so that though she dragged him to hell in shame and in despair, he would never find the strength to free himself. But where among that bastard race was the splendid desire for freedom of their fathers, the love of the fresh air of heaven and the untrammeled life of the fields?

At first glance also the cathedral seemed devoid of charm. I suppose travellers seek emotions in the things they see, and often the more beautiful objects do not give the most vivid sensations. Painters complain that men of letters have written chiefly of second-rate pictures, but the literary sentiment is different from the artistic; and a master piece of Perugino may excite it less than a mediocre work of Guido Reni.

The cathedral of Granada is said by the excellent Fergusson to be the most noteworthy example in Europe of early Renaissance architecture; its proportions are evidently admirable, and it is designed and carried out according to all the canons of the art. 'Looking at its plan only,' he says, 'this is certainly one of the finest churches in Europe. It would be difficult to point out any other, in which the central aisle leads up to the dome, so well proportioned to its dimensions, and to the dignity of the high altar which stands under it.' But though I vaguely recognised these perfections, though the spacing appeared fine and simple, and the columns had a certain majesty, I was left more than a little cold. The whitewash with which the interior is coated gives an unsympathetic impression, and the abundant light destroys that mystery which the poorest, gaudiest Spanish church almost invariably possesses. In the *Capilla de los Reyes* are the elaborate monuments of the Catholic Kings, of their daughter Joan the Mad, and of Philip her husband; below, in the crypt, are four simple coffins, in which after so much grandeur, so much joy and sorrow, they rest. Indeed, for the two poor women who loved without requite, it was a life of pain almost unrelieved: it is a pitiful story, for all its magnificence, of Joan with her fiery passion for the handsome, faithless, worthless husband, and her mad jealousy; and of Isabella, with patient strength bearing every cross, always devoted to the man who tired of her quickly, and repaid her deep affection with naught but coldness and distrust.

Queen Isabella's sword and sceptre are shown in the sacristy, and in contrast with the implement of war a beautiful cope, worked with her royal hands. And her crown also may be seen, one of the few I have come across which might really become the wearer, of silver, a masterpiece of delicate craftsmanship.

But presently, returning to the cathedral and sitting in front of the high altar, I became at last conscious of its airy, restful grace. The chancel is very lofty. The base is a huge arcade which gives an effect of great lightness; and above are two rows of pictures, and still higher two rows of painted windows. The coloured glass throws the softest lights upon the altar and on the marble floor, rendering even quieter the low tints of the pictures. These are a series of illustrations of the life of the Blessed Virgin, painted by Alonzo Cano, a native of Valladolid, who killed his wife and came to

Granada, whereupon those in power made him a prebendary. In the obscurity I could not see the paintings, but divined soft and pleasant things after the style of Murillo, and doubtless that was better than actually to see them. The pulpits are gorgeously carved in wood, and from the walls fly great angels with fine turbulence of golden drapery. And in the contrast of the soft white stone with the gold, which not even the most critical taste could complain was too richly spread, there is a delicate, fascinating lightness: the chancel has almost an Italian gaiety, which comes upon one oddly in the gloomy town. Here the decoration, the gilded virgins, the elaborate carving, do not oppress as elsewhere; the effect is too debonair and too refreshing. It is one colour more, one more distinction, in the complexity of the religious sentiment.

But if what I have said of Granada seems cold, it is because I did not easily catch the spirit of the place. For when you merely observe and admire some view, and if industrious make a note of your impression, and then go home to luncheon, you are but a vulgar tripper, scum of the earth, deserving the ridicule with which the natives treat you. The romantic spirit is your only justification; when by the comeliness of your life or the beauty of your emotion you have attained that, (Shelley when he visited Paestum had it, but Theohophile Gautier, flaunting his red waistcoat *tras los montes,* was perhaps no better than a Cook's tourist,) then you are no longer unworthy of the loveliness which it is your privilege to see. When the old red brick and the green trees say to you hidden things, and the *vega* and the mountains are stretched before you with a new significance, when at last the white houses with their brown tiles, and the labouring donkey, and the peasant at his plough, appeal to you so as to make, as it were, an exquisite pattern on your soul, then you may begin to find excuses for yourself. But you may see places long and often before they are thus magically revealed to you, and for myself I caught the real emotion of Granada but once, when from the Generalife I looked over the valley, the Generalife in which are mingled perhaps more admirably than anywhere else in Andalusia all the charm of Arabic architecture, of running water, and of cypress trees, of purple flags and dark red roses. It is a spot, indeed, fit for the plaintive creatures of poets to sing their loves, for Paolo and Francesca, for Juliet and Romeo; and I am glad that there I enjoyed such an exquisite moment.

Beggars

People say that in Granada the beggars are more importunate than in any other Spanish town, but throughout Andalusia their pertinacity and number are amazing. They are licensed by the State, and the brass badge they wear makes them demand alms almost as a right. It is curious to find that the Spaniard, who is by no means a charitable being, gives very often to beggars — perhaps from superstitious motives, thinking their prayers will be of service, or fearing the evil eye, which may punish a refusal. Begging is quite an honourable profession in Spain; mendicants are charitably termed the poor, and not besmirched, as in England, with an opprobrious name.

I have never seen so many beggars as in Andalusia; at every church door there will be a dozen, and they stand or sit at each street corner, halt, lame and blind. Every possible deformity is paraded to arouse charity. Some look as though their eyes had been torn out, and they glare at you with horrible bleeding sockets; most indeed are blind, and you seldom fail to hear their monotonous cry, sometimes naming the saint's day to attract particular persons: 'Alms for the love of God, for a poor blind man on this the day of St John!' They stand from morning till night, motionless, with hand extended, repeating the words as the sound of footsteps tells them some one is approaching; and then, as a coin is put in their hands, say gracefully: *'Dios se lo pagara!* God will repay you.'

In Spain you do not pass silently when a beggar demands alms, but pray his mercy for God's love to excuse you: *'Perdone Usted por el amor de Dios!'* Or else you beseech God to protect him: *'Dios le ampare!'* And the mendicant, coming to your gate, sometimes invokes the Immaculate Virgin.

'Ave Maria purissima!' he calls.

And you, tired of giving, reply: *'Y por siempre!* And for ever.'

He passes on, satisfied with your answer, and rings at the next door.

It is not only in Burgos that Théophile Gautier might have admired the beggar's divine rags; everywhere they wrap their cloaks about them in the same magnificent fashion. The *capa,* I suppose, is the most graceful of all the garments of civilised man, and never more so than when it barely holds together, a mass of rags and patches, stained by the rain and bleached by the sun and wind. It hangs straight from the neck in big simple lines, or else is flung over one shoulder with a pompous wealth of folds.

There is a strange immobility about Andalusian beggars which recalls their Moorish ancestry. They remain for hours in the same attitude, without moving a muscle; and one I knew in Seville stood day after day, from early morning till midnight, with hand outstretched in the same rather crooked position, never saying a word but merely trusting to the passer-by to notice. The variety is amazing, men and women and children; and Seville at fair-time, or when the foreigners are coming for Holy Week, is like an enormous hospital. Mendicants assail you on all sides, the legless dragging themselves on their hands, the halt running towards you with a crutch, the blind led by wife or child, the deaf and dumb, the idiotic. I remember a woman with dead eyes and a huge hydrocephalic head, who sat in a bath-chair by one of the cathedral doors, and whenever people passed, cried shrilly for money in a high, unnatural voice. Sometimes they protrude maimed limbs, feetless legs or arms without hands; they display loathsome wonds, horribly inflamed; every variety of disease is shown to extort a copper. And so much is it a recognised trade that they have their properties, as it were: one old man whose legs had been shot away, trotted through the narrow streets of Seville on a diminutive ass, driving it into the shop-doors to demand his mite. Then there are the children, the little boys and girls that Murillo painted, barely covered by filthy rags, cherubs with black hair and shining eyes, the most importunate of all the tribe. The refusal of a halfpenny is followed impudently by demands for a cigarette, and as a last resort for a match; they wander about with keen eyes for cigar-ends, and no shred of a smoked leaf is too diminutive for them to get no further use from it.

And beside all these are the blind fiddlers, scraping out old-fashioned tunes that were popular thirty years ago; the guitarists, singing the *flamenco* songs which have been sung in Spain ever since the Moorish days; the buffoons, who extract tunes from a broomstick; the owners of performing dogs.

They are a picturesque lot, neither vicious nor ill-humoured. Begging is a fairly profitable trade, and not a very hard one; in winter *el pobre* can always find a little sunshine, and in summer a little shade. It is no hardship for him to sit still all day; he would probably do little else if he were a millionaire. He looks upon life without bitterness; Fate has not been very kind, but it is certainly better to be a live beggar than a dead king, and things might have been ten thousand times worse. For instance, he might not have been born a Spaniard, and every man in his senses knows that Spain is the greatest nation on earth, while to be born a citizen of some other country is the most dreadful misfortune that can befall him. He has his licence from the State, and a charitable public sees that he does not absolutely starve; he has cigarettes to smoke — to say that a blind man cannot enjoy tobacco is evidently absurd — and therefore, all these things being so, why should he think life such a woeful matter? While it lasts the sun is there to shine equally on rich and poor, and afterwards will not a paternal government find a grave in the public cemetery? It is true that the beggar shares it with quite a number of worthy persons, doubtless most estimable corpses, and his coffin even is but a temporary convenience — but still, what does it matter?

Song

But the Moorish influence is nowhere more apparent than in the Spanish singing. There is nothing European in that quavering lament, in those long-drawn and monotonous notes, in those weird trills. The sounds are strange to the ear accustomed to less barbarous harmonies, and at first no melody is perceived; it is custom alone which teaches the sad and passionate charm of these things. A *malagueña* is the particular complaint of the maid sorrowing for an absent lover, of the peasant who ploughs his field in the declining day. The long notes of such a song, floating across the silence of the night, are like a new melody on the great harpsichord of human sorrow. No emotion is more poignant than that given by the faint sad sounds of a Spanish song as one wanders through the deserted streets in the dead of night; or far in the country, with the sun setting red in the cloudless sky, when the stillness is broken only by the melancholy chanting of a shepherd among the olive-trees.

An heritage of Moordom is the Spanish love for the improvisation of well-turned couplets; in olden days a skilful verse might procure the poet a dress of cloth-of-gold, and it did on one occasion actually raise a beggar-maid to a royal throne; even now it has power to secure the lover his lady's most tender smiles, or at the worst a glass of Manzanilla. The richness of the language helps him with his rhymes, and his southern imagination gives him manifold subjects. But, being the result of improvisation — no lady fair would consider the suit of a gallant who could not address her in couplets of his own devising — the Spanish song has a peculiar character. The various stanzas have no bearing upon one another; they consist of four or seven lines, but in either case each contains its definite sentiment; so that one verse may be a complete song, or the singer may continue as long as the muse prompts and his subject's charms occasion. The Spanish song is like a barbaric necklace in which all manner of different stones are strung upon a single cord, without thought for their mutual congruity.

Naturally the vast majority of the innumerable couplets thus invented are forgotten as soon as sung, but now and then the fortuitous excellence of one impresses it on the maker's recollection, and it may be preserved. Here is an example which has been agreeably translated by Mr. J.W. Crombie; but neither original nor English rendering can give an

adequate idea of the charm which depends on the oriental
melancholy of the music:

> Dos besos tengo en el alma
> Que no se apartan de mi:
> El ultimo de mi madre,
> Y el primero que te di.

> *Deep in my soul two kisses rest,*
> *Forgot they ne're shall be:*
> *The last my mother's lips impressed,*
> *The first I stole from thee.*

Here is another, the survival of which testifies to the
Spanish extreme love of a compliment; and the somewhat
hackneyed sentiment can only have made it more pleasant to
the feminine ear:

> Salga el sol, si ha de salir,
> Y si no, que nunca salga;
> Que para alumbrarme á mí
> La luz de tus ojos basta.

> *If the sun care to rise, let him rise,*
> *But if not, let him ever lie hid;*
> *For the light from my lady-love's eyes*
> *Shines forth as the sun never did.*

It is a diverting spectacle to watch a professional improviser
in the throes of inspiration. This is one of the stock 'turns' of
the Spanish music-hall, and one of the most popular. I saw a
woman in Granada, who was quite a celebrity; and the
barbaric wildness of her performance, with its accompani-
ment of hand-clapping, discordant cries, and twanging of
guitar, harmonised well with my impression of the sombre
and mediæval city.

She threaded her way to the stage among the crowded
tables, through the auditorium, a sallow-faced creature,
obese and large-boned, with coarse features and singularly
ropy hair. She was accompanied by a fat small man with a
guitar and a woman of mature age and ample proportions: it

appeared that the cultivation of the muse, evidently more profitable than in England, conduced to adiposity. They stepped on the stage, taking chairs with them, for in Spain you do not stand to sing, and were greeted with plentiful applause. The little fat man began to play the long prelude to the couplet; the old woman clapped her hands and occasionally uttered a raucous cry. The poetess gazed into the air for inspiration. The guitarist twanged on, and in the audience there were scattered cries of *Ole!* Her companions began to look at the singer anxiously, for the muse was somewhat slow; and she patted her knee and groaned; at last she gave a little start and smiled. *Ole! Ole!* The inspiration had come. She gave a moan, which lengthened into the characteristic trill, and then began the couplet, beating time with her hands. Such an one as this:

> Suspiros que de mí salgan,
> Y otros que de tí saldran,
> Si en el camino se encuentran
> Que de cosas se diran!

> *If all the sighs thy lips now shape*
> *Could meet upon the way*
> *With those that from mine own escape*
> *What things they'd have to say!*

She finished, and all three rose from their chairs and withdrew them, but it was only a false exit; immediately the applause grew clamourous they sat down again, and the little fat man repeated his introduction.

But this time there was no waiting. The singer had noticed a well-known bull-fighter and quickly rolled off a couplet in his praise. The subject beamed with delight, and the general enthusiasm knew no bounds. The people excitedly threw their hats on the stage, and these were followed by a shower of coppers, which the performers, more heedful to the compensation of Art than to its dignity, grovelled to pick up.

Here is a lover's praise of the whiteness of his lady's skin:

La neve por tu cara
  Paso diciendo:
En donde no hago falta
  No me detengo.

Before thy brow the snow-flakes
  Hurry past and say:
'Where we are not needed,
  Wherefore should we stay?'

And this last, like the preceding translated by Mr. Crombie, shows once more how characteristic are Murillo's Holy Families of the popular sentiment:

La Virgen lava la ropa,
San Jose la esta tendiendo,
Santa Ana entretiene el niño,
Y el agua se va riendo.

The Virgin is washing the clothes at the brook,
And Saint Joseph hangs them to dry.
Saint Anna plays with the Holy Babe,
And the water flows smiling by.

Ernest Hemingway: Corrida in Madrid

As a young man, Ernest Miller Hemingway (1896-1961) went on hunting and fishing trips in northern Michigan. Neither his expatriate years in Paris, nor his writing as spokesman for "the lost generation" after World War I, dampened his enthusiasm for the outdoor life. His writings reflect a strong interest in machismo—in manliness, virility, and violence. It is natural that he should have been drawn to that major vestigium of the Roman arena, the Spanish bullfight, which he examines in great detail in Death in the Afternoon *(1932). The following chapter is taken from this work. The art of the toreador, which fascinates many, but which many turn from as a barbaric relic of the past, is still a major spectacle in Spain.*

If you go first to a corrida in Madrid you can go down into the ring and walk about before the fight. The gates into the corrals and the patio de caballos are open and there in the courtyard you willl see the line of horses against the wall, and the picadors arriving on the horses they have ridden in from town, these horses having been ridden from the bull ring by the red-bloused monos or bull-ring servants to the lodgings in the town where the picadors live, so the picador, dressed in his white shirt, narrow black four-in-hand tie, brocaded jacket, wide sash, bowl-topped hat with the pompom on the side and the thick buckskin trousers that cover the steel leaf armor over the right leg, may mount and ride through the streets and in the traffic along the carretera de Aragon out to the ring; the mono sometimes riding behind his saddle, sometimes on another horse he has led out; these few horsemen in the stream of carriages, carts, taxis and motor cars serving to advertise the bullfights, to tire the horses ridden, and to spare the matador from having to provide room for the picador in his coach or motor. As you ride toward the ring the best way to go is on one of the horse-drawn busses that leave the Puerta del Sol. You can sit on the top and see all the other people who are going and if you watch the crowd of vehicles you will see a motor car pass packed full of bullfighters in their costumes. All you will see will be their heads with the flat black-topped hats, their gold or silver brocade covered shoulders and their faces. If, in one car, there are several men in silver or dark jackets and only one in gold and while the others may be laughing, smoking and joking, his face is still, he is the matador and the others are his cuadrilla. The ride to the ring is the worst part of the day for the matador. In the morning the fight is still a long way off. After lunch it is still a long way off, then, before the car is ready or the carriage comes, there is the preoccupation of dressing. But once in the car or the carriage the fight is very near and there is nothing he can do about it during all that closely packed ride to the ring. It is closely packed because the upper part of a bull-fighter's jacket is heavy and thick at the shoulders and the matador and his banderilleros, now that they ride in the motor car, crowd each other tightly when they are dressed in their fighting clothes. There are some that smile and recognize friends on the ride, but nearly all are still-faced and detached. The matador, from living every day with death, becomes very detached, the measure of his detachment of course is the measure of his imagination and always on the day of the fight and finally during the whole end of the season, there is a detached something in their minds that you can almost see. What is there is death and you cannot deal in it each day and know each day there is a chance of receiving it without having it make a very plain mark. It makes this mark on every one. The banderilleros

and the picadors are different. Their danger is relative. They
are under orders; their responsibility is limited; and they do
not kill. They are under no great strain before a fight.
Ordinarily though, if you wish to see a study in apprehension
see an ordinarily cheerful and careless picador after he has
been to the corrals, or the sorting of the bulls, and seen that
these are really very big and powerful. If I could draw I
would make a picture of a table at the café during a feria
with the banderilleros sitting before lunch reading the
papers, a boot-black at work, a waiter hurrying somewhere
and two returning picadors, one a big brown-faced, dark-
browed man usually very cheerful and a great joker, the other
a gray-haired, neat, hawknosed, trim-waisted little man, both
of them looking the absolute embodiment of gloom and
depression.

"Qué tal?" asks one of the banderilleros.

"Son grandes," says the picador.

"Grandes?"

"Muy grandes!"

There is nothing more to be said. The banderilleros know
everything that is in the picador's mind. The matador may be
able to assassinate the big bull, if he swallows his pride and
puts away his honor, as easily as any small bull. The veins of
the neck are in the same place and as easily reached with the
point of the sword. There is no greater chance of a
banderillero's being caught if the bull is big. But there is
nothing the picador can do to help himself. After the bulls
are above a certain age and weight, when they hit the horse it
means the horse goes up into the air and perhaps he comes
down with the picador under him, perhaps the picador is
thrown against the barrier and pinned under the horse, or if
they lean forward gallantly, put their weight on the vara and
try to punish the bull during the encounter it means they fall
between the bull and the horse when the horse goes and must
lie there, with the bull looking for them with the horn, until
the matador can take the bull away. If the bulls are really
big, each time they hit the horse the picador will fall and he
knows this and his apprehension when "They are big" is
greater than any the matador, unless he is a coward, can feel.

There is always something the matador can do if he keeps his nerve. He may sweat ink, but there is a way to fight each bull no matter how difficult. The picador has no recourse. All he can do is turn down the customary bribe from the horse contractor for accepting an undersized mount and insist on a good strong horse, tall enough to keep him above the bull at the start, try to peg him well once and hope for not the worst.

By the time you see the matadors standing in the opening of the patio de caballos their worst time of apprehension is over. The crowd around them has removed that loneliness of the ride with people who know them all too well, and the crowd restores their characters. Nearly all bullfighters are brave. Some are not. This seems impossible since no man who was not brave would get into the ring with a bull, but in certain special cases natural ability and early training, commencing the training with calves where there is no danger, have made bullfighters of men with no natural courage. There are only about three of these. I will go into their cases later and they are among the most interesting phenomenons of the ring, but the usual bullfighter is a very brave man, the most common degree of bravery being the ability temporarily to ignore possible consequences. A more pronounced degree of bravery, which comes with exhilaration, is the ability not to give a damn for possible consequences; not only to ignore them but to despise them. Nearly all bullfighters are brave and yet nearly all bullfighters are frightened at some moment *before* the fight begins.

The crowd starts to thin in the patio de caballos, the bullfighters line up, the three matadors abreast, their banderilleros and picadors behind them. The crowd goes from the ring, leaving it empty. You go to your seat and, if you are in a barrera, you buy a cushion from the vender below, sit on it, and with your knees pressing the wood look out across the ring to the doorway of the patio you have just left with the three matadors, the sun shining on the gold of their suits, standing in the doorway, the other bullfighters, on foot and mounted, making a mass behind them. Then you see the people around you looking up above them toward a box. It is the president coming in. He takes his seat and waves a handkerchief. If he is on time there is a burst of clapping; if he is late there is a storm of whistling and booing. A trumpet blows and from the patio two mounted men in the costume of the time of Philip II ride out across the sand.

They are the aguacils or mounted bailiffs and it is through them that all orders by the president who represents the constituted authority are transmitted. They gallop across the ring, doff their hats, bow low before the president and presumably having received his authorization gallop back to place. The music starts, and from the opening in the courtyard of the horses comes the procession of the bullfighters; the paseo or parade. The three, if there are six bulls, four, if there are eight, matadors walk abreast, their dress capes are furled and wrapped around their left arms, their right arms balance, they walk with a loose-hipped stride, their arms swinging, their chins up, their eyes on the president's box. In single file behind each matador comes his cuadrilla of banderilleros and his picadors in the order of their seniority. So they come across the sand in a column of three or four. As the matadors come in front of the president's box they bow low and remove their black hats or monteras — the bow is serious or perfunctory depending on their length or service or degree of cynicism. At the start of their careers all are as devoutly ritual as altar boys serving a high mass and some always remain so. Others are as cynical as night club proprietors. The devout ones are killed more frequently. The cynical ones are the best companions. But the best of all are the cynical ones when they are still devout; or after, when having been devout, then cynical, they become devout again by cynicism. Juan Belmonte is an example of the last stage.

After they have bowed to the president they replace their hats, settling them carefully, and go to the barrera. The procession breaks up as, all having saluted, the matadors remove their heavy gold brocaded and jewelled parade capes and send them or pass them to friends or admirers to spread along the front of the wall protecting the first rows of seats, or, sometimes, send them by the sword handler to some one, usually a singer, a dancer, a quack doctor, an aviator, a cinema actor, a politician or some one notorious in the news of the day who happens to be in a box. Very young matadors or very cynical ones send their capes to bullfight impresarios from other towns who may be in Madrid, or to the bullfight critics. The best ones send them to friends. It is better not to have one sent to you. It is a pleasant compliment if the bullfighter has a good day and does well, but if he does badly it is too much responsibility. To have an obvious allegiance to a bullfighter who through bad luck, a bad bull, some accident that makes him lose confidence, or bad nerves from coming back to the ring in poor physical shape after a goring, disgraces himself and finally makes the public so indignant that he may have to be protected by the police as he goes out of the ring, head down, under a bombardment of thrown leather cushions, makes one conspicuous when the sword handler comes dodging around the falling cushions to reclaim the cape. Or perhaps, anticipating the disaster, the sword handler has come for the cape before the last bull so that you can see the cape, so proudly received, drawn tightly around the disgraced shoulders, being carried sprinting across the ring, the cushions sailing, a few of the more violent spectators being charged by the police as they pursue your matador. The banderilleros give their capes to friends to display too, but as these capes are regal looking only at a distance, are often thin, well-sweated and lined with that same striped material that seems to form the lining for vests all over the world and as the banderilleros do not take the conferring of this favor seriously, the honor is only nominal. While the capes are being thrown and spread and the fighting capes taken from the barrera, the bull ring servants smooth the sand of the ring that has been disturbed by the procession of the mounted picadors, the harnessed mules for handling of dead bulls and horses and the hooves of the horses of the alguacils. Meantime the two matadors (it is inferred that this is a six-bull fight) who are not killing retire with their cuadrillas into the callejon or narrow passage way between the red fences of the barrera and the first seats. The matador whose bull is to come out selects one of the heavy percale fighting capes. These are usually rose-colored on the outside and yellow inside with a wide stiffened collar, and big and full enough so that if the matador should put it over his shoulders the bottom of it would fall to his knees or just below and he would be able to wrap himself completely in it. The matador who is to kill places himself behind one of the little flat plank shelters which are built out from the barrera, wide enough for two men to stand in and just narrow enough to dodge behind, the alguacils ride up to under the president's box to ask for the key to the red door of the toril where the bull is waiting. The president throws it and the alguacil tries to catch it in his plumed hat. If he does the crowd claps. If he misses it whistles. But it does not take any of this seriously. If it is not caught a bull ring servant picks it up and hands it to the alguacil who gallops across the ring and hands it to the man who stands ready to open the door of the toril, gallops back, salutes the president and gallops out while the servants smooth away the traces of the horse marks on the sand. This smoothing completed there is no one in the ring but the matador behind his little shelter or burladero and two banderilleros, one on each side of the ring, tight against the fence. It is very quiet and every one is looking at the red plank door. The president gives a signal with his handkerchief, the trumpet sounds and the very serious, white-haired, wide old man, his name is Gabriel, in a sort of burlesque bullfighter's suit (it was bought for him by popular subscription) unlocks the door of the toril and pulling heavily on it runs backward to expose the low passageway that shows as the door swings open.